Advances in
the Psychology of Religion

INTERNATIONAL SERIES IN EXPERIMENTAL SOCIAL PSYCHOLOGY

Series Editor: Michael Argyle, University of Oxford

A Related Pergamon Journal

Language & Communication

An Interdisciplinary Journal

Editor: Roy Harris, *University of Oxford*

The primary aim of the journal is to fill the need for a publicational forum devoted to the discussion of topics and issues in communication which are of interdisciplinary significance. It will publish contributions from researchers in all fields relevant to the study of verbal and non-verbal communication.

Emphasis will be placed on the implications of current research for establishing common theoretical frameworks within which findings from different areas of study may be accommodated and interrelated.

By focusing attention on the many ways in which language is integrated with other forms of communicational activity and interactional behaviour it is intended to explore ways of developing a science of communication which is not restricted by existing disciplinary boundaries.

*Free specimen copy available on request.

Advances in
the Psychology of Religion

Edited by

L. B. BROWN

PERGAMON PRESS

OXFORD · NEW YORK · TORONTO · SYDNEY · PARIS · FRANKFURT

U.K.	Pergamon Press Ltd., Headington Hill Hall, Oxford OX3 0BW, England
U.S.A.	Pergamon Press Inc., Maxwell House, Fairview Park, Elmsford, New York 10523, U.S.A.
CANADA	Pergamon Press Canada Ltd., Suite 104, 150 Consumers Road, Willowdale, Ontario M2J 1P9, Canada
AUSTRALIA	Pergamon Press (Aust.) Pty. Ltd., P.O. Box 544, Potts Point, N.S.W. 2011, Australia
FRANCE	Pergamon Press SARL, 24 rue des Ecoles, 75240 Paris, Cedex 05, France
FEDERAL REPUBLIC OF GERMANY	Pergamon Press GmbH, Hammerweg 6, D-6242 Kronberg-Taunus, Federal Republic of Germany

BL
53
.A27
1985

First edition 1985

Library of Congress Cataloging in Publication Data
Main entry under title:
Advances in the psychology of religion
(International series in experimental social psychology; v. 11)
Includes index.
1. Psychology, Religious – Addresses, essays, lectures. I. Brown, L. B. II. Series.
BL53.A27 1985 200'.1'9 84–14683

British Library Cataloguing in Publication Data
Advances in the psychology of religion.
(International series in experimental social psychology: V.11)
1. Psychology, Religious
I. Brown, L. B. II. Series
200'.1'9 BL53

ISBN 0–08–027948–1

Printed in Great Britain by A. Wheaton & Co. Ltd Exeter

Acknowledgements

THOSE who came to the meeting for which these papers were prepared covered most of their own expenses. Financial assistance from the School of Psychology at the University of New South Wales in Sydney, Australia and from the Pergamon Press in Oxford allowed meals to be provided and is very gratefully acknowledged. Wolfson College, Oxford provided the context for the meeting, which was held in the Haldane Room there. The staff of the College was most helpful. Mrs Louise Kahabka, as she always does, guaranteed the most capable secretarial assistance, especially with the preparation of the manuscripts for publication.

List of participants

Dr Verene Aebischer, University of Paris, France.

Dr Michael J. Apter, University College, Cardiff, Wales.

Dr Michael Argyle, University of Oxford, England.

The Rev. Edward Bailey, Winterbourne Rectory, England.

Professor C. Daniel Batson, University of Kansas, USA.

Dr Benjamin Beit-Hallahmi, University of Haifa, Israel.

Dr Willem Berger, Catholic University, Nijmegen, Netherlands.

Dr Dorothy Berridge, Oxford, England.

Professor L. B. Brown, University of New South Wales, Australia.

Professor Don Browning, University of Chicago, USA.

Dr John H. Clark, University of Manchester, England.

Dr John H. Crook, University of Bristol, England.

Professor Jean-Pierre Deconchy, University of Paris X, France.

Dr Leslie Francis, The Culham College Institute, Abingdon, England.

Dr John Hall, Warneford Hospital, Oxford, England.

Mr David Hay, University of Nottingham, England.

Dr Paul Heelas, The University of Lancaster, England.

Professor Malcolm Jeeves, University of St. Andrews, Scotland.

Dr Kate Lowenthal, Bedford College, London, England.

Mr Henry Lupton, St. Martin's College, Lancaster, England.

Professor H. Newton Malony, Fuller Theological Seminary, Pasadena, USA.

Professor E. F. O'Doherty, University College Dublin, Eire.

Professor Conrad Van Ouwerkerk, State University of Leiden, Netherlands.

Professor James T. Richardson, University of Nevada, Reno, USA.

Rev. Dr G. E. W. Scobie, University of Glasgow, Scotland.

Mrs Emma Shackle, London, England.

Dr Mike Smithson, James Cook University, North Queensland, Australia.

Dr Robert Towler, The University, Leeds, England.

Dr Jan van der Lans, Catholic University, Nijmegen, Netherlands.

Professor Antoine Vergote, Catholic University of Leuven, Belgium.

Introduction to the Series

MICHAEL ARGYLE

SOCIAL psychology is in a very interesting period, and one of rapid development. It has survived a number of "crises", there is increased concern with external validity and relevance to the real world, the repertoire of research methods and statistical procedures has been greatly extended, and a number of exciting new ideas and approaches are being tried out.

The books in this series present some of these new developments; each volume contains a balance of new material and a critical review of the relevant literature. The new material consists of empirical research, research procedures, theoretical formulations, or a combination of these. Authors have been asked to review and evaluate the often very extensive past literature, and to explain their new findings, methods or theories clearly.

The authors are from all over the world, and have been very carefully chosen, mainly on the basis of their previous published work, showing the importance and originality of their contribution, and their ability to present it clearly. Some of these books report a programme of research by one individual or a team, some are based on doctoral theses, others on conferences.

Social psychologists have moved into an increasing number of applied fields, and a growing number of practitioners have made use of our work. All the books in this series will have some practical application, some will be on topics of wide popular interest, as well as adding to scientific knowledge. The books in the series are designed for advanced undergraduates, graduate students and relevant practitioners, and in some cases for a rather broader public.

We do not known how social psychology will develop, and it takes quite a variety of forms already. However, it is a great pleasure to be associated with books by some of those social psychologists who are developing the subject in such interesting ways.

Contributors

Dr Michael J. Apter,
Department of Psychology,
University College,
PO Box 78,
Cardiff, Wales.

Dr Michael Argyle,
Department of Experimental
Psychology,
University of Oxford,
South Parks Road,
Oxford, OX1 3UD,
England.

Professor C. Daniel Batson,
Department of Psychology,
University of Kansas,
426 Fraser Hall,
Lawrence, Kansas, 66045, USA.

Dr Benjamin Beit-Hallahmi,
University of Haifa,
Mount Carmel, Haifa,
Israel, 31999.

Professor L. B. Brown,
School of Psychology,
University of New South Wales,
PO Box 1, Kensington, NSW 2033,
Australia.

Professor Jean-Pierre Deconchy,
Laboratoire de Psychologie Sociale,
University of Paris X,
184, Rue de la Sorbonne,
75005 Paris,
France.

Dr Leslie Francis,
The Culham College Institute,
The Malthouse,
60 East St Helen St,
Abingdon, Oxon, England.

Mr David Hay,
School of Education,
University of Nottingham,
University Park,
Nottingham N67 2RD, England.

Dr Paul Heelas,
Department of Religious Studies,
The University of Lancaster,
Bailrigg, Lancaster, CA1 4YG,
England.

Professor H. Newton Malony,
Graduate School of Psychology,
Fuller Theological Seminary,
177 N. Madison Avenue,
Pasadena, CA 91101,
USA.

Professor James T. Richardson,
Department of Sociology,
University of Nevada Reno,
Reno, Nevada 89557–0067,
USA.

Dr Jan van der Lans,
Faculteit der Sociale Weterschappen,
Psychologisch Laboratorium,
Katholicke Universiteit,
Montessorilaan 3,
Postbus 9104,
6500 HE Nijmegen, Netherlands.

Professor A. Vergote,
Faculteit der Psychologie en
Pedagogische Weterschappen,
Katholicke Universiteit Te Leuven,
Tiensestraat 102,
3000 Leuven, Belgium.

Contents

1

Introduction

L. B. BROWN

THESE previously unpublished papers were prepared for an *ad hoc* meeting of about 30 people who were invited because they were known to be actively involved with research in the psychology of religion. The meeting, which was made possible by the participants themselves, was held over the first weekend in May 1982, at Wolfson College, Oxford.

The first letter that was sent out about this meeting stressed that it would consider current work and new directions in the psychology of religion. The relationship with other social sciences, methods of study, recent findings about religious beliefs and attitudes, and about religious experience and behaviour were the topics specially mentioned. Most of the papers that were read then have been revised for this book, in the light of the discussions and with reference to the other contributions. That they might not cohere is unavoidable since they did not set out to develop a unified view.

A deliberate aim of the meeting was to gather psychologists, sociologists, anthropologists and one zoologist from Europe, the British Isles, North America and Australia. The participants were therefore from several backgrounds, with training and experience in different academic and religious traditions. While they were not equally committed to the truth or falsity of religious claims, they were agreed on the validity of a scientific or empirical psychology of religion. They also shared an openness to new ideas and a concern for the practical implications of what was discussed. Disagreements that emerged over the theories that should be developed were no greater than those which arise whenever one asks why it is that someone in either a traditional or modern society holds religious ideas and beliefs.

Michael Argyle (Chapter 2) opened the conference by commenting on previous work, and drawing our attention to some neglected aspects of both religion and psychology that could be brought together. In his paper, Paul Heelas (Chapter 4) considered the extent to which anthropologists and sociologists have relied on basically psychological explanations and theories to account for the religions that they encounter. Benjamin Beit-Hallahmi (Chapter 3) examined the way social and religious factors may have influenced the theories of religion that were developed by Freud and by Allport.

The usual definitions of religion imply adherence to some prescribed social or ideological system or accepting the truth of a set of beliefs. Michael Apter (Chapter 6), however, examined what it might mean for religion to be taken as an overriding state of mind. Religion has also been referred to an attribute, like soul or spirit, or to the awareness of particular kinds of experience, as in David Hay's analysis in Chapter 10. Vergote (Chapter 5), however, argues that an important focus for any *psychological* analysis of religion must be on the dynamic tension between belief and unbelief.

Perhaps it is because religion reminds psychology of its early history and some of its origins that progress has been slow in finding explanations for it which are supported by sound data and well-controlled observations. Yet there is no shortage of theory. The close relationships between religion and psychology are often assumed and reinforced by the popular understanding of contemporary psychology as almost "a spilt religion". This can be found in numerous paperbacks advocating self-help, and optimism about our unfulfilled potential. James Richardson's paper on the new religions (Chapter 14) examined how this search is being satisfied by social movements which straddle conventional psychology and religion. He drew attention to the direct rejection of positive evidence for the rehabilitative value of these movements, not only by those who advocate "deprogramming" for people who have been influenced by these groups. This is a striking example of the way general attitudes and values overlay assessments of research findings.

A variety of methods has been used to study religion. While most of the current work rests on descriptions and correlational analyses it was strongly argued at our meeting that we should aim for an *experimental* psychology of religion. Although experimental control allows firmer conclusions than correlational methods, many still think it unethical to "manipulate" religion for scientific, rather than religious, ends. Jean-Pierre Deconchy (Chapter 7) took up these and other questions about our research methods, arguing that new theoretical models are needed, and that experiments are possible but must be used confidently in the psychology of religion. Deconchy's (cf. 1980) own careful experiments on reactions to religious orthodoxy show what can be achieved. Beyond decisions about the methods that are to be used lies the theoretical stance of any study. Thus Newton Malony (Chapter 8) interpreted his experimental findings within the perspective of recent theology, which he argues offers insights that psychologists have neglected; Jan van der Lans, on the other hand (Chapter 9), relied on cognitive psychology to interpret the results of his experiment on meditation.

Experimental studies point up an important direction for the psychology of religion, and even if proper controls are not always possible, awareness of experimental procedures must improve the design of surveys and questionnaire-based studies. What has been achieved already suggests that we should overcome the squeamishness psychologists seem to have felt about systematically varying the conditions in studies of religion. While religious education, clergy selection and training have, with good intentions, recently been altered, as have doctrines, liturgies and styles of preaching, few assessments have been made of the effects of such changes on church-goers, beyond the intuitions of committee members and those in authority who can sanction change. Although Yeatts and Asher (1979) argued that the Church can not afford to be unsystematic in its evaluations, and should adopt a more positive attitude to experimentation, many religious people still seem to believe that scientific techniques and methods are antagonistic to the immediacy of religious claims or experience. Too few acknowledge that doubt may be an important component of trust and confidence.

The ideal experiment on religion would not, of course, expose people to something they had had no previous knowledge or contact with, although it might imply rejecting the belief that *every* outcome reflects God's intervention. Methods to resolve attributional questions about such interventions are still being developed rather tentatively, perhaps because we are not clear about what is expected. Any scientific study must be based on an analysis of the phenomenology and perhaps the history of what is being explored, for it to be ecologically valid. It is an ideological conceit, however, for psychologists to insist that their classical experimental methods are always needed to control what can be observed, and even the most careful investigator is limited by what can be understood. Studies of religion are also always hindered by implicit assumptions about what it involves. They are necessarily diverse, and we must recognize that both uni- and multi-dimensional solutions have been found to define the structure of religious attitudes and responses. That there are many orientations or ways to be "religious" derives from the work of William James (1902), and the enquiries that Gordon Allport (1950) opened up when he pursued the links between religion and prejudice, having noticed that religion both "makes and unmakes prejudice". Exploring these and other relationships, for example between religion and mental health or altruism, offers the possibility of further advance, as Batson and his colleagues show in Chapter 13. The usually negative personality traits of neuroticism, extraversion and social desirability that are considered in Leslie Francis' paper (Chapter 12), as well as the conservatism and authoritarianism of some forms of religion, are no longer blandly accepted as the most reasonable explanations of a non-specific religiousness. Focusing on the integrative or constructive functions of religion suggests further directions for work that could broaden our understanding of the psychology of religion.

While our discussions concerned the influence of religion on psychology, they neglected how psychology has been used to challenge or understand religious "faith". Such challenges occur when conflicts between scientific findings and existential judgements are unresolved, or because concepts such as suffering or desire, and the psychological theories or explanations of them, have too readily been expected to involve psychoanalytic solutions. Yet psychoanalysis as a solution, and broad epistemological questions, continue to be an important driving force among European psychologists of religion, some of whom follow Ricoeur to stress the importance of the religious texts that specify what is acceptable. Relationships between theology and psychology go both ways, and the influence of psychology on theological interpretations can be seen in the issue of *Concilium* (June 1982) on "The challenge of psychology to faith", where Adorno's remark that epistemological categories are repeatedly turned into moral imperatives is noted. While the psychology of religion explores religious concepts and behaviour agnostically, "religious psychology" necessarily accepts and pursues the validity of religious explanations. (That approach is to be found in the *Journal of Psychology and Theology*.)

In one discussion, Malcolm Jeeves, who wrote *Psychology and Christianity* (1976), drew our attention to the extent to which scientific findings, although resisted by religion at first, have directly altered beliefs about "man", nature and the cosmos, which in turn have influenced ethical judgements. He noted that social science and dynamic psychological theories have had a strong if indirect effect on religious thought, altering our understanding of, for example, prejudice and behavioural control. They also emphasize the place of psychological development, anxiety, and interpersonal relationships in shaping religious and other beliefs.

While many well-developed theories and approaches have been used to build a psychology of religion, recent discussions of feminism, political liberation and religious education suggest "new directions" that were not taken up at our meeting. That it proved impossible to find someone to read us a paper on religious development could indicate an unfortunate decline of interest in that field, unlike the great concern of 20 years ago for psychological and pedagogical work on religious education, and on the developmental psychology of religious concepts and moral education. Ronald Goldman's (1964) studies of the religious thought of children filled a vacuum then by offering both psychological and educational support for a change in the direction of religious education.

Although we now have some knowledge about many aspects of religion, and the philosophy of Thomas Aquinas has been represented as a flow diagram (Hayes, 1983), we cannot yet write computer programs to simulate what a person should do to achieve particular religious beliefs or orientations to religion. This is partly because a sudden sense of immediacy or "surprise" can alter the course of one's religious development, and because there is more than one path that can be followed. Beyond social influence, and contact with a religious tradition and with its language, it is hard to specify exactly what other preparations might be required. David Hay's paper (Chapter 10), which rests on the accounts that people have given of their religious experiences, shows that these experiences readily fit with the rest of life, at least for some people. Although a person's religious vocabulary will be limited by what particular traditions or groups allow, these external influences also shape or reflect a religious "style" or "personality". This is similar to the finding from Newton Malony's experiment that whether a religious response can be elicited by religious paintings or by their context depends on prior religious contact. Despite that, subjects are usually asked to rate, or to evaluate, religious concepts or statements in isolation, without finding, for example, whether they lie within a person's "range of convenience", or whether they are even recognized as being "religious". Brown's paper (Chapter 11) emphasizes the convergent and prescriptive nature of many studies of religious attitudes, and Deconchy's discussion of non-experimental research methods stresses the epistemological problems in directly applying concepts like locus of control to religion. Procedures that rely directly on simple verbal reactions about religious questions or issues neglect the effects of task demands, or of moderator variables like evaluation apprehension, response bias, social desirability and compliance, on the responses that are given. To emphasize that there are "no right or wrong answers" to a questionnaire is disingenuous.

The dominant concern with religious attitudes has aligned the psychology of religion with the rest of social psychology, although the extent to which attribution theory or group processes might account for the appeal of religion has hardly been considered. Questions about whether the content or the object of religious belief and thinking produce psychological effects that are different from what can be found in the domains of science or politics, have also been neglected. Although we do not yet have a psychology of science, findings from the "psychology of politics" could enliven our understanding of religion. The gaps that are also to be found in aesthetics between the language of art criticism, the psychology of art, and its actual practice might similarly clarify some of the problems of religion which involve practice, belief and contact with a tradition embodied in institutions, dogma, creeds and theological writing. The psychology of religion has neglected both the effects of responses to specific traditions and confidence in a transcendent reality, in favour of a pursuit of current orthodoxies, or reactions that are judged pathological or maladaptive.

Changes in the theoretical direction of the psychology of religion require broadened psychological perspectives. Newton Malony would move the "interface" between religion and psychology, and Deconchy would examine existing psychological models more carefully. None of that impedes the development of existing theories, as in Vergote's use of psychoanalysis and van der Lans's use of cognitive social psychology. Practical questions should also be investigated, including, for example, whether lists of religious words are learned more readily by religious than non-religious subjects, and how religious settings define the language that is to be used in them. To show whether religious material is differentially processed, and how a religious frame of reference develops, might also be useful. Most studies have adopted an external or observer's perspective, although studies of attitudes and values, conceptual development, and even the accounts of experience, might benefit from inside perspectives that look beyond "behavioural" data to intention, or the way conflicts are resolved when understanding or interpreting any religion.

Psychological theories about religion have responded to its specific content, to conclude that Christianity allows one to compensate for social disadvantage or that God is a projection of paternal images. Despite the absence of good empirical support for these views, they have become implicitly accepted theories that have formed our attitudes to the truth of religion, producing assumptions about what is "natural" or "normal". Few have asked whether, or even how, religious *disbelief* should be explained. Despite that, psychology has fostered our tolerance of deviance, mental illness and developmental disability, and it has ensured that egocentric or ethnocentric responses are treated cautiously. Attributions to spirit possession are therefore understood in a figurative or metaphoric sense, except by those who hold essentially conservative beliefs. The world has in this way been tamed by psychology, so that scientific explanations have helped to purge self-serving, primitive and concrete ideas from the religions of many people. Yet there is a wide spectrum of orientations to religion, and of beliefs about the way its demands are to be met (or discarded) that psychology has not touched, even in Western societies.

We found no reasons at our meeting for a restricted isolation from others' approaches to psychology or to religion itself. Our fields of interest were broad, not least because psychological concepts and theories have been taken into other disciplines, and quite readily used in religious apologetics. While the psychology of religion has a scientific basis for its social, cognitive, emotional, developmental or behavioural interpretations, religion itself does not always imply direct experience and an actively committed stance. There are conflicting perspectives on religion and psychology, although the concepts or values of one system can often be translated into, or reinterpreted in terms of, another. The correspondence between some aspects of psychology and religion gives to the psychology of religion an appeal that does not have to be reductionistic, although once psychology finally gave the philosophy of mind back to philosophers, psychologists seemed to prefer to stay close to behavioural analysis. That does not deal well with the conflicts in the ideas or beliefs that are found in religion, and neglects the subjective certainty about religious belief and experience that endows explicit action with transcendent qualities. That the criteria to assess the validity of reports about such experiences are essentially consensual, especially when they involve religious values or rules, brings their study within social psychology.

Before the First World War the psychology of religion was at the centre of psychology. While mental imagery and consciousness have emerged from the obscurity that Behaviourism assigned to them while it dominated American psychology, studies of religion are still slightly suspect. This could explain why there is still more study of the structure of religion than of its functions or what it achieves.

Few of the early findings (and even later ones) seem to have been counterintuitive, although the careful descriptions they require gave insight into what religion involved. We should ask ourselves how far we have moved from early attempts to understand religion "scientifically", and how we can improve our present knowledge. The discussions at our meeting suggested several lines of progress, which could be constrained by the fact that those from North America still have a more behavioural orientation to the factors in religion. That both groups share the concern for experimental methods may, however, eventually bring them together.

Any question about how the psychology of religion has recently changed should answer, "a great deal". The literature continues to grow, as does agreement about how to measure religious variables (cf. Gorsuch, 1984). These measures are not, however, religiously innocent, in that they embody items that implicitly favour particular kinds of religion or religious orientation. The implications of early work, like that of Gordon Allport on religious orientations, are still being worked out, as Batson's paper (Chapter 13) shows. Religion itself and the common attitudes to it have also changed. This can be seen by the increased strength of the ecumenical movement, and by changed religious and non-religious practices and sanctions. While social surveys may have documented a "decline in religious commitment", they also show growing support for the enthusiastic and conservative forms of religion. The psychological characteristics and effects of those groups have not yet been well documented, nor do we know how the new forms and language of the liturgy have altered the popular semantics of God's action or the responsiveness of individuals.

References

ALLPORT, G. W. *The individual and his religion.* New York: Macmillan, 1950/1962.

DECONCHY, J.-P. *Orthodoxie religieuse et sciences humaines suivi de (Religious) Orthodoxy, rationality and scientific knowledge.* The Hague: Mouton, 1980.

GOLDMAN, R. *Religious thinking from childhood to adolescence.* London: Routledge & Kegan Paul, 1964.

GORSUCH, R. L. Measurement: the boon and bane of investigating religion. *American Psychologist,* 1984, **39**(3), 228–236.

HAYES, B. Computer recreations. *Scientific American,* 1983; **249**(6), 11–16.

JAMES, W. *The varieties of religious experience.* New York: Collier, 1902.

JEEVES, M. A. *Psychology and Christianity: the view both ways.* London: Inter-Varsity Press, 1976.

YEATTS, J. R. and ASHER, W. Can we afford not to do true experiments in the psychology of religion: a reply to Batson. *Journal for the Scientific Study of Religion,* 1979; **18**(1), 86–89.

2

New directions in the psychology of religion

MICHAEL ARGYLE

IN THE last few years the psychology of religion has made considerable advances; in particular a great number of excellent empirical studies have been published on a variety of topics. Meanwhile the religious scene has also been changing and, for example, we have seen the rise of many new sects and cults, together with an increased use of drugs and of meditational techniques. Psychology has been changing even more, and there are a number of developments in psychology which are relevant to the psychology of religion, some of which have not yet been exploited. It is perhaps unfortunate that the psychology of religion has tended to be rather parasitical on mainstream psychology, but the time may come when this is reversed, with findings in the psychology of religion seen to be of general importance for other psychologists. This has started to happen. Social psychologists have become interested in religious sects and their conversion techniques, and cognitive psychologists are interested in religious experience.

Recent developments in psychology which are relevant to the psychology of religion

If we are to be parasitical on other branches, let us see what can now be used from developments in personality and social psychology.

Techniques of cognitive analysis

There have been important and now familiar advances in the methods available for studying cognitions. The first of these was the semantic differential (Osgood *et al.*, 1957), and quite a lot of use has been made of it in studying how people conceive God, to test the psychoanalytic theory that God is a projected parental image (e.g. Godin and Hallez, 1964). These findings can be summarized by saying that God is seen as rather similar to parents, espcially to the preferred and opposite-sex parent, and that attitudes to God and to parents are also similar (Argyle and Beit-Hallahmi, 1975, p. 184f.). A

8

better possible test of the Freudian theory that God is a substitute parent figure could, however, be made by establishing whether children suddenly become more religious when they leave home or when their parents die. Ullman (1982), who compared converts with "religiously affiliated non-converts" to various theistic faiths, found that the converts had higher levels of absent fathers, and a history of bad relations with their fathers; there was much less difference for mothers. Cognitive research could be pressed a lot further to ask, for example, how people view the Holy Spirit or the after-life. Other methods of cognitive analysis which have not yet been fully used to study religious ideas and beliefs include the Repertory Grid Technique (Fransella and Bannister, 1977). This is a way of assessing cognitions in terms of the dimensions or constructs that are used by the subjects, rather than using those imposed by the investigator (Todd, 1977). Multidimensional scaling provides a method of showing how concepts are related to each other, and along which dimensions they are seen as similar or different (cf. Brown and Forgas, 1980). The use of these methods on a range of religious ideas, and in different religious or non-religious groups, could be very illuminating. They would enable a more refined analysis of, for example, ideas about the after-life than was possible when Gorer (1955) found from open-ended questions that it was seen as rather similar to this life and as a kind of reincarnation, although for some of his English sample it involved "no sex, no dogs barking, and no washing up".

Personality–situation interaction

It is now well documented that personality systems are not active all the time, and that people behave very differently in different situations (Argyle *et al.*, 1981). There are certainly situations in which many people behave and feel "religious", just as there are "religious" persons. One British survey asked which situations made respondents think about religion (ITA, 1970). The replies were very striking: e.g. making love 2 per cent, holidays 2 per cent, death and serious illness 64 per cent. These respondents were also asked whom they would see if they had different kinds of trouble. For a wide range of problems they said they would see their general practitioner. Almost the only problems for which priests or clergy were thought suitable were death (usually of relatives or a fear of their own death) and marital problems. Of course some people are influenced by religion in a very wide range of situations, which itself might be a useful index of religious concern.

Non-verbal communication

It is now well established that emotions are expressed primarily by non-verbal signals, especially in facial expression and tone of voice (Argyle, 1975). Religious ideas and feelings are also expressed non-verbally by music, darkness, candles, incense and bodily postures, and these religious expressions are similar in different religions, suggesting that there may be some signals universal to mankind here. A lot of religious music seems to have a special blend of emotions, as in the kind of joyful melancholy exemplified in J. S. Bach's religious works. Music has been described as "the language of the emotions" (Langer, 1953). Singing hymns is a widespread group religious activity which combines non-verbal music with words that contain religious ideas, expressed in a poetic way. This combination arouses further emotions.

Sex differences

One of the best-known findings in the psychology of religion is the greater religiosity of women, in the Christian world at least. The extensive research on sex differences (Maccoby, 1966) has done little to explain why this should be so. Women have also been found to be more expressive in general and to be better senders of non-verbal signals (Rosenthal et al., 1980). Women are found to form closer attachments to each other, both as friends and within their families, and to do more for their husbands' health and happiness than the latter do for them. The explanation of these results still eludes us. It may be because women are socialized into a nurturant role or because they are biologically predisposed to care for children and their families, or perhaps it is because the verbal and non-verbal parts of female brains are better interconnected than they are in male brains.

Social skills

While all religions instruct their adherents to love their neighbours, they do not always give very specific guidance on how to do it, apart from a few examples or parables. It is therefore easy to get this wrong. For example, when a German mental hospital introduced nuns as nurses in a schizophrenic ward the nuns were so "loving" that the patients became progressively worse and ended up staying in bed and being fed by hand. Research on the most effective social skills for different roles and in different settings has provided detailed information about what is needed to function in them (Argyle, 1981a,b). Just as an effective doctor needs medical skills – and an effective nurse, teacher or parent needs social skills – anyone who is trying to love his neighbour also needs social skills. What difference does a positive religious attitude make here? Perhaps it simply strengthens a concern for the welfare of others, or it could help people to make a greater effort, by using the skills which have been found to work well. A great deal of recent research into "social support" has also found that it produces great benefits for health, happiness, mental health and length of life (Lynch, 1979). Such social support may be similar to what is known as "love" in Christian circles, its main components being tangible help, emotional support, listening to problems, giving advice, and integrating others into a social network (Gottlieb, 1981).

Identity achievement

Recent work in the tradition of Erik Erikson by Marcia and his collaborators (Bourne, 1978), has shown that young people in North America often have to struggle to achieve a sense of personal identity. This has been found to have several components, such as choosing a career and attitude to sex, while positive decisions about religion have been found to be central in the sense that they predicted the rest of the identity system (Slugoski et al., 1984). It has, however, been pointed out that a long process of identity formation which lasts into the 20s is only possible for the more privileged youth in affluent societies. Those who have to start work at 16 or earlier probably have less difficulty in finding their identity. This state of affairs could perhaps explain the great interest among middle-class people in new religious movements, in encounter groups like EST, and in other therapeutic programmes. It looks as if achieving a religious point of view, or at least a coherent outlook on the world, is now a crucial part of the maturation of many young people in the modern world.

The effects of religion on behaviour

Many studies have been made of the effects of religion on non-religious behaviour, to establish differences between religious and non-religious people in morality, moral judgement, and so on. There are some areas in which religious people do well. They are more helpful to strangers, give more to charity, and have a reputation for kindness and honesty (Argyle and Beit-Hallahmi, 1975; Batson and Ventis, 1982). On the other hand they have been widely found to be more racially prejudiced, unless they are particularly committed to their religion, and to be more hostile to, and hence unforgiving of, criminals, the unemployed, unmarried mothers, and the like. In other words, religious folk don't like sinners. This looks like a failure of religion to work, although it is largely explicable in terms of intergroup processes. In order for members of a group to keep up their self-esteem, they tend to exaggerate the merits of their own group and the failures of members of rival groups on relevant criteria (Tajfel, 1981). It would therefore be expected that those who are trying to live a good life would naturally contrast themselves with those who are not. In the case of Christianity, however, this produces behaviour which is in conflict with the Christian ethic.

One area in which religion has had an immense effect on people's lives, especially in the past, is that of sexual behaviour. The Catholic church still forbids the use of artificial forms of contraception, although many Catholics no longer obey this injunction, and this has had an effect on the sexual behaviour of married (and unmarried) Catholics, and on their feelings of guilt (Westoff and Ryder, 1971).

Religion also has effects on the health and happiness of church members. They get divorced less often, and claim to be more happily married (e.g. Chesser, 1956). If this is a genuine result it could show that pressures on couples to persevere with their marriage could lead to beneficial results. Church-goers are also found to be in better health, partly or even wholly because they drink and smoke less, and engage in less promiscuous sex (Comstock and Partridge, 1972). Their suicide rate is half that of non-church-goers, and their level of neuroticism has been found to be lower. Old people, especially those who are single or widowed and also religious, show quite marked advantages in health and adjustment. Moberg and Taves (1965) suggest that social support may be a crucial factor here.

Psychological theories of religion

Fear of death

Of the traditional psychological theories about the origin of religion, fear of death continues to receive strong support. Studies of the terminally ill have shown that believers are less anxious than non-believers (Hinton, 1972) and that many old people look forward positively to death (Swenson, 1961). This is a most important finding since it shows that religious belief for these people is a serious matter and more than just poetry or metaphor. It is still puzzling, however, that so many people say they believe in Hell (17 per cent in the UK, 65 per cent in the USA – Argyle and Beit-Hallahmi, 1975), although they may not believe in it as a place for themselves. This could reflect the influence of some kinds of evangelical teaching, the popularity of the belief in a "just world", or strong guilt feelings and a related wish to be punished. In the past, Hell has been an important Christian doctrine, and its fear an incentive to obeying the rules.

Sexual repression and sublimation

It has often been suggested that religious activities are in some way a sublimation of sex. A number of studies have supported this: for example in Christian countries, at least, religious people engage in less sex, even if they are married (Kinsey, 1948, 1953). If there were a causal relationship here, the "sexual revolution" should have led to a decline in religion. In fact, there has been a slow general decline in Church membership over a long period, and while the nonconformist churches in Britain have declined most and Catholics have hardly declined at all there has been a greatly increased interest in sects and in cults. Perhaps the nineteenth-century pattern of early conversion, which was partly linked to sex, has been replaced by other forms of religious activity.

Social construction of reality

Some sociologists regard religion as part of the "social construction of reality", or of a group's shared way of looking at the world (Berger and Luckmann, 1963). It is not only the young who want explanations of why we are here, who made the world, and the purpose of life. These are questions to which no single branch of knowledge provides an answer, and there appears to be no tendency for those who are intelligent or well-educated to be less religious than any others. Furthermore, doctors quite often come across problems in medical ethics which cannot be answered from within a medical framework alone. The same is true in other branches of science and one function of a religious outlook is to deal with such questions.

Theories of religious experience

A number of studies have shown that mescaline, LSD and similar drugs can produce religious experiences, at least in religious people and in a religious setting. This is consistent with Schachter's (1959) two-factor theory of emotion, that specific emotions are produced by a combination of physiological arousal and appropriate cognitions which allow the arousal to be interpreted as a particular emotion. While one criticism of this theory has been that different emotions are accompanied by different physiological states (Levanthal, 1980), we also know that only certain physiological states produce religious experience. Coffee does not, and there is little evidence that alcohol does; it is the hallucinogenic drugs which work best, although they need the right setting and the right people. Pahnke's study (1966) of a Good Friday meditation by theological students who had been given psilocybin is a good example of this combination working successfully.

What is the connection then between drug-induced religious experiences and those reported, mostly without the aid of drugs, by 36 per cent of the British population (Hay, 1981)? A few of them may have been among schizophrenics whose disturbed body chemistry is similar to the effects of LSD. Others may have been a result of illness of fasting. Meanwhile this is an important question for further research.

Experiments with drugs have been shown to involve attribution processes; and religious attributions may similarly be given to some unusual experiences. Further instances of religious attribution occur where people think that an illness is a punishment from God, or that their recovery depends on God's approval. Some people believe that the decisions they reach are a result of divine guidance.

A quite different account of religious experience has been put forward by Jaynes (1976) who suggests that the Greeks at the time of Homer, and the Jews in early Old Testament times, had a "bicameral mind". The right cerebral hemisphere may have been responsible for auditory hallucinations which the left hemisphere interpreted as the voices of the gods. Hearing such voices is less common now, being mainly restricted to schizophrenic patients and to some religious people. Jaynes argues that the bicameral mind broke down between 2000 and 1000 BC due to increased trading, contact with other peoples, and the discovery that different gods said different things. The development of writing also weakened the authority of inner voices. In terms of this theory, present-day religious experience could therefore be interpeted as a remnant of past traditions or modes of awareness.

New topics in the psychology of religion

The new cults

Early studies of Protestant sects found that they appealed mainly to working-class people and to members of racial minority groups, and that they had a high predominance of women. As those sects became better established and their membership became more middle-class a new generation of cults has developed. Some of these are Christian, or partly so, like the Jesus people, and the Moonies. Others, including Transcendental Meditation and Rajneesh, are Indian in origin. Some which originated in California, like EST and Exegesis, are really therapeutic movements.

The early Protestant revival movements engaged in evangelical activities, and produced conversions typically but not exclusively among the young. The new sects appeal to a very different clientele, and their members, typically in their 20s and from the middle class, are more equally male and female. Some of these sects appeal to, and aim to attract, dropouts, and have been successful with alienated young people who are on drugs (cf. Chapter 14 by Richardson, in this book). While earlier sects forbade premarital sex, and aroused feelings of guilt over former sexual activities, some of the new sects make sex freely available. Traditional sects had enthusiastic and even ecstatic meetings; the new ones practise meditation and group therapy. The old sects were closely knit and required a high level of commitment, while some of the new cults have loose boundaries and make minimal demands on their members. Some observers have even regarded the new sects as an exotic consumer item, with little relevance to everyday life. Others think they help people to cope with the lack of community and the conflicting values in modern society. Whether the needs of most of their members are just outside the sphere of psychiatry needs to be carefully explored, as does the role of these sects in providing an identity and a purpose in life (Robbins and Anthony, 1979).

The nature of religious belief

In earlier times religious beliefs were taken to be like beliefs in the physical world, with Heaven and Hell regarded as definite places, and God a fatherly person. Under the influence of philosophers like Wittgenstein, educated people in the West now make a sharp distinction between propositions about the physical world which are directly or indirectly verifiable, and religious propositions which cannot be verified in that way, but depend on authority or on consensus. Although Thouless (1935) showed that religious and factual beliefs operate in different ways, what exactly are religious propositions and beliefs like psychologically? One suggestion is that they are plans for behaviour, though they clearly contain definite images and cognitions as well. Others have said that religious beliefs are metaphors, analogies, or a kind of poetry (Frye, 1982). Some theologians have "demythologized" religion so that "I believe in god" is taken to mean "I take a generally positive and optimistic attitude towards the universe". However, we can readily find people who take religion much more seriously than this, being quite literally afraid of Hell or dependent on divine assistance. Such religious beliefs seem to embody values and fundamental views about existence and are able to control behaviour.

The nature of religious communication

We have seen that non-verbal communication plays an important role in the expression of religion, and that a special set of emotions may be involved here. We also saw the peculiar potency of non-verbal religious signals when they are combined with words. Religious language, however, has a rather different use from the language that is applied to the physical world. As Farrer (1958) has argued, religious language contains some very compelling images, like the shepherd and his sheep or a father and his wayward son, and is typically couched in terms of parables, analogies and metaphors. We argued above that religion is not just a set of metaphors, but perhaps its additional meaning is conveyed by the powerful non-verbal and contextual signals that accompany those metaphors and messages. A further component may be found in religious exhortations, and the rules for a good life, which can be expressed in quite ordinary words. One of the reasons why religious language takes its particular form is that, especially when adopting the vernacular, it takes words usually applied to the physical world and expects them to deal adequately with transcendent religious concerns.

The limits of reductionism

Much recent work in the psychology of religion has assumed a reductionist point of view, supposing that religious phenomena can be explained in terms of the same psychological processes that apply to any other sphere of social behaviour. This was not the point of view of the founders of the psychology of religion. William James and C. G. Jung, for example, both supposed that a further spiritual reality was involved. On the other hand, a reductionist approach is not adopted by psychologists for mathematics or chemistry, and it is accepted that mathematical truth is hardly a matter for psychological analysis. To put this differently, there is no psychology of mathematicians or chemists that doubts or questions the validity of the object of their study. With music, literature and the arts, psychologists are more cautious, but they believe that they can partly explain how aesthetic experiences are generated, while not denying the importance of these experiences.

Music students take courses in physics, not to be told that music is bunk but to enable them to understand the acoustics and physics of sound, so that they may handle it better. Furthermore, physics as such does not distinguish between good and bad music. To do that requires a particular kind of aesthetic or critical expertise about music itself. Similarly, horticulturalists who know what kinds of manure and fertilizer will produce good roses do not see this knowledge as explaining away, or detracting from, the beauty of their roses. These examples suggest a less reductionist model for the psychology of religion, especially if psychology were to use its explanations of religious responses to show how to produce them to order, or more effectively. These spheres of religious knowledge and expertise are no more reducible to psychology than music simply obeys the rules of mathematics or physics.

Can psychology learn from religion?

It has often been assumed, especially in the past, that there is a lot which religion could learn from psychology. But what about the converse process? After all, psychology and religion are almost in the same line of business, explaining and offering a guide to life. And many more people have so far accepted religious solutions than have ever heard of psychology. The ideas and practices of religion clearly have a wide appeal, and in this sense represent some truths about human nature. Perhaps religious experts, gurus and spiritual directors possess such expertise and have access to a body of knowledge that psychologists ought to know about. To identify this is yet another task for the psychology of religion.

References

ARGYLE, M. *Bodily communication.* London: Methuen, 1975.
ARGYLE, M. (ed.) *Social skills and health.* London: Methuen, 1981a.
ARGYLE, M. (ed.) *Social skills and work.* London: Methuen, 1981b.
ARGYLE, M. and BEIT-HALLAHMI, B. *The social psychology of religion.* London: Routledge and Kegan Paul, 1975.
ARGYLE, M., FURNHAM, A. and GRAHAM, J. A. *Social situations.* Cambridge: Cambridge University Press, 1981.
BATSON, C. D. and VENTIS, W. L. *The religious experience: a social-psychological perspective.* New York: Oxford University Press, 1982.
BERGER, P. L. and LUCKMANN, T. Sociology of religion and sociology of knowledge. *Sociology and Social Research*, 1963; **47**, 417–427.

BOURNE, E. The state of research on ego identity – a review. *Journal of Youth and Adolescence*, 1978; **7**, 223–251 and 371–391.

BROWN, L. B. and FORGAS, J. P. The structure of religion: a multi-dimensional scaling of informal elements. *Journal for the Scientific Study of Religion*, 1980; **19**, 423–431.

CHESSER, E. *The sexual, marital and family relationships of the English woman.* London: Hutchinson, 1956.

COMSTOCK, G. W. and PARTRIDGE, K. B. Church attendance and health. *Journal of Chronic Diseases*, 1972: **25**, 665–672.

FARRER, A. *The glass of vision.* London: Dacre, 1958.

FRANSELLA, F. and BANNISTER, D. *A manual for Repertory Grid Technique.* London: Academic Press, 1977.

FRYE, N. *The great code: the Bible and literature.* London: Routledge and Kegan Paul, 1982.

GODIN, A. and HALLEZ, M. Parental images and divine paternity. In A. GODIN (ed.), *From religious experience to a religious attitude.* Brussels: Lumen Vitae, 1964.

GORER, G. *Exploring English character.* London: Cresset, 1955.

GOTTLIEB, B. (ed.) *Social networks and social support in community mental health.* New York: Sage, 1981.

HAY, D. *The journey within.* Harmondsworth: Penguin, 1981.

HINTON, J. *Dying.* Harmondsworth: Penguin, 1972.

I.T.A. *Religion in Britain and Northern Ireland.* London: Independent Television Authority, 1970.

JAYNES, J. *The origin of consciousness in the breakdown of the bicameral mind.* Boston: Houghton Mifflin Company, 1976.

KINSEY, A. C., POMEROY, W. B. and MARTIN, C. E. *Sexual behavior in the human male.* London: Saunders, 1948.

KINSEY, A. C. *et al. Sexual behavior in the human female.* London: Saunders, 1953.

LANGER, S. K. *Feeling and form.* London: Routledge and Kegan Paul, 1953.

LEVENTHAL, H. Toward a comprehensive theory of emotion. *Advances in Experimental Social Psychology*, 1980; **13**, 140–247.

LYNCH, J. J. *The broken heart.* New York: Basic Books, 1979.

MACCOBY, E. E. (ed.) *The development of sex differences.* Stanford, Calif.: Stanford University Press, 1966.

MOBERG, D. O. and TAVES, M. J. Church participation and adjustment in old age. In A. M. ROSE and W. A. PETERSON (eds.) *Older people and their social world.* Philadelphia: F. A. Davis, 1965.

OSGOOD, C. E., SUCI, G. J. and TANNENBAUM, P. H. *The measurement of meaning.* Urbana, Ill.: Illinois University Press, 1957.

PAHNKE, W. N. Drugs and mysticism. *International Journal of Parapsychology*, 1966; **8**, 295–314.

ROBBINS, T. and ANTHONY, D. The sociology of contemporary religious movements. *Annual Review of Sociology*, 1979; **5**, 75–89.

ROSENTHAL, R. *et al. Skill in nonverbal communication: Individual differences.* Cambridge, Mass.: Oelgeschlager, 1980.

SCHACHTER, S. The interaction of cognitive and physiological determinants of emotional states. *Advances in Experimental Social Psychology*, 1959; **1**, 49–80.

SLUGOSKI, B. R., MARCIA, J. E. and KOOPMAN, R. F. Cognitive and interactional characteristics of ego identity statuses in college males. *Journal of Personality and Social Psychology* **47**, 646–61.

SWENSON, W. M. Attitudes towards death in an aged population. *Journal of Gerontology*, 1961; **16**, 49–52.

TAJFEL, H. *Human groups and social categories.* Cambridge University Press, 1981.

THOULESS, R. H. The tendency to certainty in religious belief. *British Journal of Psychology* 1935; **26**, 16–31.

TODD, N, *Religious belief and personal construct theory*, Ph.D. thesis, Nottingham University, 1977.

ULLMAN, C. Cognitive and emotional antecedents of religious conversion. *Journal of Personality and Social Psychology*, 1982; **43**, 183–192.

WESTOFF, C. F. and RYDER, N. B. *Reproduction in the United States.* Princeton University Press, 1971.

3

Religiously based differences in approach to the psychology of religion: Freud, Fromm, Allport and Zilboorg

BENJAMIN BEIT-HALLAHMI

THE QUESTION we are dealing with here is part of the field of the sociology of psychological knowledge (Buss, 1975; Homans, 1979). It is not just an academic question, but also a question that touches on the basic methodological limitations of the study of religion. As Homans (1979) stated: 'The line separating a sociology of psychological knowledge and a psychology of psychological knowledge is not as sharply drawn as one might first suppose. Both explore an infrastructure of the superstructure of existing, conscious, and rationally explicated ideas' (p. 370). This infrastructure includes a variety of ideological approaches to the psychological study of religion.

The psychology of religion, just like any other branch of psychology, aims at achieving generalizations and discovering the universals in human behaviour. And that is why we regard religiously based differences in approaches to the psychology of religion as a problem. We are all ethnocentric to the extent that our notions of what religion is are based on a culturally skewed sample, and to the extent that our research questions, and answers, are determined by our cultural exposure to religion.

Any discipline studying religion is forced to deal with the validity of religious claims because religion typically makes rather strong and unusual claims which often enjoy a privileged status within the individual scholar's own culture. The attitude of the psychologist toward the claims of religion does have a bearing on the way it is going to be studied. Most of those who are engaged in the academic study of religion, including psychologists, have a religious axe to grind. Many are outright apologists, or reformers who want to remodel religion in order to help it survive in the modern world (Beit-Hallahmi, 1974, 1977).

Given the findings on the indifferent or negative attitudes of most social scientists and psychologists toward religion and the lack of professional interest in it, we would expect those psychologists who are interested in religion as a topic of study to be different from most of their colleagues. The stereotype of the psychologist who is interested in religion, at least among his academic colleagues, embodies the notion of strong religious commitments or frustrated theological ambitions. This stereotype seems to have much truth to it. Ragan, Malony and Beit-Hallahmi (1980), found that members of the APA who study religion tend to be religious themselves. Commitment to religion among such scholars is clear (Allport, 1950, 1978), and many see their main contribution in terms of helping religion become better and stronger (Dittes, 1967). Many have been ordained as ministers or priests and are affiliated with divinity schools, theology schools, or departments of religious studies. Personal statements by psychologists who have been involved in writing in the area of the psychology of religion (Clark, 1978; Dittes, 1978; Gorsuch, 1978; Malony, 1978; Strunk, 1978) show quite clearly that a commitment to a religious viewpoint is an important part of the motivation for their work as psychologists. Religious psychologists treat their subject-matter differently because they accord a special status to religious claims, religious institutions and individual experiences in religion. The religious psychologist will admit the similarity between religion and other belief systems, but will also emphasize the correctness of religion.

Searching in a university library for a book entitled *The Psychology of Religion*, the naive reader is likely in most cases to find a volume which is more religious than psychological. The specific religious orientation can, in most cases, be simply deduced from the author's institutional affiliation and the publisher's identity. The religionists' contributions to the psychology of religion may contain useful insights, but they are hampered by the excess baggage of theology, which to most psychologists may seem strange. The theological language used by such authors is not likely to be shared with readers outside particular traditions, while the psychological language may well be. Some of these books are scholarly, in the sense of demonstrating an excellent knowledge of psychological literature. However, the melange resulting from the combination of theology and psychology is likely to be exasperating to most psychologists. An example of such writing is Oates' (1973) book, which is a compendium of psychological theories and findings from a variety of sources, presented rather clearly but unsystematically, together with Biblical quotations and theological assertions.

In addition to apologetics in the defence of one's particular religion, there is also the phenomenon of apologetics in the defence of religion in general. This is a unique historical development, which has to be seen in its own context. It can be encountered most often in the US, and is a part of the American context. The ecumenical approach to apologetics is thoroughly American, and reflects very much the American, as opposed to the European, view of religion (Argyle and Beit-Hallahmi, 1975). It is a defence of religion as a world view and a general way of life, reflecting the notion that some religion is always better than no religion. The literature of apologetics via psychology, or "religious psychology" of all kinds, is in itself as important as a subject-matter of research for psychologists, sociologists, or historians of religions.

The literature on the psychology of religion can usefully be divided, according to its ideological bent, into the religious and the irreligious. As I have already said (Beit-Hallahmi, 1977), most psychologists who study religion are themselves religiously committed. This has obviously affected the whole tenor of the field of psychology of religion, and has contributed to its difficulties. The difference between a religious psychology and a psychology of religion is that between defending religious beliefs and explaining them. Psychology of religion treats religion as a phenomenon for systematic psychological study, while religious psychology aims at promoting religion through the adaptation and use of psychological concepts. Our division of the literature into religious psychology and psychology of religion is based on works rather than individuals. The same psychologist can be engaged in both, though in reality this is not often the case, although Allport, for example, has contributed to both aspects.

The influence of religious traditions may be reflected in the psychology of religion in three ways:

(1) a cultural influence, which determines the way religion is defined and analysed, and the kind of phenomena to be studied;
(2) exposure to specific religious phenomena, which are then generalized and regarded as universal;
(3) religious apologetics.

One's religious tradition is going to have an effect on one's work as a psychologist of religion in terms of the choice of questions for research, the interpretation of findings, and the formulation of a general theory of religion. A specific kind of religious behaviour, with which the researcher is most familiar, may become the model for religion in general, and the basis for a general theory of religion. There is no easy way of predicting a psychological theorist's approach to religion on the basis of cultural and personal background factors. We can attempt an analysis after the fact, taking into consideration long-standing cultural traditions, family and personality factors and historical developments within the theorist's lifetime that affected his particular generation.

Psychology of religion and religious background – the case of Sigmund Freud

Freud's theories of religion are certainly the most discussed and most analysed in the literature of the psychology of religion. In a particular context, two questions have been raised. First, the more general and most often raised is whether psychoanalysis in general is "Jewish" in some sense, because of

Freud's cultural background. Less often mentioned is a second question: whether Freud's views of religion have been formed by his own experiences with religion, especially of Judaism.

To what extent is psychoanalysis a product of, and reflection of, Jewish culture? This question has given rise to an enormous body of literature and scholarship, with a wide range of answers (Bakan, 1965; Jones 1953–57; Klein, 1981; Miller, 1981). Jung's comment about psychoanalysis being a "Jewish psychology" is well-known and often quoted but justifiably dismissed as a bit of anti-Jewish prejudice, and nothing more. Klein (1981) concludes that psychoanalysis in its beginning under Freud was a Jewish movement. First, because all the members of Freud's group in the early years were Jews, and they were Jews feeling alienated and threatened because of rising anti-Semitism around them. Psychoanalysis was their way of asserting themselves against a hostile world. Freud himself had no hesitation in proclaiming and asserting his Jewish identity, though this identity was more cultural than religious. He stands also for a total alienation from his ancestors' religion and identity, and for a complete alienation from religion as a cultural institution (Klein, 1981). He therefore represented a whole generation, or perhaps several generations, of secularized Jews. Homans (1982) suggests that Freud underwent a personal struggle against religious traditions, an active process which enabled him to create his own general theory of psychology. Such a struggle must have affected the way in which he viewed religion as an object of analysis for his theoretical system.

The question in this particular context is not the particularly "Jewish" nature of psychoanalysis, but the effects of Freud's own personal knowledge of religion on his theory. In other words, to what extent is Freud's work the result of his being exposed to particular religious traditions? Nobody can accuse Freud of being an apologist for any religion, or for religion in general. The issue in regard to Freud is whether his theory of religion is a reflection of his own familiarity with certain religious traditions. Bellah (1965) attempted to demonstrate the cultural limits of the Freudian interpretation of religious traditions by showing the similarities and differences between Christian and Confucian tradition in regard to father–son relations; he showed the greatness and the limitations of Freud's interpretations. Freud put the theory of the projection of family relations at the centre of his theory of religion and Bellah examines the Freudian model of father–son relations in religion as it holds up for the different cases of Christianity and Confucianism. His conclusion is that the Freudian model is found wanting when dealing with Chinese traditions; but this conclusion is not totally convincing. Bellah concedes that the basic Freudian idea has much merit in the understanding of Western culture, and that in China matters are more complicated. Freud's ethnocentrism (actually Europocentrism) can be easily pardoned in this case. He obviously did not have the familiarity, which Bellah demonstrates, with Chinese traditions, but still claimed universality for his theories. Despite obvious background limitations, it is clear that for most academic students of religion Freud's theory has remained paramount.

Religious metaphors for Freud's work can be sometimes paradoxical. Thus, G. Zilboorg (1967) says that "Like a true Christian, Freud loved and pitied man. But also like a true Jew, he was always proud of man in a melancholy way and rather serenely anxious when he contemplated the biological strivings and limitations of man and his inordinate aggression" (pp. 21–2). Freud had known best the two religious traditions of Judaism and Catholicism since, curiously enough, he was not only exposed to Judaism as a child, but also to Roman Catholicism. According to Jones (1953), Freud's nurse ". . . was a Catholic and used to take the young boy to attend the church services. She implanted in him the ideas of Heaven and Hell, and probably also those of salvation and resurrection. After returning from church the boy used to preach a sermon at home and expound God's doings" (p. 6). G. Zilboorg (1967) suggests that when Freud discussed religion ". . . he seems to have had foremost in his mind the Catholic Church; he lived most of his long life in Vienna and in the atmosphere of ancient Catholic traditions" (p. 30).

The one question that has not been dealt with adequately, in my opinion, by the many scholars who have studied the relationship between Freud's Jewish background and his theory, is that of Freud's actual Jewish education. While there is no doubt that Freud was at home with Jewish folklore, he was essentially a secularized Jew, whose schooling in formal Judaism was limited. Freud's familiarity with the Old Testament as a child, attested to by many sources (Klein, 1981), is not an indication of Orthodox schooling, but just its opposite. Orthodox schooling, even for children, means in Judaism the teaching of the Talmud, which is the essence of rabbinical Judaism. Thus, Freud's exposure to Judaism was that of a child in a family undergoing secularization, and he was sent to a general school. Nevertheless, Freud was more "at home" with Judaism than with any other tradition, and it was bound to affect his conceptions of religion in general.

If you are mainly familiar with Judaism, a tradition with little asceticism or mysticism, and with little dogma or theology, your understanding of religion in general may become slanted. It is possible that Freud substituted Old Testament mythology for the missing dogma and theology in Judaism, and thus created a framework for the work of his followers. Freud's work on religion concentrates on the phenomena of mythology and ritual, while William James started with the phenomena of individual mystical experiences. This might easily be seen as a reflection of the different religious phenomena Freud and James were exposed to. We may be certain that it was the peculiar nature of Judaism, as a religion of legalistic, compulsive practices, that led Freud to his brilliant observations on the similarities between religious and individual compulsive behaviour (Freud, 1907).

The literature of psychoanalysis, following Freud, has concentrated on religious mythology and ritual, rather than on religious experiences as its subject matter (Beit-Hallahmi, 1978). The major qualitative characteristic of psychoanalytic interpretations of religion is that they deal more often with the substance of religious beliefs and myths and less often with function and structure. A quantitative analysis of psychoanalytic writings (Beit-Hallahmi, 1978) shows that mythology is a major topic, while religious experience receives less attention that it gets from other theoretical approaches. Out of about 400 psychoanalytic studies dealing with religion along classical lines, less than 10 per cent have for a topic individual religious experiences. About 50 per cent deal with mythology, and the rest with dogma and ritual.

Methodologically, most psychoanalytic studies of religious phenomena can be characterized by their structure and style. "Modal articles" can be identified by several common characteristics, including the choice of a myth or belief to be discussed, rather than individual experience, and the use of material taken from anthropology, comparative religion, or archaeology. Often clinical material is introduced after the analysis of historical material, to show parallels between individual and cultural processes. The model for this mode of analysis is the clinical analysis of a dream or a symptom. The religious belief or behaviour is selected as the segment of human action to be analysed, in order to discover an unconscious meaning (or at least a meaning unknown to the person involved). The assumptions behind this approach are that religious acts are always psychologically meaningful, and that the same rules apply to the analysis of individual and cultural products. The psychoanalytic style of studying religion them becomes very similar to the style of clinical discussion. Nevertheless, everything said so far about Freud's theory of religion in relation to his own background is only a tentative approximation. It is somewhat frustrating to admit that Freud's interpretation of religion is a personal one, and cannot completely be predicted on the basis of background factors. Freud's case proves again (if such proof be needed) that it is impossible to predict the personal odyssey of a theorist, because there must be idiosyncratic causes for the selection of certain materials for analysis. The causes become less cultural and more personal when the cultural tradition is rejected, as in Freud's case.

We realize how paradoxical the outcomes of exposure to religious traditions may be, and how unpredictable they are, when we look briefly at the case of Erich Fromm as a psychoanalyst who chose his own way. Fromm (as his name paradoxically indicates) came from an orthodox Jewish family, which means that he had a thorough training in Judaism, and was a promising Talmudic scholar. His intimate knowledge of Jewish culture is evident in his writings. Later on, as a young man, he rejected Judaism completely, embracing, in its place, both Marxism and psychoanalysis. Given this background and development, how can we predict Fromm's attitude towards religion? The answer is that we cannot. Despite Fromm's rejection of Judaism and of Jewish identity, unlike Freud his attitude towards religion on the whole is conciliatory and even complimentary (Fromm, 1950). Freud, who knew Jewish traditions more superficially, found in them and analysed, ritual and mythology. Fromm, with his strict Talmudic training, found in Judaism (and in all other religions) an ethical concern worth preserving, and not much else. His early analysis of the beginnings of Christianity (Fromm, 1963), in itself a brilliant Marxist exercise, was something he neglected later on, as he chose to read more and more humanistic messages in religious mythology (Fromm, 1966). Fromm has become a representative of liberal Protestantism, and indeed he has been associated with this movement. Unlike Freud, Fromm came out strongly against the religious practice of his own family, which was very orthodox. But his final conception of religion was unique, especially when viewed in relation to his own early experience. He came to adopt a view of religion as an ethical system, completely remote from orthodox Judaism, as he had known it, and much closer to liberal Protestantism. The case of Erich Fromm may be put somewhere between Freud and Allport, as a person, and a theory, both Americanized, or, as some would put it, sanitized and sterilized. In moving from his initial Marxism and psychoanalysis, in their radical forms, to a later version of liberal Protestantism the case of Fromm should provide much stimulation, and more work for historians of ideas and for biographers.

Psychology of religion and religious background – the case of Gordon W. Allport

The psychology of religion in its American beginnings (Beit-Hallahmi, 1974) between 1880 and 1930, was the study of Protestant religious experience, with adolescent "conversion" becoming its modal behaviour expression. The writing of William James, the academic psychology of religion, and the work of Gordon W. Allport can all be regarded as growing out of an American Protestant tradition. Both James and Allport represent liberal American Protestantism in the process of becoming more individualized and more psychologized.

William James can be viewed as a representative of liberal Protestantism when describing religion as a totally individual experience. James's 1902 (1961) famous definition of religion embodies this approach as "... the feelings, acts, and experiences of individual men in their solitude, so far as they happen themselves to stand in relation to whatever they may consider the divine" (p. 42). Parenthically, I might mention that Maslow's (1964) concept of peak experiences is another idea typical of American liberal Protestantism, although one presented by a secularized Jew. There is still plenty of room for research on Maslow and on his religious background and transformations.

Allport's *The individual and his religion* (1950) is a masterpiece in the William James tradition, and deserves a place among the classics in the psychology of religion. In it Allport emphasizes that individual, subjective religious feelings are richer and livelier than is institutional religion, and that these uniquely individual experiences should be the subject-matter of the psychology of religion. The kind of material that a theorist selects for analysis is clearly the basis for his theory of religion. Freud selected mythology, and the image of God the father as the subject-matter for his analysis of religion. Allport, in the Jamesian tradition, selected individual, conscious experiences, in which the self is the centre. Against the Freudian concept of a dark and childish unconscious which creates the myth of an omnipotent father, Allport proposed to observe the sunny, mature self, confronting the world as it is.

Allport can rightly be seen as the antithesis to Freud: a man at peace with his ancestors' faith, carrying on old traditions with optimism and liberalism. Against Freud's Old World pessimism, Allport is an American of Protestant, Positive Thinking, a secure insider to Freud's outsiderliness in relation to every tradition. Allport's attitude towards religion is best expressed in the concluding paragraph of his *chef d'oeuvre*: "A man's religion is the audacious bid he makes to bind himself to creation and the Creator. It is his ultimate attempt to enlarge and to complete his own personality by finding the supreme context in which he rightly belongs" (Allport, 1950, p. 142).

Allport is pro-religious, but not, to use his own term (cf. Allport and Ross, 1967) "indiscriminately pro-religious". He is not in favour of every kind of religion, but in favour only of his own kind, a liberal religiosity. Allport therefore favours a mature, "healthy" religion, which is how he defines it: ". . . a disposition, built up through experience, to respond favourably, and in certain habitual ways, to conceptual objects and principles that the individual regards as of ultimate importance in his own life, and as having to do with what he regards as permanent or central in the nature of things . . ." (1950, p. 56). This indeed reflects the liberal Protestant theology of "ultimate concerns", the height of "healthy-minded" abstraction in its flight from folk religion, with its mythology, and its retreat before the advance of science. This definition is indeed so abstract, and so healthy-minded, that it can cover any kind of "ultimate concern", from that of a sports team to a political ideology. Despite the generality, which makes it useless to other theorists, this definition is important in conveying Allport's sincerity and optimism.

Some of the differences between Allport and Freud can be tied to historical differences between Europe and the United States. The nature of dominant traditions and the different place of religious institutions in society led to the gap between Freud's pessimism and Allport's (naive, to some) optimism, and to the gap between conceptions regarding the role of religion in individual and social life. Allport came out in defence of liberal Protestantism and against conservative Protestantism in his work on religiosity and social prejudices. The whole issue of the relationship between modes of religiosity and society's prejudices, which has received so much attention in the literature since the Second World War (Allport and Kramer, 1946; Allport and Ross, 1967; Gorsuch and Aleshire, 1974) is merely a question of the self-image of liberal

Protestant American psychologists when confronted with the realities of their society.

Religious psychologists are preoccupied with questions of the positive and negative effects of religious beliefs and practices, and with the effects of religion on personality functioning. The latter can be seen as the legacy of Jamesian pragmatism and the functionalist school in psychology, combined with the stand of an apologist. The differences in approach between religious psychology, the psychology of religion and the social psychology of religion can be best illustrated with a concrete example from questions about the correlation between religiosity and prejudice.

The history of research on this question is well known (cf. Argyle and Beit-Hallahmi, 1975). There has been a great number of studies since 1945 showing that in the English-speaking world there is usually a positive correlation between conventional religiosity and holding various social prejudices, including racial prejudice. Religious psychologists react to this finding with disappointment, and distinguish between those who are both deeply religious and less prejudiced, and the majority of conventionally religious people, who are prejudiced (Allport and Ross, 1967). Irreligious psychologists deal with this question as part of the social psychology of religion by pointing to a variety of factors in religion as an institution, and in the society around it. Argyle and Beit-Hallahmi (1975) present a social psychological view, which emphasizes the correlational nature of these findings and their social context. Their view is that religion does not cause prejudice, but that religiosity is, in most cases, part of a social psychological complex which includes some overall conventionality and conservatism. While the social-psychological findings remain the same, their interpretation changes so that church members become more prejudiced than non-church members for social reasons. Yet religious psychologists have put much effort into showing that "good religion" is correlated with less prejudice, although "good religion" represents only a small social minority and does not affect the general correlation. But this question, which grew out of ethnocentric interests and a specific cultural situation, turned out to have a general significance, and according to Allport's (1966) and Freud's (1922) formulations may have much to do with the basic nature of religion as a group orientation. When studied in other contexts the same relationships have been found. Thus, what started as a parochial issue has become almost a universal for the psychology of religion.

Apologetics: psychoanalysis as the stimulus

The literature on religious apologetics in relation to psychology, with its variety of headings, is enormous and complex. Apologetic literature on the psychology of religion, and especially through psychoanalysis, attempts to reconcile religious traditions and modern secular views. In the case of psychoanalysis the job may be objectively difficult, but is not insurmountable for the true apologist. Psychoanalysis, as a general personality theory, and through its specific treatment of religion, has been the stimulus to a flood of reactions from individual believers and religious institutions (Beit-Hallahmi, 1978, 1984). These have been of two kinds: one rejecting and the other conventionally apologetic. Thomas Merton (1948), for example, rejected psychoanalysis completely and denounced its basic approach. R. S. Lee (1948), on the other hand, found that although Freud was wrong about religion, his ideas on other subjects were actually supportive of Christian doctrine.

What makes psychoanalytic apologetics so interesting is the fact that it embraces psychoanalysis, while rejecting psychoanalytic views of religion. When a religionist rejects psychoanalysis altogether, no effort is involved and little intellectual energy is spent. The situation becomes more complex, and more interesting, when psychoanalysis is accepted as an essentially valid theory except in regard to religion. The further step is then taken of trying to prove that psychoanalysis actually supports one's religion. Everything, or almost everything, psychoanalysis says is shown to be prefigured in the religious traditions involved. The typical psychological apologist for religion appears to say that "Freud was right on everything, except religion." It seems rather strange that a theory is accepted as valid for the general understanding of human behaviour, and considered totally invalid for understanding a specific behaviour which seems so much a part of the general theory.

Gregory Zilboorg – a case study of Christian psychoanalytic apologetics

Gregory Zilboorg[1] who was born in Russia of Orthodox Jewish parents in 1890, abandoned his parents' faith in his 20s, and became a member of the Society of Friends after moving to the US at the age of 29. After becoming a psychoanalyst, and a leading scholar of the history of psychiatry, he flirted with the Episcopal (Anglican) Church, but found himself more strongly attracted to Roman Catholicism, which he officially joined in 1954, only 5 years before he died. In his wife's words "Gregory died a good psychoanalyst and a good Catholic" (M. S. Zilboorg, 1967, p. ix). Being a brilliant man and a serious scholar, Zilboorg's writings on psychoanalysis and religion over the last 20 years of his life constitute fascinating material for the understanding of apologetics in psychology. Zilboorg was not just an apologist for Catholicism. he was defending religion as a cultural institution against the psychoanalytic approach.

His solution to the challenge of modern psychology in general, and of psychoanalysis in particular, is to maintain that the soul exists, in addition to the psychic apparatus, and ". . . that what is true in psychology may not be true in traditional apologetics, Catholic, Protestant or secular, and *vice versa* – that the psychic apparatus is not the soul and the soul is not the psyche" (G.

Zilboorg, 1967, p. 14). So what is involved here is not only the defence of religion, but a defence of the soul. And, moreover, according to Zilboorg, "Unless . . . a truly scientific differentiation between psyche and soul is made, a proper understanding and acceptance of psychoanalysis is practically impossible" (p. 17).

As an apologist, Zilboorg takes the familiar step of discovering that there is actually no contradiction between psychoanalysis and religious tradition, for the former actually supports the latter. This is done by reinterpreting psychoanalysis and bending it slightly. To quote G. Zilboorg (1967):

> Let us take as a simple example St. Thomas's assertion that sensuality is the source of evil and misuse of reason. The scientific findings of Freud demonstrated that hedonism and infantile sexuality, if persisting beyond a certain period of life leads to mental illness and other forms of maladjustment. Here we have the scientific corroboration of the claims made by both Aristotle and St. Thomas.

And further:

> What does matter is that Freud, unconcerned with ethics or religion, arrived at the conclusion that the life of man is based on creative love, on constant domestication of his aggression, on constant harmonization of the animal within him with his humanness, on the constant living of his life on the basis of love and reason instead of hate and impulse. The conclusions imposed themselves upon Freud by the very evidential force of the psychological phenomena which he observed clinically. It is not necessary to call upon complex philosophical speculations or to exercise much logical strain to see that Freud, unbeknown to himself, thus established an empirical basis of life which is in total conformity with the Christian ideal (p. 38).

And further:

> One should not overlook the fact that even the concept of original sin or of the original fall of man finds its empirical counterpart in the findings of psychoanalysis . . . [for] without knowing it in advance, Freud soon discovered that he was studying the psychological reactions of man in the state of sin; he was at once confronted with . . . man's perennial, unconscious sense of guilt (p. 45).

It may occur to us that the logic of the case may be slightly different, since Freud does indeed represent and follow the accepted ideals in Western civilization of broader cultural traditions, which in turn have been influenced by Christianity.

In Zilboorg's world-view there can be no contradiction, by definition, between religion and psychological theories, or between religion and science:

> Psychoanalysis itself, like physics or mathematics, permits of a number of generalizations and syntheses; but not a single one of these scientific disciplines, nor all these disciplines taken together, can be made into a philosophy of life. It is the mass of empirical data which these disciplines offer to philosophy and religion which represents their true contribution to philosophy and religion. In this respect, despite its desultory excursions into materialistic philosophy and even antireligious intellectualism, psychoanalysis has made a major contribution to the greater understanding of religious life. This again is as it should be, because no true empirical findings of facts in human nature can contradict the fundamental religious truths; what is more, the more correct and the more fundamental these facts are the more they are bound to support rather than to contradict the religious truths dealing with the destiny of man (p. 68).

Zilboorg quotes Pope Pius XII in his message to Catholic psychologists (1953):

> In your studies and scientific research, rest assured that no contradiction is possible between the certain truths of faith and established scientific facts. Nature, no less than revelation, proceeds from God, and God cannot contradict Himself. Do not be dismayed even if you hear the contrary affirmed insistently, even though research may have to wait for centuries to find the solution of the apparent opposition between science and faith (p. 277).

A typical accusation of religious apologists against Freud is that he had selected unrepresentative samples in his study of religious phenomena. Zilboorg therefore accuses Freud of concentrating too much on religious ritual and states that "It would appear the religion Freud had in mind was not really religion but the somewhat sentimental, somewhat anxious attitude toward God on the part of the man in the street. It is the anxious, cowering belief, of the little man, who feels the burden of what Freud calls 'the forcible imposition of mental infantilism' " (p. 221). It seems that not only Freud, but all psychologists of religion are primarily interested in "the man in the street" and his experiences, and only to a lesser extent in the experiences of some theological elite (Beit-Hallahmi, 1984).

Moreover, G. Zilboorg (1967) claims that Freud was unconsciously attracted to ". . . the Christian faith to which he seemed to gravitate so intensely and which he wished to deny just as intensely" (p. 154). In all fairness, it should be recognized that Zilboorg was a brilliant scholar, and in his writings made substantive contributions not only to apologetics, but also to the psychoanalytic understanding of religion.

Jewish psychoanalytic apologetics

Jewish apologetic literature is no different from any other kind of apologetics, and as an example of modern Jewish apologetics in response to, and in debt to, psychoanalysis, we can take Spero's (1980) collection of essays. The treatment of psychoanalysis in this book is typical of the literature of apologetics. Spero's approach to psychoanalysis is that of the apologist who desires the use of psychoanalytic theories of personality, and psychoanalytic techniques of psychotherapy, but rejects Freud's application of psychoanalysis to the understanding of religion.

Moreover, Spero shows an amazing misunderstanding of what the psychoanalytic theory of religion is all about; amazing because Spero obviously has read widely in psychoanalysis. Thus he states that "In the Freudian view, what is most neurotic about the individual who dons *tefilin* ten times a day is not this single compulsion, but rather his overall interest in religion" (p. 194). This is a clear misstatement of the Freudian position, and I doubt very much whether any psychoanalyst would subscribe to it. Religion, in the Freudian view, is not a matter of private neurosis and religious individuals are no more likely to be neurotic than are other individuals. The individual interested in religion reflects a cultural problem, not an individual one.

Topics discussed in Spero's book include "sin and neurosis", dream psychology, substance abuse, homosexuality (which is, according to the author, still both a sin and a neurosis), countertransference, contraception and abortion. In every case the concept, or the problem, is discussed from the point of view of the *halakha*, often starting with Talmudic sources, and then studied from the point of view of psychology, mostly psychoanalysis. In many cases an attempt is made to show that Talmudic insights are anticipations of later psychological notions, and in all cases an attempt is made to reconcile the two traditions. Spero attempts to show that most of the good ideas in modern psychology were already known to Talmudic sages. Such attempts are not usually very convincing. The Talmudic literature is indeed a treasury of brilliant observations on human behaviour and human history, and of profound wisdom and shining wit. Still, this does not mean, as Spero seems to believe, that every single modern idea has been anticipated by the Talmudic sages. Unsystematic anticipations of many modern ideas are often found in ancient writings, but these disparate anticipations are not equivalent to coherent theories. If you look hard enough, you will find anticipations of Keynesian economics, psychoanalysis, and quantum physics in ancient literature, but the ancient sages were not economists, psychologists or physicists.

Ethnocentrism – inevitable, avoidable, and useful

Our pervasive and inevitable ethnocentrism may be most in evidence when we attempt to produce a general theory, valid for all cultures, or when we examine a culture other than our own. There are four types of ethnocentric errors in the interpretation of another culture.

Type I, in which the ethnocentric observer expresses his amazement at the other culture, while ignoring the existence of the same amazing elements in his own culture.
Type II, in which the observer generalizes from his own culture to the whole of mankind.
Type III, in which the observer creates the finding by his own idiosyncratic behaviour, which in turn leads "the natives" to act in a special way, then perceived as normal for the native culture.
Type IV, in which the observer misinterprets an item by not knowing its cultural context.

If there are indeed universal elements in religious behaviour, then ethnocentrism is an easier problem, because we are always sampling the universal. If there are no universals in religion, then ethnocentrism is indeed a true Procrustean bed.

Bellah (1965) has given us a warning against ethnocentrism, together with an example of how it should be recognized and handled. Being aware of one's ethnocentric viewpoint is the beginning of wisdom. The best antidote for our inevitable ethnocentrism is our awareness of it and our collaboration with other scholars studying religion, in the fields of anthropology, sociology and history. Before formulating any general notions about a psychological theory of religion, we should develop our "anthropological consciousness" and our historical awareness, thus keeping the psychology of religion among the human and humane sciences.

There is room and need for further research on the relationship between the personal religious background of a researcher and the content of research in terms of themes, formulations, questions and answers. We may even limit ourselves, and this could be a useful scholarly exercise, to the various definition of religion adopted by scholars. We should then relate specific definitions to their proposers' experiences with religion.

Ethnocentrism, in the sense of being familiar with one religious tradition by dint of one's own cultural background, is inevitable. It should be recognized and then utilized to our advantage as psychologists, as we struggle to interpret that which we know well. Freud's greatness lies in his being able to do just that. We all aim at interpreting the universals of religion, while we inevitably know only the particular and the immediate. Ethnocentrism can become an advantage as we delve deeper into what we are familiar with. Each one of us should openly acknowledge our own ethnocentrism or anthropocentrisms and then proceed to use that familiarity as an important weapon. Being thoroughly familiar with one religious tradition is a source of strength if it enables us to capture its essence. If indeed there are universal elements in religious traditions, then they should be in evidence in all traditions. Being an expert on one religion thus becomes the source of a potential universalism, rather than a hindrance, as long as we are cautious in generalizing from specifics. Looking for the general in the particular rather than generalizing from particulars should be our preferred method.

References

ALLPORT, G. W. *The individual and his religion.* New York: Macmillan, 1950.
ALLPORT, G. W. The religious context of prejudice. *Journal for the Scientific Study of Religion,* 1966; **5,** 447–457.
ALLPORT, G. W. *Waiting for the Lord: 33 meditations on God and man.* New York: Macmillan, 1978.
ALLPORT, G. W. and KRAMER, B. M. Some roots of prejudice. *Journal of Psychology,* 1946; **22,** 9–39.

ALLPORT, G. W. and ROSS, J. M. Personal religious orientation and prejudice. *Journal of Personality and Social psychology*, 1967; **5**, 432–443.
ARGYLE, M. and BEIT-HALLAHMI, B. *The social psychology of religion*. London: Routledge & Kegan Paul, 1975.
BAKAN, D. *Sigmund Freud and the Jewish mystical tradition*. New York: Shocken, 1965.
BEIT-HALLAHMI, B. *Research in religious behavior: selected readings*. Belmont, California: Brooks/Cole, 1973.
BEIT-HALLAHMI, B. Psychology of religion, 1880–1930: the rise and fall of a psychological movement. *Journal of the History of the Behavioral Sciences*, 1974: **10**, 84–90.
BEIT-HALLAHMI, B. Curiosity, doubt and devotion. The beliefs of psychologists and the psychology of religion. In H. N. MALONY (ed.), *Current perspectives in the psychology of religion*. Grand Rapids, Michigan: Eerdmans Publishing Company, 1977, pp. 301–391.
BEIT-HALLAHMI, B. *Psychoanalysis and religion: a bibliography*. Norwood PA: Norwood Editions, 1978.
BEIT-HALLAHMI, B. Psychology and religion. In M. H. BORNSTEIN (ed.), *Psychology and other disciplines*. Hillsdale, NJ: Lawrence Erlbaum Associates, 1984.
BELLAH, R. N. Father and son in Christianity and Confucianism. *The Psychoanalytic Review*, 1965; **52**, 236–258.
BUSS, A. R. The emerging field of the sociology of psychological knowledge. *American psychologist*, 1975; **30**, 988–1002.
CLARK, W. H. A follower of William James. In H. N. MALONY (ed.), *Psychology and faith: the Christian experience of eighteen psychologists*. Washington DC: University Press of America, 1978, pp. 85–96.
DITTES, J. E. *The Church in the way*. New York: Scribner's, 1967.
DITTES, J. E. An enabling ministry in academics and administration. In H. N. MALONY (ed.), *Psychology and faith: the Christian experience of eighteen psychologists*. Washington, DC: University Press of America, 1978; pp. 212–218.
FREUD, S. Obsessive acts and religious practices. *Collected Papers*, London: Hogarth Press, 1924 (1907).
FREUD, S. *Group psychology and the analysis of the ego*. London: Hogarth Press, 1922.
FROMM, E. *Psychoanalysis and religion*. New Haven: Yale University Press, 1950.
FROMM, E. *The dogma of Christ*. New York, Holt, 1963.
FROMM, E. *You shall be as Gods*. New York: Holt, 1966.
GORSUCH, R. L. Research psychology: An indirect ministry to the ministers. In H. N. MALONY (ed.), *Psychology and faith: the Christian experience of eighteen psychologists*. Washington, DC: University Press of America, 1978; pp. 220–232.
GORSUCH, R. L. and ALESHIRE, D. Christian faith and ethnic prejudice: A review and interpretation of research. *Journal for the Scientific Study of Religion*, 1974; **13**, 281–307.
HOMANS, P. The case of Freud and Carl Rogers. In A. R. BUSS (ed.), *Psychology in social context*. New York: Irvington, 1979, pp. 367–393.
HOMANS, P. A personal struggle with religion: significant fact in the lives and work of the first psychologists. *Journal of Religion*, 1982; **62**, 128–144.
JAMES, W. *The varieties of religious experience*. New York: Collier, 1961 (1902).
JONES, E. *The life and work of Sigmund Freud*, 3 vols. London: Hogarth Press, 1953–57.
KLEIN, D. E. *Jewish origins of the psychoanalytic movement*. New York: Praeger, 1981.
LEE, R. S. *Freud and Christianity*. London: Clarke & Co., 1948.
MALONY, H. N. The psychologist–Christian. In H. N. MALONY (ed.), *Psychology and faith: the Christian experience of eighteen psychologists*. Washington, DC: University Press of America, 1978.
MASLOW, A. *Religions, values and peak experiences*. Columbus: Ohio State University Press, 1964.
MERTON, T. *The seven storey mountain*. New York: Harcourt, Brace, 1948.
MILLER, J. Interpretations of Freud's Jewishness, 1924–1974. *Journal of the History of the Behavioral Sciences*, 1981; **17**, 357–374.
OATES, W. A. *The psychology of religion*. Waco, TX: Word Publishers, 1963.
PIUS XII, *Acta Apostolice Sedis*, 1953, 45.
RAGAN, C., MALONY, H. N. and BEIT-HALLAHMI, B. Psychologists and religion – Professional factors and personal beliefs. *Review of Religious Research*, 1980; **21**, 208–217.

SPERO, M. H. *Judaism and psychology*. New York: Ktav, 1980.
STRUNK, O., Jr., All things hold together. IN H. N. MALONY (ed.), *Psychology and faith: the Christian experience of eighteen psychologists*. Washington, DC: University Press of America, 1978, pp. 234–242.
ZILBOORG, G., *Psychoanalysis and religion*. London: Allen & Unwin, 1967.
ZILBOORG, M. S. Introduction. G. Zilboorg, *Psychoanalysis and religion*. London: Allen & Unwin, 1967.

4

Social anthropology and the psychology of religion

PAUL HEELAS

. . . the necessity, to which nearly every science is subject, of making assumptions belonging to the domain of another science (Rivers, 1916, p. 3).

Introduction

According to Evans-Pritchard, one of the most influential anthropologists of religion, ritual is,

a creation of society, not of individual reasoning or emotion, though it may satisfy both; and it is for this reason that Durkheim tells us that a psychological interpretation of a social fact is invariably a wrong interpretation (1965a, p. 46).

Yet social anthropologists, intent on defending the autonomy of their discipline, have in the main adopted a negative attitude towards the threat of psychological "reductionism". A social or cultural phenomenon, so the orthodoxy runs, should be explained by reference to other phenomena of the same social or collective standing. The point of view formulated by Needham is widespread: "it seems fairly certain that causal argument in terms of sentiments (or any other psychological factors) have not been of pragmatic value in sociological analysis" (1962, p. 122). In short, and I cannot resist citing Lewis on the matter, psychology and psychoanalysis have become "increasingly remote realms, into which only the brave (e.g. John Layard and Gregory Bateson) – or very foolish (if not 'mad') – have dared to venture from time-to-time" (1977, p. 3).

So what possible justification is there for including a chapter on social anthropological accounts of religion in a volume designed to consider the current status of the psychology of religion? Justification is in fact easy to provide: whatever anthropologists might have said about the unprofitable consequences of turning to psychology, they have actually made frequent recourse to psychological assumptions and theories. Psychology has been much more important than most anthropologists have been prepared to acknowledge. The "psychology of religion" is in fact alive and reasonably well in the hands of avowedly anti-psychological social anthropologists.

34

As well as discussing why this should be so, I shall summarize the nature and scope of psychological theorizing in anthropological accounts of religion.[1] My intention is twofold: to provide psychologists of religion with a guide to the main ways in which anthropologists, so to speak, work as psychologists of religion and to consider the status of this work. The second of these intentions is the more difficult to fulfil. It involves examining the debate within anthropology as to the validity of psychological explanations, as well as how the application of psychological theory is to be gauged from the perspective of psychology itself. It involves, in short, all the issues raised when one asks how psychological theories can be successfully applied to explain ethnographic material.

A guide to psychological explanations

Rather than attempt to survey the numerous ways in which anthropologists have applied psychological assumptions and theories to explain religious phenomena, I will concentrate on paradigmatic cases which illuminate the characteristics of more important applications. I also concentrate on the work of the anthropological "school" I know the best, that is the British social anthropological tradition. Space does not permit consideration of the American culture and personality theorists, American psychological anthropologists, or the current French interest in psychoanalytic approaches. I will, however, make reference to one psychological anthropologist, Spiro, because he is unusually exact in his discussion of the different ways of using psychology.

Another introductory observation concerns my use of the term "religion". When I use this term I have in mind a somewhat broader range of phenomena than the term connotes for us in the West. I include discussion of magic, witchcraft, rituals of rebellion, superstitions, and so on, on the grounds that phenomena of this variety cannot be distinguished from what is more explicitly "religious" in most societies.

Finally, and by way of introduction, I need to say something about the way I have classified psychological explanations. When anthropologists turn to psychology to help explain religious phenomena they almost invariably think in terms of such notions as "origin", "ground", "basis", "cause", "persistence", "process", "motivation", and "function". They are asking, "How does this ritual function?", or "Why do participants persist in practising (erroneous) magical activities?" To clarify things, I make an initial distinction between theories which treat religion as the consequence of antecedent conditions, and theories which treat religion as an antecedent state of affairs (thereby having consequences for participants and their institutions). This distinction is not the same as that between religion as caused and religion as functioning, since I agree with those who hold that "functional" *explanations*

N.B. [1]Notes to this chapter on page 51.

actually take a causal form. Thus the explanations to be discussed are all causal in nature.

A second distinction is between endogenous and exogenous theories. The former direct attention to inherent psychological processes and states; the latter to psychologically mediated but external states of affairs, most usually social experiences. It should be borne in mind, however, that few if any theories belong in their entirety to one camp or the other. It is a matter of emphasis.

Religion as a consequence

Endogenous explanations of origins

Durkheim wrote that "every time a social phenomenon is *directly* explained by a psychological phenomenon, we may be sure that the explanation is false" (orig. 1895, 1964, p. 104, with my italics). "Directly" means that social phenomena are being explained in terms of what now would be called the "sociobiological approach". Durkheim pilloried theories which sought the origins of religion in innate (endogenous) drives, needs, emotions, desires, or instincts. Thirty years later, however, Malinowski advanced just such a psychological explanation of magic:

> We have seen that all the instincts and emotions, all practical activities, lead man into impasses where gaps in his knowledge and the limitations of his early power of observation and reason betray him at a crucial moment. Human *organism* reacts to this in *spontaneous* outbursts, in which rudimentary modes of behaviour and rudimentary beliefs in their efficacy are engendered. Magic fixes upon these beliefs and rudimentary rites and standardizes them into permanent traditional forms (1925, p. 82, my italics).

Sociobiological-cum-psychological theorizing is not uncommon, as the following examples show. Beattie's explanation of magic argues that magic is primarily expressive (e.g. of wishes) and he explained the instrumentality of magic in terms of a psychological process involving "the imputation of causal efficacy to the symbolic expression itself" (1970, p. 241). Needham explained witch images in terms of "the unconscious generation of the archetypes . . . [and] the likelihood that these complex images are the products of genetically inherited predispositions" (1978, p. 49). Lévi-Strauss' explanation of myth and the "savage mind" argued that the savage mind is dominated by "intellectual requirements, rather than instead of satisfying needs". He writes of the "demand for order" which underlies much primitive thought, and treats myth as the expression of fundamental properties of the human mind (1962, pp. 11, 10). Spiro's explanation of religious beliefs was that "everywhere man has a desire to know, to understand, to find meaning, and I would suggest . . . that religious beliefs are *held* . . . because, in the absence of competitive explanations, they satisfy this desire" (1966, p. 110 (my italics); cf. Horton,

1967), and Kennedy's explanation of witchcraft regarded it as "primarily a manifestation of strongly held negative emotions" (1967, p. 223).

Exogenous explanations of origins

The most cursory reading of Durkheim's *The elementary forms of the religious life* (1912) shows it to be peppered with psychological claims, but of an exogenous variety. His approach is clearly stated in *The rules of sociological method* (1895) where we read that "collective representations, *emotions*, and tendencies are caused not by certain states of the consciousness of individuals but by the conditions in which the social group in its totality is placed" (1964, p. 106, my italics). Emotions as well as collective representations are generated by antecedent conditions found in the social realm. In fact it is the generation of emotions which is held to provide the mechanism whereby social experiences are transformed into, or create, religious representations:

> We have seen that if collective life awakens religious thought on reaching a certain degree of intensity, it is because it brings about a state of effervescence which changes the conditions of psychic activity. Vital energies are over-excited, passions more active, sensations stronger . . . A man does not recognize himself; he feels himself transformed and consequently he transforms the environment which surrounds him. In order to account for the very particular impressions which he receives, he attributes to the things with which he is in most direct contact properties which they have not, exceptional powers and virtues . . . In a word, above the real world where his profane life passes he has placed another . . . (Durkheim, 1915, p. 422).

It is interesting to note that Durkheim's theory of religion is essentially the same as Freud's. There *are* differences since the latter is more sophisticated psychologically, and emphasizes familial rather than general social contexts, but both saw religion as a psychologically mediated response to social experiences. Whether derived from Durkheim or from Freud, exogenous explanations of origins are quite frequently met in the anthropological literature. For example, Fortes, in his illuminating analysis of Tallensi religion, comes to the conclusion that "all the concepts and beliefs we have examined are religious extrapolations of the experiences generated in the relationships between parents and children" (1959, p. 78). Favouring Durkheim rather than Freud, Radcliffe-Brown treated rites as "the regulated symbolic expressions of certain sentiments" and suggested that "religion is everywhere an expression in one form or another of a sense of dependence on a power outside ourselves, a power which we may speak of as a spiritual or moral power" (1952, p. 157).

Finally, mention can be made of Hallpike's recent theory which, deriving as it does from Piaget, combines the exogenous with the endogenous. Hallpike's intention was to elucidate the "foundations" of primitive thought, and he argues, for example, that Dinka religion is largely explicable if it is hypothesized that members of this society think as young children. Dinka therefore function at a pre-operational level. Supposedly unable to differentiate between or dissociate the psychical and the physical, the knower and the known, they ascribe what we would call "external reality" to "subjective mental events" (1976, p. 259; cf. 1979). Such conceptual realism explains why the Dinka lack mentalistic notions (such as "mind" itself) and why they seem to envisage their "mental" processes and states as being under the control of external agencies or religious Powers.

Endogenous and exogenous explanations of persistence and motivation

In a widely cited paper, "Religion: problems of definition and explanation" (1966), Spiro accepts that theories of origins cannot be tested, and turns instead to establish the antecedent conditions "in whose absence the variable to be explained could not exist" (*ibid.*, p. 99). In other words, rather than conjecturing how religious beliefs and practices come into existence in the first place, he asks why, especially in closed societies, each new generation comes to believe and practise in a traditional fashion.[2] Looking more closely at his theory of motivation (that is, why people come to act in a religious way), we find his basic assumption is that "all human behavior, except reflexive behavior, is purposive; i.e. it is instigated by the intention of satisfying some need" (*ibid.*, p. 106). What then are the needs which motivate religious behaviour? They are the needs which, in the absence of alternative means of satisfaction (notice the role of this exogenous factor) are best satisfied by engaging in available religious activity. As an example, Spiro asks us to consider societies in which social organization and morality results in repressed hostility. These demand satisfaction or catharsis (notice the role of this endogenous, Freudian, assumption). Satisfaction is facilitated by malevolent superhuman beings, since

> Repressed hostility motives can be displaced and/or projected in beliefs in, and rituals designed for protection against, these malevolent beings. Prevented from expressing his hostility against his fellows, the religious actor can satisfy this desire symbolically through religion (*ibid.*, p. 116).

And, of course, what is satisfying is likely to encourage engagement and persistence.

Motivational explanations are perhaps most commonly encountered in attempts to explain changes of frequency in religious activity. Lewis, for example, argues that there is a connection between the incidence of stress and possession by malevolent spirits. People "allow" themselves to be possessed because it is to their advantage.

> We have traced the widespread ascription of misfortune and illness to amoral peripheral spirits which plague the weak and down-trodden. Those men and women who experience these afflictions do so regularly in situations of stress and conflict with their superiors, and, in the attention and respect which they temporarily attract, influence their masters. Thus adversity is turned to advantage, and spirit possession of this type can be seen to represent an oblique strategy of attack (1971, p. 117).

Social psychological explanations of the incidence of witchcraft accusations provide another illustration of motivational analyses. Accusations are held to increase when individual tensions and anxieties rise, especially during periods of social unrest. In terms of the frustration–aggression hypothesis, frustration then increases and is vented on socially acceptable targets which have proved satisfactory (or cathartic) and so are selected more often during periods of repression (see Trevor-Roper, 1967, and Bohannon, 1958).

Religion as an antecedent

From this perspective, more closely associated with the social psychology of Weber than with that of Durkheim, religion is taken as the "given" and attention is paid to its psychological effects on participants (and, through their psychology, on other institutions). This perspective is often discussed under the heading of "functional theory" but, as I indicated earlier, any genuinely functionalist explanation is really a causal theory. However, this is not to say that there are no functionalist accounts in which the functions or impact of religion are simply described. After considering some accounts of this variety, I will turn to explanations which focus on the psychological processes held to cause the observed psychological effects of religious life.

Functionalist descriptions

Radcliffe-Brown urged that "we must try to discover the effects of active participation in a particular cult, first the direct effects on the individuals and then the further effects on the society of which these individuals are members" (1952, p. 169). He supposed that religions function to inculcate socially valuable sentiments. Thus religious ceremonies are:

> the means by which the society acts upon its individual members and keeps alive in their minds a certain system of sentiments. Without the ceremonial these sentiments would not exist, and without them the social organization in its actual form could not exist (1948, p. 324).

Radcliffe-Brown (1952) was prepared to specify several such sentiments, including the anxiety instilled by religious taboos in connection with Andaman childbirth and the sense of dependence in connection with ancestor worship. Unfortunately, he gives remarkably little evidence to support these and similar assertions.

More unfortunately, and I shall return to this point, the supposedly exact ethnographic accounts of a great many anthropologists who have "recorded" the impact of religions on their participants are similarly devoid of the degree of rigour which is elsewhere demanded by anthropologists, let alone by psychologists.

Explanations of psychological impact

An essential feature of the ethnographic task should be to describe, as accurately as possible, the impact of religious life on the motivations, sense of identity, emotions, and so on, of participants. It is also important to explain any observed impact. So what progress has been made in developing causal theories to account for the psychological changes which have been "reported"?

Until recently anthropologists basically had two options to turn to to find their theories, in the psychoanalytic and the behavioural traditions. Given the greater relevance and theoretical interest of the former, it is not surprising to find widespread reliance on psychodynamic theory.

For Malinowski, as for Freud, magic is a way of satisfying desires (and the anxieties attendant until they are satisfied): what cannot be done in reality (e.g. making it rain) is obtained by means of the spell (so that it is then believed that it will rain). In this way release of tension or catharsis occurs, and hope is restored (see Malinowski, 1925). For Gluckman, rituals of rebellion in south-east Africa work to sustain the social order by virtue of a psychologically efficacious cultural mechanism: rebellions facilitate catharsis, both in the sense of purging anti-social emotions and, apparently, purifying socially desirable ones (see Gluckman, 1963, esp. p. 126). And for Spiro, religion allows "the disguised expression of repressed motives" and so, among other functions, "reduces the probability of psychotic distortion of desires, thereby providing a society with psychologically healthy members" (1966, p. 121).

It would be tedious to list any more examples of the application of psychodynamic theory, especially as so many hinge on the hypothesis that religion facilitates the relatively safe (because, in Spiro's sense "disguised") expression of repressed emotions, thus in turn facilitating their catharsis and their dissipation or satisfaction. It is interesting to note, however, the appeal exercised by the catharsis hypothesis; even such an avowedly anti-psychological anthropologist as Evans-Pritchard makes use of it (1937; 1965b, p. 95).

As I have already implied, behavioural theory has been little used by anthropologists of religion. But there is today a third option for those seeking to explain the impact of religion on its participants, which was formulated by Schachter (1964). This is basically a cognitive theory which maintains that cognitive appraisal performs a crucial function in the constitution of emotional states. Anthropologists have in fact predated Schachter, in that they have for long *claimed* that religions provide cultural appraisal models. And not simply anthropologists, since Radcliffe-Brown refers to later Confucian philosophers, to comment that "the chief point of their theory is that . . . rites serve to 'regulate' and 'refine' human feelings". He also cites Loisy, who claimed that "man is so made that he becomes more firmly fixed in his sentiments by expressing them" (Radcliffe-Brown, 1952, pp. 159, 174).

Geertz has played an important role in lending credibility to what he has called the "model for" view of religion, and he argues that religious symbols

both express the world's climate and shape it. They shape it by inducing in the worshipper a certain distinctive set of dispositions (tendencies, capacities, propensities, skills, habits, liabilities, pronenesses) which lend a chronic character to the flow of his activity and the quality of his experience (1966, p. 9).

To the extent that this argument bears on moods and emotions, it accords with Schachter's experimentally based finding that the way states of physiological arousal ("raw" emotions) are interpreted or modelled is a crucial component of the constitution and management of the emotions themselves. More recent writers can go further than Geertz, Radcliffe-Brown, and others in that they have been able to refer to Schachter's experimental research to explain how a religious expression or formulation of emotion works on the emotions. A good illustration is to be found in Robarchek's article, "Frustration, aggression and the nonviolent Semai" (1978). Couched in terms of the traditional frustration–aggression hypothesis, his explanation also relies heavily on Schachter's theory. Consider the Semai notion *pehunan*, referring "to a state of being unfulfilled, unsatisfied, or frustrated in regard to some specific and strongly felt want" (*ibid.*, p. 767). As Robarchek continues: "the conditions for the occurrence of *pehunan* are virtually identical with Dollard's and Berkowitz's definition of frustration: interference with an instigated goal-response sequence" (*ibid.*). Now, according to Berkowitz's formulation, *pehunan* should result in anger and an increased likelihood of aggressive behaviour. But this would hardly suit a culture with comprehensive taboos on aggressive display. Robarchek argues that the beliefs associated with incurring *pehunan* (and similar rules) explain why it is that frustration does not result in aggression; why it is that the Semai can be frustrated but not aggressive. The beliefs in question entail that those who have incurred *pehunan* are "in danger of attack by supernaturals or animals, accidental injury, illness and, ultimately, death" (*ibid.*). Applying Schachter's theory, it is thus possible to claim that "Semai learn to perceive the state of general arousal itself as threatening" (*ibid.*, p. 775). In short, religious beliefs and moral rules function to ensure that fear, not anger and aggression, is the response to frustration. Semai culture therefore shapes Semai emotions.

The status of psychological explanations

Having illustrated how anthropologists of religion have used psychology, I turn now to consider the validity of their psychological theorizing. The first issue to be settled is whether social anthropologists are justified in using psychological theories. This issue is raised by the fact, as I indicated at the beginning of the chapter, that anthropologists have often raised objections to using psychology. The main point I shall make is that although not all social anthropological accounts of religion need refer to psychological assumptions and theories, the validity of using psychology is assured in that a range of questions cannot be adequately answered in a non-psychological fashion. This explains why explanations of a psychological variety should have proved important enough to have been applied by practitioners of a discipline which is supposedly anti-psychological. The second point I want to make is addressed more specifically to psychologists of religion. I want to indicate the extent to which the psychology of religion has taken root in the anthropological context. I do this by contrasting psychological and non-psychological approaches, thereby providing a general context in which to gauge the importance and scope of psychological theorizing.

I then examine the status of specific applications of psychological theory to explain religious phenomena. To be successful, a psychological explanation should rest on firm psychological grounds, be demonstrated in its application, and contend successfully with other interpretations. Discussion of these issues leads to my final point. There is an urgent need for greater psychological expertise, in effect for a more broadly developed *psychology of religion*, if the anthropological use of psychology is not to remain largely conjectural.

The general standing and scope of psychological theories

The importance of psychological explanations

The most obvious question which social anthropologists ask, and which demand psychologically couched solutions is, "What are the consequences of religious activity?" Any consequence – whether it be with respect to other sociocultural institutions, responses to the natural world, or the human self – must be mediated by the impact of religion on those who participate in it. In Brown's words, "Psychological theories overlap with . . . sociological theories . . . which *entail* psychological concepts because any analysis in terms of social norms or institutional pressure implies some response from those who are involved or influenced" (1973, p. 9). It goes without saying that the study of the impact of religion on participants is a psychological matter; it should also go without saying that religious institutions do not influence other institutions directly, but rather do so by virtue of how they influence the cognitions, values and emotions of the participants.

The second question demanding a psychological answer is "What, in scientific terms are the grounds of religious belief and practice?". Most social anthropologists who have addressed this question have followed Durkheim and sought the grounds of religion in social experiences. Unlike Durkheim, who, as we have seen, did not maintain that what is sociocultural operates in a *sui generis* (non-psychological) fashion but instead saw religion as a psychologically mediated response to social experiences, these descendants have tried for "ideological" reasons to minimize the role accorded to psychological processes. Radcliffe-Brown was sometimes "driven" to use psychology, but he tried to resist the temptation by arguing in terms of teleological (causal) functionalism, couched in terms of latent functions and needs. Society has certain necessary needs (in particular the maintenance of social sentiments) and religion functions to satisfy these needs. Since society cannot exist unless these requirements are satisfied, and since religion is a necessary condition for their satisfaction, social needs cause the existence of religion (see Radcliffe-Brown, 1952, pp. 153–177). Although this argument is not entirely devoid of psychology (religion functions to sustain social sentiments), religion is not taken to be generated by the psychological responses of participants to their experiences of society. The Durkheimian theory is replaced by the obscure teleological theory that latent *social* needs can generate a religious response, which is an appropriate response because of the latent functions performed by religion.

Other examples of this kind of explanation are to be found in the work of Fortes (who explains the Tallensi ancestor cult by reference to the fact that "their social structure demands it" (1959, p. 66)) and Evans-Pritchard (who, it will be recalled, speaks of ritual as "a creation of society" (1965, p. 46)). I agree with Spiro (1966, p. 108) that explanations of this kind are inadmissible. Another way in which anthropologists have tried to avoid psychology is by simply avoiding the issue of explaining the connection between social experiences and religious life. Thus Douglas draws attention to the "ranges of symbolic behaviour in which a tendency to replicate the social situation is observed" and speaks of "the *principle* of symbolic replication of a social state" (1970, pp. 81, 82; my italics). We are told extraordinarily little about the nature of this "principle", although, and this is significant, she turns to psychology when on rare occasions she tackles the matter:

> The scope of the body as a medium of expression is limited by controls exerted from the social system. Just as the experience of cognitive dissonance is disturbing, so the experience of consonance in layer after layer of experience and context after context is satisfying. I have argued . . . that there are pressures to create consonance between the perception of social and physiological levels of experience (*ibid.*, p. 70).

What all this comes down to is that unless the investigator is to remain content with teleological explanations, or with simply being non-explanatory, he has to develop a psychological theory to explain why social experiences should be replicated (or compensated for) at the religious level.

Another question leading to psychology is: "What motivates participants to believe in and engage in culturally provided religious systems?". As Spiro points out, the fact that religious "beliefs" are cultural phenomena,

> is not a sufficient basis for the belief that these propositions are true. Children are taught many things which, when they grow up – often, before they grow up – they discard as so much nonsense (1966, pp. 101–102).

The persistence of religious belief and practice, the facts that some participants are more religious than others or that, for example, the incidence of witchcraft accusations varies with time, are issues requiring psychological investigation. Our attention is directed to the subject of motivation (see Spiro, 1966, pp. 98–117).

Finally, and equally briefly, there are two more reasons for introducing psychological explanations. The first is that the more constant a religious phenomenon across cultures, the more likely it is to be a product of some basic psychological process or state of affairs. Discussing the image of the witch, Needham claims that "amid a welter of contingent social facts . . . this complex construction of the imagination displays a very remarkable constancy" (1978, p. 33). Constancy directs attention away from contingent sociocultural facts, and favours explanation in terms of fundamentals of the human mind (cf. Levi-Strauss on primitive classification and myth (1962)).

The remaining point is well made by MacIntyre:

> the explanation of rational belief terminates with an account of the appropriate intellectual norms and procedures; the explanation of irrational belief must be in terms of causal generalizations which connect antecedent conditions specified in terms of social structures or psychological states – or both – with the genesis of beliefs (1971, p. 247).

To draw an analogy: if I point to a white wall and say it is white, I am using the word "white" correctly and, in so far as explanations of everyday life are concerned, there is no need for further explanation. But if I say that the wall is exuding red pores, and I insist that this is really the case, I am likely to end up with a psychiatrist or with someone else trying to make sense of what is occurring. Returning to anthropology, it has seemed to many that apparently irrational or erroneous beliefs and activities are better explained in terms of emotional or expressive processes than in terms of intellectual norms and procedures (see, for example, Beattie, 1970, p. 246).

The limitations of psychological explanations

Psychological explanations, I have argued, are required if anthropologists are to make progress in answering a number of questions. But there are other questions which do not lead to psychological theorizing. I briefly discuss these to help psychologists of religion appreciate the limitations on the scope of anthropological psychologizing, and, more importantly, to pave the way for my discussion of how to assess the validity of the application of psychological theories to explain particular ethnographic phenomena.

Non-psychological approaches are generally brought to bear on religion when it is treated as a semantic phenomenon. To regard religion as a component of culture directs attention to examining it "as an assemblage of texts" (Geertz, 1972, p. 26). As a text or an arrangement of meanings, the religion calls for interpretation, analysis, "decoding", and the application of structural and intra-religious approaches (see Heelas, 1977a). To make sense of a myth, to analyse the symbolism of witch images, to show that a ritual symbolizes social values, to interpret a perplexing metaphor, to find recurrent patterns or structures in religious symbolism, or to show how the moral values articulated in sacrifice fit in with broader socio-cultural themes is to remain at the level of semantic investigation. As the explorations of meaning, psychological (causal) theories have little to offer (see Winch, 1971), although of course such exploration might prompt psychological questions, as when Turner decodes Ndembu ritual symbols to find sensory and ideological referents. The juxtaposition of such referents raises psychological issues (Turner, 1967).

The status of specific applications of psychological theory

The distinction I have drawn between questions prompting psychological explanation and questions prompting semantic inquiry can be mapped onto that between extra- and intra-religious explanations (see Heelas, 1977b). In the first case scientific theories are applied to explain religions by reference to the non-religious psychological and sociological domains; in the second case interpretive procedures are applied to examine the religious in terms of what religious "systems" of meaning themselves imply. That the two general approaches are based on different questions (finding functions and causes as opposed to exploring meanings and finding structures) does not, however, always imply that the two approaches do not compete. Having argued that psychological explanations have a *generally* assured role in the anthropological study of religion, I now examine the first of the three issues I raised in connection with assessing applications of psychological theories – namely *specific* cases where anthropologists have argued that psychological explanations of religious phenomena cannot successfully compete with (supposedly) non-psychological accounts.

Cases of competition

Consider Radcliffe-Brown's alternative to Malinowski's psychological theory of magic (the latter holding, in essence, that magic is a response to anxiety). Radcliffe-Brown is discussing the taboos associated with childbirth amongst the Andaman Islanders. He writes:

> In a given community it is *appropriate* that an expectant father should feel concern or at least should make an appearance of doing so. Some suitable symbolic expression of his concern is found *in terms of* the general ritual or symbolic *idiom* of the society ... (1952, p. 150, my italics).

The childbirth taboos are not the product of parental anxieties; they are explained in terms of the symbolic idiom of the society as a whole. This explanation, it should be noted, is not entirely devoid of psychology since cognitive consistency is implied, but it is certainly much more weakly psychological than Malinowski's psychodynamic explanation.

Similar cases of competition are to be found in theories of witchcraft (Kennedy, 1967; Gluckman, 1968; Selby, 1974), discussion of the abominations of Leviticus (Douglas, 1966), explanations of totemism (Lévi-Strauss, 1963), and magic (Jarvie and Agassi, 1970; Beattie, 1970). Rather than dwell on these complicated debates, I hasten to consider what is involved in demonstrating the application of psychological theories regardless of whether or not there are contending non-psychological explanations of the same ethnographic material.

Demonstrations of application

I have just added the proviso "of the same ethnographic material" because a number of debates have occurred within anthropology in which non-psychological explanations have scored over psychological ones, because semantic investigation has shown that the psychological applications have been made in terms of erroneous understanding of the phenomena in question. In other words, there are cases in which psychological explanations have been discredited by showing that they address phenomena which do not really exist.

Gluckman, for example, treats the Swazi *Incwala* ceremony as a ritual of rebellion. Treating the ritual as an enactment of conflict of interests, he is able to apply catharsis theory, and so claims that the rite banishes the threats to disunity imposed by the conflicts (1963). Beidelman, however, shows quite conclusively that

> the main theme of the *Incwala* is not rebellion or the expression of aggression and conflict . . . but the separation of the king from the various groups within his nation so that he is free and fit to assume the heavy supernatural powers of his office as king-priest of the nation" (1966, p. 401).

Beidelman's detailed examination of the ethnographic material, not so much his use of a non-psychological structuralist approach, is what discredits Gluckman's theory. A similar debate is that between Leach (1961) and Spiro (1966), the former providing ethnographic evidence to discredit Spiro's psychological explanation of Trobriand "virgin birth" beliefs.

A great deal could be said of what is involved in substantiating the application of psychological theories (see e.g. Bateson, 1958, especially p. 115; Heelas, 1983). The only point I will make for the present is that anthropologists have been remarkably lax in seeking evidence to support their psychologizing. It is true that a certain amount of correlational research has been done to test the Durkheimian and Freudian causal theories (see Swanson, 1968; Whiting, 1961; Spiro and D'Andrade, 1958), but in the main, anthropologists have provided little evidence that, for example, rituals work in Schachterian fashion (see Hanson's (1981) comments on Ortner (1978)).

Psychological validity

Finally, it is clear that a successful anthropological application relies on the anthropologist using psychologically acceptable theories. Given the controversy in psychology over, for instance, the validity of the catharsis hypothesis (cf. Heelas, 1982) and the validity of Schachter's theory (see Leventhal, 1980), and given problems to do with extrapolating from experimental conditions to what goes on in the real (ethnographic) world (see Berkowitz and Donnerstein, 1982), it is by no means certain that anthropological theorizing has always rested on firm psychological grounds.

Conclusion

The reader will have noticed that as this chapter has progressed I have become increasingly critical of anthropological psychologizing. Without concurring with Evans-Pritchard's anti-psychological position, I agree with virtually all the specific criticisms he makes in *Theories of primitive religion* (1965a). Perhaps it is not surprising that anthropological psychologizing is so open to criticism. Few anthropologists are well-versed in psychology, which means that their psychological theorizing tends to suffer from naïvety. And this tendency has been encouraged by those anthropologists such as Gluckman who have urged their colleagues that it is not their role to be anything but naïve with respect to psychology (1964).

There are some recent signs of a greater psychological sophistication among anthropologists. One can think of Sperber (1975) and his use of cognitive theory to argue that symbols do not "mean", but function to store and organize knowledge, and one thinks of Hallpike's use of Piagetian theory (1979) or of Robarchek (1978). And there is in general an increasing appreciation of the view expressed by Kennedy, that,

> all sociological analyses are based upon a set of psychological assumptions – an implicit, and therefore often gross, theory of mental and emotional processes. ... One obvious implication of such a realization is that the implicit assumptions should be made explicit, so that their validity may be judged, and their ramifications followed out. A further and perhaps more important implication is that a sophisticated psychological model be employed by the student of social behaviour. These implications are quite formidable and we cannot blame individual scholars who quail before the difficult labour entailed by the Pandora's box of psychologies which is thereby immediately opened (1967, p. 224).

Opening this Pandora's box would be made easier if psychologists were to concern themselves more with the issues raised by anthropological psychologizing. Unfortunately, few psychologists of religion have turned their attention to the issues raised by anthropologists. Not only does the anthropological study of religion suffer from this, for so too does the psychology of religion. At the moment, psychologists of religion seem to restrict themselves to such traditional topics as the relationship between conservative social attitudes and the Christian tradition. It is difficult not to conclude that the discipline of the psychology of religion would benefit from a greater interest in cross-cultural matters. This would broaden the scope of the discipline which might then, if this is not too controversial, fulfil its potential.[3]

Jahoda, whose views have helped me greatly, states that his "firm belief is that the disciplines of anthropology and psychology can be of mutual help to each other" (1970a, p. 38; see also 1970b). Rather than speaking of disciplines, I am inclined to argue that progress could be made, both in the "psychology" and the "anthropology" of religion, by a synthesis: to produce psychologists-cum-anthropologists and anthropologists-cum-psychologists. There are signs of this happening. Ness is a psychologically trained but anthropologically minded researcher. His investigation of "The impact of indigenous healing activity: an empirical study of two fundamentalist churches" (1980) paves the way for further work. If he can demonstrate that particular rituals in Newfoundland fundamentalist churches have demonstrable effects on the distressful emotions of these participants there is no longer any justification for anthropologists to remain content with impressionistic accounts of the impact of ritual (cf. Richardson, Chapter 14, in this volume; and see Kleinman (1980)). Wills is another socially minded psychologist. In his article, "Downward comparison principles in social psychology" (1981), he argues that people who experience negative affects can enhance their subjective well-being by comparing themselves with those who are less fortunate (the process taking either active or passive forms). Wills uses that principle to explain scapegoating in that "Downward comparison can be achieved through active derogation of another person, thereby increasing the psychological distance between the self and the other" (*ibid.*, p. 246). Anthropologists have often seen witchcraft accusations as a form of scapegoating, and have explained it in terms of psychodynamic theory. Perhaps Wills' cognitive theory can offer new insights. As a final illustration of the synthesis under discussion, Schweder uses experimental work on how personality judgements are made, to find a new approach to the problem of explaining magic. Experimental research shows that "the concept of correlation is often replaced by intuitive notions such as resemblance and likeness when estimates are made about what goes with what in experience" (1977, p. 647). Schweder claims that the same applies to magical acts and beliefs in primitive societies: "magical thinking is an expression of a universal disinclination of normal adults to draw correlational lessons from their experiences, coupled with a universal inclination to seek symbolic and meaningful connections (likeness) among objects and events" (*ibid.*, p. 637). It is certainly arresting to be told that "Magical thinking seems to be no more a feature of Zande beliefs that ringworm and fowl excrement go together than of our own beliefs that self-esteem and leadership do" (*ibid.*).

Psychological theories, I have argued, are an integral component of a comprehensively envisaged anthropology of religion. To emphasize a key point, psychological theories have frequently been used by anthropologists, but rarely have they been applied vigorously enough for their explanatory status to be other than what Evans-Pritchard liked to characterize as that of a "just-so story". This is a field crying out for more sophisticated forms of investigation. There is ample scope for more naturalistic "experimental" work, in particular with respect to questions of efficacy. What exactly do particular rituals *do* to participants? There is also scope for developing better ways of answering the question, *how* do rituals achieve what they have been shown to do? One strategy here is to argue that laboratory experiments result in a certain end, for example in the cathartic reduction of aggression; this is also the consequence of a particular ritual; by extrapolation, the process hypothesized to account for the result obtained in the laboratory can be held to account for the result demonstrated in the field; and this extrapolation is further justified if it can be shown that the experimental design and the ritual have features in common (e.g. instigated display of emotions with regard to the catharsis process). Finkelstein *et al.* have recently argued in this fashion to explain the apparently efficacious psychological techniques employed by the "est" organization (1982; see also Ness, 1980).

Just-so stories might also be transformed into valid explanations if it can be demonstrated that a particular psychological process is occurring in a particular naturalistic setting, on the grounds that alternative psychological processes cannot account for what is ethnographically the case (see Heelas, 1983). Another way to make progress involves more cross-cultural experimental work: to investigate the presence of Piagetian stages, for example, thereby putting Hallpike's theory to the test (see Harris and Heelas, 1979). And there is a need for more correlational research. Concerning Malinowskian-like theories positing a connection between anxiety-inducing circumstances and magical activities, common sense tells us that occupations involving risk, uncertainty or fear, are likely to be surrounded by superstitions. But as Jahoda points out, "as far as I know, there have been no systematic studies of the differential incidences of superstitions for people in different occupations" (1970b, p. 128).

More exact examination of the consequences of religious life, of the means whereby demonstrated consequences are obtained, the ethnographic evidence counting for or against particular explanations, and of the psychological options in terms of which explanations might be offered is required if the hinterland between psychology and anthropology is to be developed. Finally, anthropological research shows that religions have their own models of human nature, their own indigenous psychologies (see Heelas and Lock, 1981). Anthropologists, such as Lévi-Strauss, have investigated fundamental structures of the mind by means of the analysis, of, for example, myth. What anthropologists and psychologists have paid less attention to is the role of psychologically explicit religious formulations of models in organizing and constituting psychological states and processes. The ways religions specifically address the motives, emotions, decisions, and so on, of participants have not yet been systematically explored.

References

BATESON, G. *Naven*. Stanford: Stanford University Press, 1958.
BEATTIE, J. On understanding ritual. In B. WILSON (ed.), *Rationality*. Oxford: B. Blackwell, 1970, 240–266.
BEIDELMAN, T. Swazi royal ritual. *Africa*, 1966; **36**, 273–405.
BERKOWITZ, L. and DONNERSTEIN, E. External validity is more than skin deep. *American psychologist*, 1982; **37**(3), 245–257.
BOHANNON, P. Extra-processual events in Tiv political institutions. *American Anthropologist*, 1958: **60**, 1–12.
BROWN, L. B. (ed.) *Psychology and religion*. Harmondsworth: Penguin, 1973.
DITTES, J. Psychology of Religion. In G. LINDZEY and E. ARONSON (eds.), *The handbook of social psychology*, vol. 5. Addison-Wesley, 1969, pp. 602–659.
DOUGLAS, M. *Purity and danger*. London: Routledge & Kegan Paul, 1966.
DOUGLAS, M. *Natural symbols*. London: Barrie & Rockliff, 1970.
DURKHEIM, E. *The elementary forms of the religious life*. London: George Allen & Unwin, 1915.
DURKHEIM, E. *The rules of sociological method*. London: Collier-Macmillan, 1964.
EVANS-PRITCHARD, E. *Witchcraft, oracles and magic among the Zande*. Oxford: Clarendon Press, 1937.
EVANS-PRITCHARD, E. *Theories of primitive religion*. Oxford: Clarendon Press, 1965a.
EVANS-PRITCHARD, E. *The position of women in primitive societies and other essays in social anthropology*. London: Faber & Faber, 1965b.
FINKELSTEIN, P., WENEGRAT, B., and YALOMI, I. Large group awareness training. *Annual Review of Psychology*, 1982; pp. 515–539.
FORTES, M. *Oedipus and Job*. Cambridge: Cambridge University Press, 1959.
GEERTZ, C. Religion as a cultural system. In M. BANTON (ed.), *Anthropological approaches to the study of religion*. London: Tavistock, 1966, pp. 1–46.
GEERTZ, C. Deep play: notes on the Balinese cockfight. *Daedalus*, Winter, 1972, pp. 1–38.
GLUCKMAN, M. *Order and rebellion in tribal Africa*. London: Cohen & West, 1963.
GLUCKMAN, M. (ed.) *Closed systems and open minds: the limits of naivety in social anthropology*. Edinburgh: Oliver & Boyd, 1964.
GLUCKMAN, M. Psychological, sociological and anthropological explanations of witchcraft and gossip: a clarification. *Man (J.R.A.I.)*, 1968; **3**(1), 20–34.
HALLPIKE, C. Is there a primitive mentality? *Man*, 1976; **11**, 253–270.
HALLPIKE, C. *The foundations of primitive thought*. Oxford: Clarendon Press, 1979.
HANSON, F. The semiotics of ritual. *Semiotica*, 1981; **33**(1/2), 169–178.
HARRIS, P. and HEELAS, P. Collective representations and psychic unity. *European Journal of Sociology*, 1979; **XX**, 211–241.
HEELAS, P. Intra-religious explanations. *Journal of the Anthropological Society of Oxford*, 1977a; **VIII**(1).
HEELAS, P. Semantic anthropology and rules. In P. COLLETT (ed.), *Social rules and social behaviour*. Oxford: B. Blackwell, 1977b, pp. 109–131.
HEELAS, P. Anthropology, violence and catharsis. In P. MARSH and A. CAMPBELL (eds.), *Aggression and violence*. Oxford: B. Blackwell, 1982, pp. 48–61.
HEELAS, P. Anthropological perspectives on violence: universals or particulars? *Zygon* 1983; **18**(4), 375–404.
HEELAS, P. and LOCK, A. (eds.) *Indigenous psychologies*. London: Academic Press, 1981.
HORTON, R. African traditional thought and western science. *Africa*, 1967; **37**, 50–71, 155–187.
JAHODA, G. A psychologist's perspective. In P. MAYER (ed.), *Socialization: the approach from social anthropology*. London: Tavistock, 1970a, pp. 33–50.
JAHODA, G. *The psychology of superstition*. Harmondsworth: Penguin, 1970b.
JARVIE, I. and AGASSI, J. The problem of the rationality of magic. In B. WILSON (ed.), *Rationality*. Oxford: B. Blackwell, 1970, pp. 172–193.
KENNEDY, J. Psychological and social explanations of witchcraft. *Man*, 1967; **2**, 216–225.

KLEINMAN, A. *Patients and healers in the context of culture.* London: University of California Press, 1980.

LEACH, E. Golden bough or gilded twig? *Daedalus,* 1961.

LEVENTHAL, H. Toward a comprehensive theory of emotion. In L. BERKOWITZ (ed.), *Advances in experimental social psychology,* 1980; **13,** 140–194.

LEVI-STRAUSS, C. *The savage mind.* London: Weidenfeld & Nicolson, 1962.

LEVI-STRAUSS, C. *Totemism.* Boston: Beacon Press, 1963.

LEWIS, I. *Ecstatic religion.* Harmondsworth: Penguin, 1971.

LEWIS, I. (ed.) *Symbols and sentiments.* London: Academic Press, 1977.

MACINTYRE, A. *Against the self-images of the age.* London: Duckworth, 1971.

MALINOWSKI, B. Magic, science and religion. In JOSEPH NEEDHAM (ed.), *Science, religion and reality.* London: Sheldon Press, 1925.

NEEDHAM, R. *Structure and sentiment.* London: University of Chicago Press, 1962.

NEEDHAM, R. *Primordial characters.* Charlottesville: University Press of Virginia, 1978.

NESS, R. The impact of indigenous healing activity: an empirical study of two fundamentalist churches. *Social Science and Medicine,* 1980; **148**(3), 167–180.

ORTNER, S. *Sherpas through their rituals.* Cambridge: University Press, 1978.

RADCLIFFE-BROWN, A. *The Andaman islanders.* Cambridge: University Press, 1948.

RADCLIFFE-BROWN, A. *Structure and function in primitive society.* London: Cohen & West, 1952.

RIVERS, W. Sociology and psychology. *Sociological Review,* 1916; **9,** 1–13.

ROBARCHEK, C. Frustration, aggression, and the nonviolent Semai. *American Ethnologist,* 1978, pp. 762–779.

SCHACHTER, S. The interaction of cognitive and physiological determinants of emotional state. In L. BERKOWITZ (ed.), *Advances in experimental social psychology,* Vol. 1. New York: Academic Press, 1964.

SCHWEDER, R. Likeness and likelihood in everyday thought: magical thinking in judgements about personality. *Current Anthropology,* 1977, **18**(4).

SELBY, H. *Zapotec deviance.* London: University of Texas Press, 1974.

SPERBER, D. *Rethinking symbolism.* Cambridge: University Press, 1975.

SPILKA, B. The current state of the psychology of religion. *The Council on the Study of Religion Bulletin,* 1978; **9**(4), 96–99.

SPIRO, M. Religion: problems of definition and explanation. In M. BANTON (ed.), *Anthropological approaches to the study of religion.* London: Tavistock, 1966, pp. 85–126.

SPIRO, M. and D'ANDRADE, R. A cross-cultural study of some supernatural beliefs. *American Anthropologist,* 1958, **60.**

SWANSON, G. *The birth of the gods.* Michigan: University Press, 1968.

TREVOR-ROPER, H. *Religion, the reformation and social change.* London: Macmillan, 1967.

TURNER, V. *The forest of symbols.* London: Cornell University Press, 1967.

WHITING, J. Socialization process and personality. In F. HSU (ed.), *Psychological anthropology,* Homewood, Ill.: Dorsey Press, 1961.

WILLS, T. Downward comparison principles in social psychology. *Psychological Bulletin,* 1981; **90**(2), 245–271.

WINCH, P. *The idea of a social science and its relation to philosophy.* London: Routledge & Kegan Paul, 1971.

Notes

1. I do not apologize for including so many quotations in this paper. The most reliable and convincing way of summarizing the theories discussed is by letting the authors present their key points in their own words.
2. However, I have had to include Spiro in the category of endogenous origins theory because he at times shifts from explaining the appeal of religion to the existence of what appeals. This is implied in the extract already given; it is even clearer in his exogenous explanation, Freudian in emphasis, of the "basis of religious belief" (1966, p. 103).
3. This applies even if one does not agree with Dittes' judgement that the psychology of religion is in a "primitive state" (1969, p. 603). For the fact remains that the psychology of religion is narrow in scope and weak on theory (Spilka, 1978, p. 97), and would benefit from encounters with anthropological material and theory.

5

Psychology of religion as the study of the conflict between belief and unbelief

A. VERGOTE

TO INTRODUCE my topic I would raise a critical question concerning the scope and the field of the psychology of religion. It seems to be a prevailing intention of psychologists of religion to know *why* people engage in religion. Often psychologists go on to elaborate this question, as the overwhelming project for explaining religion as such. That step seems obvious and one fears that to raise a critical question about this conception of the psychology of religion might be done for the wrong reasons. Not to accept it would seem to maintain the obscurantist view that the mysteries of religion, and of the psyche, should not be treated scientifically. I will take the risk of incurring this suspicion. I fear that the project of making a general explanatory theory of religion has been in a muddle, and has encumbered the whole history of the psychology of religion.

On the other hand, I conceive of psychology of religion as the inquiry into lawlike regularities in the field of religious behaviour or belief, and see why-questions as a pre-scientific intention that has to be defined by the findings. This then opens the question of the general framework for the psychology of religion that I have in mind.

The distinguished cultural anthropologist, Evans-Pritchard, who very rigorously studied some primitive religions and then made an inquiry into the theories about them, writes that "I have to conclude that I do not feel that on the whole the different theories we have reviewed, either singly or taken together, give us more than common-sense answers, which for the most part miss the mark" (1965, p. 120). I would say the same about the theories of non-primitive religions. Theories which intend to elaborate a general psychological explanation proceed like a tailor who would make a whole suit from a button. The buttons here have "need-motivation" as a basic term, together with the vague concept of projection, or the idea of function and emotional experience. All these elements are to be found in religion, but there are even more. What Freud said about psychoanalysis should also be said of psychology: "There

52

are no grounds for fearing that psychoanalysis which first discovered that psychic acts and structures are invariably overdetermined will be tempted to trace the origins of anything so complicated as religion to a single source" (Freud, 1955, p. 100).

Most psychologists who maintain the project of explaining religion admit that until now psychology has failed to do so. Is that for a lack of scientific maturity? I think that this failure actually shows that the project itself is a mistake and that it has often hindered the pursuit of valuable inquiries.

I wonder if the personal attitude of many psychologists towards religion is not largely responsible for the conception of the psychology of religion that I would criticize. It is well documented that many psychologists are convinced that there is a contradiction between religious belief and the scientific study of religion. The belief of a religious man is for them an illusion. Consequently they wish to *explain* religion, which for them is an alien behaviour and belief. Mainstream psychology studies mental or psychic processes. But the psychology of religion, in order to explain religion, should study processes and content. In other words it should explain religious beliefs as they exist, develop and operate.

One may think that this is the only neutral scientific attitude. But I would ask the question: "Is this not, on the contrary, a philosophical preconception, and a scientific fallacy?" It is interesting to observe Freud's contradictory attitude in these matters. On the one side, he states that psychology, as a science, is not a *Weltanschauung*, not even a complete anthropology, and is consequently neutral with respect to religion. Nonetheless, transgressing this strongly stated scientific principle, he sets out to explain and to demystify religion.

The specific difficulty of the psychology of religion is that it is almost impossible to be neutral with respect to religion. The solution has been to think that unbelief and consequently the aim of explaining religion coincides with scientific neutrality. Language, art and sex are obviously objective and universally human data, and a psychologist of art, language, sexuality or love will not try to elaborate a general theoretical explanation of them. He would feel this pretentious and preposterous, and everybody would think it ridiculous to identify scientific neutrality with an abstinence from art, sex, love or language.

I would defend the idea that both the cultural reality of religion and the scientific status of psychology require that the psychologist, as psychologist, accepts a third alternative beyond the two opposed attitudes that produce either a psychology of religion (in the way I have discussed) or a religious psychology (where religion determines the viewpoint but not the object).

The third alternative is an agnostic suspension of judgement concerning the ultimate meaning and nature of religion, with a consequent reformulation of the aim of the psychology of religion. With this perspective a dynamic psychology of religion would involve the investigation of how and why, in a given cultural context, persons are, or become or do not become, religious.

Actually, in western civilization, the object of psychology of religion will be quite specific and for the great part an investigation of the tension or conflict between religious belief and unbelief. The rationale which supports that opinion is, first, that religion is an observable phenomenon.

The nature of religion

Religion is a cultural phenomenon, and a fact of subjective consciousness and individual behaviour. It also belongs to the collective consciousness, and is a social institution. There are clear data about this. However, it would be an error to consider religion as belonging only to the field of psychology and/or to the field of sociology, and therefore to explain it with reference to psychology or to sociology. I do not invoke a supernatural origin of religion since that is the point of view of religion itself, not of science. But I oppose the false contrast that advances either a religious explanation, or an explanation in terms of the human sciences. Religion is a symbolic system that belongs to what K. Popper (1979) calls the third world. It is present in humanity as an ensemble of languages, references and meanings, symbols, modes of symbolic behaviours and prescriptions. Affective experiences, as William James himself finally had to accept, have only a religious meaning because the cultural system of religious symbols and language gives individuals articulating references that fill some experiences with religious meaning. The same holds for motivation. When Freud explained religion as a father-nostalgia, he was well aware that he did not explain the transference of this nostalgia on to God as such. His ethno-psychological study in *Totem and Taboo* is, as far as I know, the only attempt to present a genetic and psychological theory of religion which takes into account the cultural evolution of mankind, tries to base itself on ethnological data, and which develops a psychological interpretation of them. Freud was aware that the psychology and sociology of contemporary religion do not produce an explanation, because religion is a cultural heritage. But his genealogical and naturalistic psychological theory of the origins and the cultural development of religion is a grandiose failure, not only because of his erroneous ethnological references and the faulty descriptions of religion and its history but also because of the incapacity of psychology to generate that which it would explain genetically. This is obviously an inherent deficiency. Psychological explanations of origins must presuppose what is to be explained. I agree with Evans-Pritchard whom I have already quoted: "origins, with respect to culture, are not a possible object for science" (1965, p. 120). A psychology that would explain contemporary religion by retracing the history of culture, and explain the history of culture by referring to contemporary mankind, turns around the paradox of a popular old German song: "Saint Christopher carries the Christ child. The Christ child carries the world. Where upon does Saint Christopher place his feet?"

The second rationale which supports my opinion involves the status of psychology. A consequence of my former remarks is that the first problem of religion is to examine what in religion, as in other domains, is psychological. If it is an unjustified prejudice to start with the heuristic idea that every cultural phenomenon is psychological, then the main scope of psychology should be to detect what is psychological, and what can be explained by psychology. That is a very difficult task, for we cannot easily separate psychological from cultural factors. All that is human is psychological and nothing is merely psychological: therefore all human sciences make psychology – sometimes doing it better than psychologists.

Parental images

Let us briefly consider an example. If we examine the mother or father images of a subject or population, we observe the interaction of different factors. One is the result of an ongoing personal experience of the real father or mother. But this experience is also determined by the complex structure and triangular relationships among at least three subjects: the ego, the mother, and the father. That structural relationship is not the sum of individual relationships, nor is it determined by the individual characteristics of the subjects involved. Even more is the meaning of these complex relationships co-determined by cultural ideas of the father and the mother. This can be clearly observed in the expression, "I had no real father or mother." When we try further to elaborate the psychology of a religious relationship lived in relation to a God-father, the affair is still more complex (Vergote and Tamayo, 1981). The ideas involved here have been proposed to the subject in a complex religious language and by models of behaviour. It is the language, with its different connotations, which shapes to a large extent subjective ways of reacting to God and which will more or less influence behaviour towards other people, and even towards oneself. The God-representation proposed by a religion therefore assumes in different ways images of the human father and mother. There are also elements of transference, and of metaphoric transformation, and even of conflictual doubling. One never knows *a priori* what the connections are and which components are brought by each individual, although there must be a psychodynamic substratum to this type of religious relationship. But a psychodynamic patterning cannot ground the observed religious fact on a simple causal substratum such as the need for protection or for power. A psychology which involves one mechanism, such as projection, remains not only hopelessly vague and incomplete, but is simply mistaken, for it reduces a complex interaction of different sorts of elements to a causality that is one-directional. Consequently it is irrelevant, for it will never encompass every specific content of the relationship and there will be an immense gap between what is reconstructed by the explanation and the accurately observed explanandum. I sometimes think that if academic psychologists had experience of in-depth clinical work, they would not search for *the* model in a psychology of religion, since such contact with human realities would dissipate that idea as an illusory dream. Psychology puts religion to the test, but inversely religion, as an observable phenomenon, puts psychology to the test. The psychological study of religion is an inquiry into the interaction between an individual and an objective religion, as a symbolic system. That interaction is, of course, determined by the cultural context, and by the opinions, ideologies, cultural values, behavioural and mental schemes that any group shares to a greater or lesser degree.

As for the psychological point of view, one general notion can be extracted which undoubtedly allows at least some specification: psychology examines the meaning of religious conduct or action insofar as it is found to be influenced by reasons which do not belong to the significance explicitly recognized and affirmed by the subjects, but derives from elements interior to the personality and which underlie the consciously entertained significations. Psychological factors to some extent determine the modality of religious behaviour and, on the other hand, the religiously symbolic data contribute to a structuring of the personality. Every psychological explanation is therefore an interpretation with two entries. I have previously tried to apply this interactive scheme in an explanation of phenomena such as stigmatization, visions, etc. (Vergote, 1978).

The psychology of religion

An important consequence of this view is that the task for a psychology of religion, as a study of the relationship between data of a psychic order and religious data, leads me to define the psychology of religion as a *psychology which studies religious belief together with unbelief.* The heading, "psychology of religion", itself leads to misunderstandings, because it causes one to think that religion represents a domain set apart, radically different from unbelief and thereby calling for particular psychological explanations. Two attitudes are then possible. Either one can associate religion with psychological resources foreign to normal psychology, as when the psychology of religion is approximated to para-psychology in, for example, the study of altered forms of consciousness. Or one seeks to explain how people create an enigmatic universe of supernatural beings. In that case the non-religious person is the basic personality-type and an attempt is made to understand the processes by which a typical personality, or a religious person, is constituted.

The reasoning in both these orientations fails to recognize the real religious situation. If religious behaviour is developed as a response to the symbolic system of religion it is necessary to accept positive religious attitudes *and* unbelief, as two positions with respect to the network of religious significations. The ensemble they form is then the domain of the psychology of religion. If unbelief – or secularization, whatever it is called – is not the pure absence of religious questions and interests, it is equally a response to the call of the religious dimension in culture to humanity. This operates in the same way as science, ethics, politics or a love-language. Beyond any intellectual reasons, a negative response also results from reasons of a psychological order, in the same way as does religious faith.

Yet it would be a mistake if reality were recognized simply as the juxtaposition of negative and positive responses. A little bit of human experience teaches us that questions regularly arise about religious attitudes, questions that are motivated psychologically as well as intellectually, and which sit a believer before the choice of adhering to religion or refusing it, or of transforming previous or earlier religious intentions and behaviours. That which sustains one type of religion can, at other times and for some other subjects, be transformed into reticence or into its opposed attitude.

Religion is presented to a subject by the cultural milieu. It reverts to psychology to see whether any person produces a religion for himself, and to find what it is, subjectively, that receives, selects, transforms, deforms or suppresses the messages sent by the symbolic system of a religion. It is for psychology to look at what it is in humanity that comes to meet religion, and to observe how a person integrates that experience subjectively and relates to it conflictually.

The nature of religious life

Religious life is not a sum of practices to be observed, of experiences to be described, nor an ensemble of statements to which persons consent. It composes a significant individual and social history that is made of tensions, crossroads and vicissitudes. It passes through conflicts and is transformed by their solution. At least that is so within our present culture. Religion offers a possible response to human desires, and awakens desires. It engenders conflicts, being a stumbling block with respect to human desires. Accordingly, its development is invariably tortuous, and results either in a subjectively confirmed religious attitude, or in a doubt which partially suspends engagement and leaves an interior division, or rejection, that may be provisional or definitive. Thus, it is necessary to understand religious belief and unbelief with reference to each other since, while they are opposed in their point of view, each is for some part interior to the other, especially in their formation and in their transformation.

Let us take a simple example. If one observes that the lack of an answer to a prayer of petition leads to the declaration that religious faith is an illusion, one can try to understand the motivation determining the prayer as well as the representation of God that supports it. One could also develop Freud's argument in *The future of an illusion*, and disengage the underlying motives and the more or less unconscious representations that are transferred to the religious word "God". That may explain the psychological nature of *this* belief and explain its dissipation through the experience of receiving no response, as a conflict between representation and reality. If a psychologist observes that other subjects modify their conception of God and their practice following such a deceptive experience, a fragmentary law about the ambivalent effect of an experience of deception could be extracted. A psychologist could also identify from these facts a major element of religion, in that God is a hidden God, who clashes with spontaneous desires and representations, and that belief, as it is proposed by religion, is achieved through an experience of disillusion.

Psychology should also examine what it is in the person and in religion that makes the transformation to a new form of belief possible. When this happens, as has often been observed, it is of course partly because the signifier, God, within the context of religious language, conveys more numerous and other significations than the subject interiorized or accepted at first. On the other hand, what psychological factors are at work in that transformation? This is a most intricate question. There must also be some psychological factors that correspond with the newly discovered meaning of the God-idea. This could be some kind of pre-religious experience, like a sense of the mystery in nature or in the cosmos. Or there could be a sense of fundamental happiness with the divine presence that would be similar to a love-satisfaction.

Belief and unbelief

A study of the belief *and* unbelief in an after-life, or, within the Christian context, in resurrection, should be done in the same manner. The question to be asked is not simply "Why do some believe?" but also why do a large number of those who declare themselves to be Christian not believe in a major doctrine of their religion? Let me first mention that fear of death can lead one to repress the idea of death and consequently to reject the idea of an after-life that is linked with it. The same fear can sustain the belief of others. When elderly people come to believe this more strongly, is it because they fear death or because younger people have not yet recognized, or repress, the reality of death? There are as many non-religious illusions as there are religious ones. My main contention is that psychodynamic concepts should refer "to generative or transformative mechanisms relating underlying structures to particular behavioural episodes" (Cheshire, 1975). As one particular behavioural episode we could think of the observations that have just been mentioned where religious doubt or unbelief follows a disappointment with respect to prayer or to the experience of the loss of a loved person. Here we have the psychodynamic fact of a conflict between expectation and experienced reality.

Petitionary prayer is a demand. Since a demand is a specific behaviour I propose to consider demand as a psychodynamic concept. In religion there are different kinds of prayer including expressions of debt, praise, and so on, which implicitly include a form of demand. One might also infer from demand the typical psychological concept of need. But I prefer to consider need as an underlying dynamic structure, since needs are not sufficient to account for a demand, which also supposes a recognition that one cannot, oneself, satisfy the need. Furthermore, a demand implies an underlying confidence. This confidence presupposes the psychological, but not yet the religious, representation of another who is powerful and helpful. Confidence and the representation of this other person belong to the underlying psychological structure that is formed by early experience. Those psychological conditions for the demand are not, however, always present. To be religious, the demand supposes the representation of a God who is similar to the mentioned psychological representation. This representation of God, however, stems from the religious language that the subject has appropriated.

The concept of need should still be reduced to a more specific psychological factor, like the drive to self-preservation (as in cases of extreme poverty or illness), or a drive to realize oneself (as in prayers for the success of a human enterprise). The generative mechanism for such a link between religion and behaviour is therefore a complex structure of need-drive, confidence and representation. This mechanism does not generate religion as such, although in a religious context it generates this religious behaviour.

The conflict between prayer and the experience of reality produces a transformation into an altered belief, or into unbelief. What then, is the underlying structure and what is the transforming mechanism? It is easier to analyse a transformation into unbelief than into a new form of belief, which invokes some rationale of imaginary representations. But the process is usually very complicated for there is often, between the demand and the unbelief, an episode of revolt or even of hatred, which is a negative passion. That is more difficult to analyse, although in religion it supports the attribution to God of an evil intention.

There is a wide range of such conflict situations that the psychology of religion could investigate, including conflicts between autonomy and authority, autonomy and hope, sexual pleasure and a recognition of God, the experience of evil and good, open and closed mindedness, the maternal and paternal components of the God-idea, and so on.

As the psychology of religion cannot limit itself to a set of particular observations and interpretations, there must be some principle for assembling them into a structured whole. This idea guides psychologists who look for a model. But can such a principle or model be derived from psychology? The object of the study of psychology is usually human behaviour, with a specific content that is not purely psychological. The principle or model that may operate will always be co-determined by the field of behaviour and by the psyche. In the psychology of religion any principle or model should therefore be at the junction between psychology and religion as a cultural or symbolic system. Religions are however, specific. An objective look at the Christian religion shows us that belief in God is the core and that this core is the dynamic centre of the different contents of belief and of various behaviours and their expression. That is not the case in primitive religions where the word "belief" may not even exist, or which do not invite a belief *in* anything. The general principle for ordering these different observations and their psycho-dynamic explanations cannot therefore be the same in different religions. If they were, the psychological model would merely be an artificial construct.

As one general dynamic principle, I would propose for the psychology of religion in a Christian context the dynamic development or the becoming of belief and/or of unbelief. And I would examine how different behavioural episodes contribute to that development, or are expressions of it, since behaviour must to a large extent be expressive and neither merely motivated nor consequential. This focus on belief accords with the observation that what Glock and Stark (1965) called (misleadingly) the ideological dimension, is the essential part of religion. This dimension, I would insist, is the essentially *dynamic process* in religion.

A psychologist in our contemporary Christian context should not disregard the essential fact that the Christian religion, by its claim upon belief, intends to bring about a dynamic process, and that there is a multifaceted tension between a culture of enlightment or of self-realization and religious belief; this cultural tension enhances the dynamic nature of belief and unbelief. In this context I would also consider the self-defensive attitude of some believers as a dynamic process that produces intolerance and authoritarianism. For me that is a functional pathology of belief, which I would explain with psychodynamic concepts and the underlying structures of psycho-pathology. The dynamic process of belief versus unbelief or of unbelief versus belief is not the only principle for organizing the data of religious psychology in a Western milieu, although it is the most important axis. The nature of the process depends upon the prevailing cultural and religious references. For those who refer mainly, for example, to an Eastern religion, the psychologist should examine their specific dynamic processes. When there is a syncretistic compound of religious references, the psychological problem of selection and rejection should be examined. The psychology of religion is also an agent of change. Some think it will produce secularization. Why cannot that effect also be a transformation of religion? Religious literature itself develops an intrinsic criticism of what it regards as the too-human motivations and representations. In that context, consider only the Biblical Wisdom literature and the mystics. It would also be interesting to investigate whether psychology provokes a crisis among believers, and how any such conflicts can be resolved.

Conclusion

To conclude, I would compare a dynamic psychology of religion with cultural anthropology. There are at least two important types of research in cultural anthropology. One involves the investigation of how a person becomes initiated into his culture and gets his identity through the many facets of initiation, among them initiation rites. The other is the process of transformation and change through interactions between cultures. If a psychology of the contrasts between belief and unbelief did not adopt that same view, and did not analyse the processes with the same neutral accuracy, it would be irrelevant.

References

CHESHIRE, N. M. *The Nature of Psychodynamic Interpretation*. London: John Wiley & Sons, 1975.

CLAYTON, R. R. 5-D or 1. *Journal for the Scientific Study of Religion*, 1971; **10**(1), 37–40.

EVANS-PRITCHARD, E. *Theories of Primitive Religion*. Oxford: University Press, 1965, p. 120.

FREUD, S. *Totem and Taboo*, 2nd edn. London: Hogarth Press, 1955, Vol. XIII.

GLOCK, C. Y. and STARK, R. *Religion and Society in Tension*. Chicago: Rand and McNally, 1965.

POPPER, K. *Objective Knowledge. An Evolutionary Approach*, 5th edn. Oxford: University Press, 1979.

VERGOTE, A. *Dette et désir. Deux axes chrétiens et la dérive pathologique*. Paris: Editions du Seuil, 1978.

VERGOTE, A. and TAMAYO, A. *The Parental Figures and the Representation of God, A Psychological and Cross-Cultural Study*. The Hague, Netherlands: Mouton, 1981.

6

Religious states of mind: a reversal theory interpretation

MICHAEL J. APTER

Religion as a state of mind

It is probably safe to say that most people, whether themselves religious or not, understand the meaning of the distinction between doing something in a genuinely religious state of mind and merely "going through the motions". This means that there would seem to be something about religious activity which requires that it be performed in a particular spirit and that, unless this is the case, the activity cannot be said to be truly religious, however correctly performed in other respects. The implication of this is that psychological studies of religion which restrict themselves to overt behaviour alone are likely not only to be rather limited in scope but to miss the very essence of the phenomenon itself. This is particularly the case where the religious activity consists entirely in the search for, and attainment of, certain kinds of experience, especially since there may be little overt behaviour to observe in these cases at all. This does not mean that much of psychological interest may not be learned from the usual kinds of objective observational and experimental studies, but simply that they are unlikely to throw light on the peculiar and special nature of religious activity. The thrust of this argument is that the crucial psychological questions about religion (even about overt religious behaviour, as Loewenthal, 1975, has pointed out) can only be approached from a phenomenological perspective. And this is of course necessarily true of the most basic question of all which can be asked about religion by a psychologist: namely, what is the nature of religious experience and how does it differ from other kinds of experience?

In the history of the study of religion, the key feature of religious experience has generally been taken to be something like an awareness of, or belief in, supernatural forces of some kind which interact with the natural world. In other words, the religious state of mind involves the experience of something which is felt to be sacred, holy, divine, spiritual or, to use Rudolf Otto's (1923) term, "numinous". Thus E. B. Tylor in his pioneer study, *Primitive culture* (1871), suggested as a "minimum definition" of religion that it was "a belief in

62

spiritual beings". William James in *The varieties of religious experience* defined it as ". . . the feelings, acts, and experiences of individual men in their solitude, so far as they apprehend themselves to stand in relation to whatever they may consider the divine" (1960 edn., pp. 31–32). Elsewhere he argues that "Religion means primarily a universe of spiritual relations surrounding the earthly practical ones, not merely relations of 'value', but agencies and their activities" (Brown, 1973, p. 124). Indeed, the term "religion" itself comes from the Latin "religio" meaning "the awe felt in the presence of a spirit or god" (Ninian Smart, 1971, p. 325).

There are, however, a number of problems involved in defining religion or the religious state of mind in terms of some "content" of that state of mind, however special this content may be thought to be.

(1) It is possible to be aware of, or believe in, supernatural agencies and events without being in a religious state of mind while doing so. A scientific investigator of paranormal phenomena, for example, even if he believed in their supernatural origin, would not necessarily be (or even be likely to be) in what one would want to call a religious state of mind; nor would any of us when we are being merely superstitious – for example touching wood, or avoiding walking under ladders. In a rather different way, it is arguable whether someone who is carrying out occult practices is genuinely religious. And what about someone who believes in God but who, at a given time, is defiant and blasphemous: is he in a truly religious state of mind at that time? One might try to get around this problem by saying that someone in a religious state of mind must be aware of, or believing in, the existence of some particular type of supernatural entity – God, for example – and treating it with respect. Unfortunately, there is no single belief which is common to all the great world religions which could be unequivocally identified to define the state. Even the concept of God is not universal: for instance, no use is made of it in Buddhism.

(2) Defining religious experience in terms of the content of that experience does not bring out the close affinity which such experience seems to have to other experiences which do not involve the awareness of anything supernatural, including, for example, certain feelings of supreme contentedness, or of oneness with the natural world. Research on both meditation and peak experiences seems to show that such feelings as these are not necessarily interpreted by the subject in sacred or divine terms.

This is not to deny that some supernatural content is an essential part of a complete religious experience. But something else seems to be involved as well (and this something else seems to be involved in some other kinds of experiences too). In other words, supernatural content is a necessary but not sufficient part of a definition of "religious states".

If this "something else" cannot be identified in terms of content, it must have to do with *the way in which* this content is experienced or with the nature and quality of the experience itself, rather than with what is experienced. In

Husserl's phenomenological terms, it must be connected with "noesis" rather than "noema", "noesis" referring to the experience of psychological acts, such as judging, and noema to the experience of that which is acted on, or to that which is judged. For those who like computer analogies, this distinction is like the difference between the data on which a program can act and the program itself. (Of course a program itself can be changed by data, but it still formally remains different from the data which it is processing). What is being suggested here, therefore, is that the religious state of mind must be specified not just in terms of religious content, but also in terms of a "higher level" at which religious content is interpreted, organized, structured or processed in the phenomenal field. The implication is that the same content may be interpreted in different ways (just as a weight may be judged to be heavier one day than the next, or a picture as ugly on one occasion and beautiful on another), and that religious experience involves a particular way of relating to, and interpreting, the special content provided by religious systems.

The psychology of religion, as it has developed, has very little to say about religious states of mind conceived in this way. Indeed, since a large part of the modern psychology of religion has been influenced by the orientation of methodological behaviourism, it has had difficulty in dealing with the subjective aspects at all, although the use of questionnaires, attitude scales and the like has allowed religious experience to be approached in an indirect way. But even then the orientation has tended to be towards the "content" of the experience – what is believed, types of religious affiliation, and so on – rather than to the nature of the experience itself. So the whole thrust of modern experimental psychology in relation to religion has systematically tended to by-pass one of the central and most important questions of all: that concerning the nature and quality of religious "feeling", i.e. of religious experience itself as distinct from the specific beliefs, perceptions and allegiances which enter into it.

There is an important exception here, and this is the study of what one might term "strong" religious experiences through interviews, written descriptions etc., as carried out by Sir Alister Hardy and his team (e.g. Hardy, 1979) and latterly by David Hay (1982). These in turn relate to studies, including those carried out under the influence of humanistic psychology, of the *special* states of consciousness of a religious or quasi-religious type such as peak experiences and the experiences obtained during meditation (as in the review by Hetherington, 1975). However, religious states of mind are not confined to such special and strong experiences. Rather are the majority of religious experiences of a fairly mundane kind: the sort of experience which genuinely religious people will have experienced regularly at times throughout the day – for example while praying, or during church services. Very religious people are likely to be in this state of mind more frequently through everyday life than others, but this does not necessarily mean that any of these experiences are of a peak kind. Of course, studies of such special states of awareness may throw light on the more normal types of religious experience, by throwing some of its properties into strong relief. But one must not equate religious states of mind with such unusual states, or assume that genuinely religious people are necessarily regularly subject to overpowering experiences of this kind.

Clearly what is needed, then, is a psychological approach which is centred around different states of mind, where the term "state of mind" is understood to refer to the noetic properties of experience rather than to its noematic properties at a given time – in other words, which refers to the structure of the experience rather than to its content. Such an approach has been referred to as "structural phenomenology" (Apter, 1981) and defined as the search for pattern and structure in the nature and quality of experience. A particular structural–phenomenological theory of states of mind has in fact been developed by the writer with Dr K. C. P. Smith and other colleagues, and is known as "reversal theory". This identifies a number of distinct phenomenological states, each with its own characteristic way of structuring certain aspects of the phenomenal field. The theory was not developed initially to deal with problems in the psychology of religion, but rather to help in understanding various kinds of clinical problems (e.g. see Apter and Smith, 1979a,b; Svebak and Stoyva, 1980; Murgatroyd, 1981), and to provide a new conceptual framework for approaching research problems in the psychology of motivation, affect, and personality (e.g. see Apter, 1976; Murgatroyd *et al.*, 1978; Fontana, 1981; Svebak *et al.*, 1982). Nevertheless, certain of the states which have been identified seem to provide a "good fit" to structural aspects of what I have been calling "religious states of mind". The rest of this paper will therefore examine the religious state of mind from the reversal theory perspective.

Reversal theory: some basic concepts

It will not be possible here to provide anything but the very briefest sketch of some of the concepts of reversal theory. A detailed and extended account will, however, be found in *The experience of motivation* (Apter, 1982).

What reversal theory does is to define a set of pairs of states, each of which consists of two opposite ways of structuring or interpreting the content of the phenomenal field in some respect. At any time *one* member of each of these pairs is involved in organizing experience in this way. In other words, the pairs are complementary, but the members of each pair are mutually exclusive. Since the members of each pair are discretely different from each other, change between pairs is necessarily discontinuous and involves a type of switching which, since the members are opposite, may be thought of as a *reversal*. The use of the term "reversal" in the name of the theory highlights the central place which this switching process has in its explanations. (To continue the computer analogy, this would be like a computer which has a number of different programs for processing data in an on-line way, and which can switch from program to program while processing the same continuous data flow.)

Although these pairs of states determine many different aspects of the interpretation of the phenomenal field, they are defined at the outset in terms of different ways of interpreting aspects of the experience of motivation. They are therefore referred to as *metamotivational states.* Switches between the members of a pair of such states can be induced in a number of different ways which have been discussed in detail elsewhere (especially in Apter, 1982), including environmental events and social cues of different kinds. They also occur from time to time, if reversal does not occur for other reasons, as the result of a type of satiation. In other words, they are not situation-specific in any simple way and the same situation (over a period of time, or at different times) may therefore be encountered through the mediation of different combinations of metamotivational states. Which states are operative at a given time will often be recognizable from overt behaviour, but this is not necessarily the case and sometimes actions which appear to an external observer to be the same will nevertheless be performed in different states. Similarly an "inventory" of the contents of the phenomenal field would not necessarily disclose the metamotivational state, since the contents can be the same in different states.

Let us now look at some of the characteristics of three pairs of metamotivational states.

Telic and paratelic states

These are in fact complex states which can be distinguished in a number of different ways. One way is in terms of the relative status of means and ends, i.e. of goals, and activities which may lead towards goals. In the telic state the goal is primary in the sense that it is felt to be essential and unavoidable. (The word "telic" comes from the Greek "telos" meaning "goal" or "end"). Here, any activity which is undertaken acquires its meaning from the goal; and the activity is relatively flexible in that if one approach does not seem to work, then another is adopted. In the paratelic state, in contrast, the activity is primary in that it is undertaken for its own enjoyment; the goal, if there is one, is felt to be simply an excuse for the activity. In this case the goal is relatively flexible in that if the activity does not lead to one goal then a different goal may be adopted. Furthermore, in the telic state there is a linking tendency, so that activities are seen as leading to goals which in turn lead to yet other goals, and so on. Another way of putting this is by saying that in the telic state there is a search for significance, present goals being seen in the widest possible context of progress towards the future (and indeed achieving their "essential" status in this way). In contrast, in the paratelic state the activity is unlinked from its implications, is "encapsulated" and performed for itself, so that it has little or no significance beyond itself. The simplest way of putting all this is to say that the telic state is serious, the paratelic state playful.

One other aspect of the telic and paratelic states which should be mentioned is the way in which arousal is interpreted in each state. In the telic state, high arousal is felt as unpleasant and is avoided as far as possible. In this state it is in fact felt as some degree of anxiety. In the paratelic state, high arousal is felt as pleasant and is sought out. In this latter state it is felt as some degree of excitement. Part of the complexity of the two states derives from the interaction between the need for significance and the need for arousal in each state. In the telic state the feeling of high significance which is itself pleasant is at the same time likely to raise arousal to an uncomfortably high level; in the paratelic state one way to achieve pleasantly high arousal is to increase feelings of significance, but these are, as already noted, inimical to this state. The individual must therefore develop techniques for reconciling these contradictions within each state.

Conformist and negativistic states

The negativistic state is one in which the person feels a desire to act against some perceived requirement, e.g. some rule or expectation which is salient in the situation. The conformist state is the more usual one in which the individual is happy to act in conformity with the requirements of the situation as it is perceived. To gain satisfaction in the negativistic state, then, one must act in a way which is construed by oneself to be awkward, "difficult" or defiant, whereas in the conformist state one will feel uncomfortable if one sees oneself to be causing difficulties, breaking taboos, etc. These states are metamotivational since they are about the way in which individuals interpret their own reasons for their actions, and in principle many actions can be perceived in either way: for example, a teenager may wear long hair in order to defy the rules of those in authority or in order to conform to the expectancies of his or her peers.

Sympathy and mastery states

These two metamotivational states involves two different ways of seeing "self–other" relations, and, in each, self's motivational needs in relation to the other are felt differently.

In the sympathy state, self is felt to be open to other, and indeed there is felt to be a need for what one might call *mergence* with other. (The term "mergence" is used because it is neutral as to whether self or other is active in bringing this about, and it is neutral as to whether the other is living or is some non-living situation; in the latter case one is thinking of the so-called "oceanic feeling".) The word "love" refers to strong feelings of a need of this type. In the mastery state, self is felt to be closed to other and the tendency is towards further separation rather than a coming together. This does not preclude the other being "attached" to self, or possessed by self. But this implies an *assertiveness* by self, which only makes sense if self is different from other. The mastery state, then, is characterized by self's attempt to dominate an alien other.

These two ways of seeing self–other relations lead respectively to two different ways of seeing transactions between self and other. In the sympathy state one sees transactions as nurturant, i.e. one sees oneself to be nurturing, or nurtured by, other. In the mastery state one sees the transactions between self and other as to do with power and control, i.e. one sees oneself to be controlling, or being controlled by, other. The states are metamotivational since the same actions can frequently be seen either way. For example, a parent's guidance of a child can be seen by the parent (or the child for that matter) either as nurturant or as controlling, and indeed will probably be seen in each of these ways at different times. (This third pair of states is a recent addition to the theory and no reference will be found to this pair in Apter, 1982. They are described fully in Apter and Smith, in press.)

Although, as already noted, the conceptualization of these three pairs of states has been developed in the first instance in order to deal with certain traditional problems in the psychology of motivation and personality, and to provide insight into certain clinical phenomena, nevertheless one finds that light can also be thrown on the nature of the religious state of mind by reference to them. Specifically, it quickly becomes apparent that the genuinely religious state of mind is characterized by a combination of one particular member of each pair of metamotivational states: namely, the telic, the conformist and the sympathetic states.

Furthermore, the thesis will be that the supernatural content of these three allows each metamotivational state to be experienced in a peculiarly satisfactory way, and a way which is difficult to achieve by other means. That is to say, the "religious" content allows the believer the possibility of experiencing unusually high levels of significance and low levels of arousal in the telic state, exceptionally high levels of conformity in the conformist state, and provides him or her with extreme experiences of mergence and nurturance in the sympathetic state. Indeed, the "fit" of descriptions of religious experiences to these metamotivational states, and to preferred levels of the salient variables in these states, was quite unexpected to the writer until he examined the relevant literature. On doing so he was amazed by how often the key words of reversal theory occurred: such words as telos, significance, and mergence.

Let us now look at each of these metamotivational states in turn in the religious context: i.e. at the psychology of "faith, hope, and charity", which some might characterize as conformist, telic, and sympathetic respectively.

The religious state of mind as telic

One obvious feature of the religious state of mind is that it is *serious*. Or to put it the other way around, it eschews frivolity or triviality: rather, it is about that which the individual holds to be dearest and most important in his life. As William James put it: "For common man 'religion', whatever more special meanings it may have, signifies always a *serious* state of mind. . . . It favours gravity not pertness; it says 'hush' to all vain chatter and smart wit" (James, 1960 edn., p. 38; the italics are his). In this respect, then, the religious state is obviously telic rather than paratelic, and its goals tend to be the most serious and far-ranging ones there can possibly be: overcoming personal death, coming to terms with suffering and bereavement, and finding a positive meaning in life.

What different religions do is to provide, each in its own way, the promise that such goals *can* be achieved, and guidance as to *how* they can be achieved. As Bowker (1973) has put it: ". . . religions should be conceived as route-finding activities, mapping the general paths along which human beings can trace their way from birth to death and through death . . ." (p. 82). Thus the Christian prays that "we may so pass through things temporal that we finally lose not the things eternal" (Hebrews 13, 14).

This means that the adherents to a religion can derive from it enormous feelings of significance in relation to their activities, because they can be seen as linked to the ultimate goals of existence. To quote William James again: "And let the orientalists and pessimists say what they will, the thing of deepest – or, at any rate, of comparatively deepest – significance in life does seem to be its character of *progress* . . ." (James, 1907, p. 294).

This relationship of the religious state with the telic state comes out particularly clearly in the writings of Kierkegaard. As Mullen (1981) says in discussing Kierkegaard's "Concluding Unscientific Postscript":

> First, to the question of what it means to be a religious person in the abstract. The formula is: a religious person is one who has developed an absolute relationship to the absolute telos. Another expression of this is that the religious person has made his eternal blessedness the absolute telos of his life (p. 137).

It will also be realized that those religions which are essentially historical religions, like Judaism, Christianity and Islam, also tend to foster the idea of progress on earth towards some new state of man, e.g. at the second coming. So current actions are given significance not only in terms of the individual's progress to some kind of personal salvation, but also in terms of the progress of all mankind, or at least of those who believe in the religion, towards some future state of greater perfection when "God's will is done".

It was pointed out earlier that one of the arguments of reversal theory is that the aim of the telic state is not only to experience high significance in relation to one's actions, but also low arousal (i.e. relaxation). It is notable in this context that those activities which are likely to increase arousal to high levels and which are typically performed for this reason in the paratelic state, for example sexual activity and joking, are generally felt to be inappropriate and incongruous in the religious state; the psychological reason for this will now be apparent. Unfortunately, as has already been pointed out, a strong feeling of significance may itself raise arousal to an unpleasantly high level: if each action which a person performs is felt to relate to ultimate goals, then that person is likely to feel extremely anxious about such actions. Indeed, words stronger than "anxiety" – words like "awe" (which comes from an old Norse word meaning "fear") and "dread" – are sometimes used to describe this feeling in the religious state of mind. But now we come to one of the key features of religion: typically, belief in a religion provides the believer concurrently with feelings of high significance and low arousal. In other words, religions reconcile the inherent conflict in the telic state between these two kinds of need, allowing the possibility of a simultaneous optimization of both felt significance and felt arousal. This is one of the things which is so special and satisfying about the religious state of mind, at least if advantage is taken by the individual of the possibility to which belief gives rise. And in sociological terms this may be one of the pivotal reasons for the continuing success of religious institutions.

How do religions achieve this? They do so by offering not only ultimate significance but also, in some sense, ultimate reassurance. This is achieved through the promise of individual salvation (and also perhaps of the eventual advent of some kind of utopia on earth). Sometimes this promise is unconditional: e.g. we are all saved through God's mercy, or through Christ's death. But more typically it is conditional: we are saved (and this is guaranteed) if we believe certain things, or if we behave in accordance with certain rules, or if we perform certain ritual actions on a regular basis, or if we can bring ourselves to feel certain kinds of sentiment (e.g. love of God). In Eastern religions this is expressed in terms of progress through a series of incarnations governed by the law of Karma: if one is good in this life, then inevitably the next life will be better than the present one, and, provided one continues to do good and be good, one will continue on a path of upward progress until eventually one attains a supernatural state of ultimate bliss.

The religious state of mind as conformist

The stoics believed that wisdom lay in conforming to the laws of the universe, and all the major world religions have also required, from their adherents, obedience to laws of various kinds which are believed to be laid down at some supernatural level. Such obedience is of course particularly required in the monastic orders which the great faiths have given rise to; but compliance to at least certain fundamental principles is also demanded of secular adherents. In the words of the fourteenth-century *Theologia Germanica*: "Man is created for true obedience, and is bound of right to render it to God" (see extract in Happold, 1970, p. 296). Indeed, the word "pious" comes from the Latin "pius" meaning "dutiful". (It is notable, too, that the word "Islam" means "submission" and "Muslim" means "the submissive"). The necessity for obedience, and the dire consequences of a lack of obedience, are also made clear in some of Man's greatest myths: for example, the story of Adam's defiance of God's rule in the Garden of Eden, and the myth of Prometheus who disobeyed the Gods in bringing fire to Mankind.

This, then, is the second structural–phenomenological characteristic of the religious state of mind: it is conformist rather than negativistic. As already indicated in discussing telic aspects of the religious state, personal salvation according to all the major religions can be achieved only through compliance with what are seen as essential rules; and the pursuit of salvation through these rules typically gives rise to both feelings of great significance and to feelings of security and reassurance and, as a concomitant, a generally relaxed state of mind. However, it is argued in reversal theory (for reasons which cannot be developed here) that the feeling that one is conforming is itself pleasant in the conformist state of mind (just as the perception that one is acting defiantly is pleasant in the negativistic state). Conformity therefore becomes a value in its own right, and makes its own contribution to the special feeling of well-being which religious people can achieve.

There are generally three types of rules required in relation to behaviour by religious systems. Ideally they must all be complied with, although the first type is the most important:

(1) Moral rules, such as those represented by the Ten Commandments.
(2) Rules for everyday practice, e.g. about what may or may not be worn under which circumstances, and what may or may not be eaten.
(3) Rules for special ritual activities, e.g. concerning religious services or pilgrimages.

Such rules are not restricted to overt behaviour, but also govern "right thinking". Again, they can be discerned at three levels:

(1) Rules of belief, such as those embodied in the Christian creeds. The central significance of "faith" becomes apparent here.
(2) Rules about beliefs in relation to everyday life, e.g. that every action, however small, is recorded in some way and may determine such matters as entry into heaven or hell.
(3) Rules for special religious thinking, e.g. during prayer or meditation.

So the religious state of mind is not only a state which, through interaction with certain ideas about supernatural forces, gives rise to extreme feelings of satisfaction in relation to the telic state. It also allows, again by means of a certain kind of religious "content", the possibility of extreme feelings of pleasure in relation to the conformist state.

The religious state of mind as sympathetic

The third structural–phenomenological characteristic of the religious state of mind is that it is sympathetic in the sense defined earlier.

The key part which the feeling of "mergence" plays in religion is denoted by the word "religion" itself, the root of which is based on the Latin word "ligare" meaning "to bind". It is also interesting that the word "Holy" comes from an old English word meaning "whole" and that "atonement" means, literally, "at one-ment". In other words, the religious state of mind involves more than just the recognition of spiritual or supernatural forces: there is also frequently some feeling of mergence or union with such forces. As Starbuck wrote in his classic, *The psychology of religion* (1901): "The individual learns to transfer himself from a centre of self-activity into an organ of revelation of universal being, and to live a life of affection for and oneness with the larger life outside" (p. 147). This may be experienced as entering into these forces or being entered by them. There is therefore no place in this state of mind for selfishness, conceit, individualism, self-glorification, etc.

This means that the truly religious person attempts to live his or her life in such a way as to be in the sympathy rather than the mastery state for as long as possible and, when in the sympathy state, to try to fulfil the needs of that state by feeling at one with supernatural forces – either directly or through sympathy with other people or situations. The extremely devout person will, of course, avoid interactions with the natural world which might tend to induce the mastery state. Indeed it is for this reason that chastity and poverty are extolled in the major religions: both of these help the individual to avoid feelings of possessiveness and also of a tendency to "manipulate" things and other people. And the ultimate aim of life is typically seen as complete and permanent "oneness" with supernatural forces, whether this is expressed as oneness with God, as Heaven or as Nirvana.

When the orientation of the sympathy state is more towards active transactions between self and other, rather than simply passive feelings, these transactions are experienced as forms of nurturance or love, so one feels oneself to be nurturing and/or being nurtured, loving and/or being loved, giving or being given, cherishing or being cherished. This of course contrasts with the feelings that go with transactions in the mastery state: dominating or submitting, controlling or being controlled, manipulating or being manipulated, taking or having taken away. Such feelings of nurturance can be expressed towards the supernatural forces themselves; for example, through religious ritual like church services; and the feelings experienced are described by such words as reverence, devotion and worship. But they can also, of course, be expressed towards other people, perhaps on behalf of supernatural forces.

The need to love is, of course, central to Christianity, with Christ setting the new "commandment" of love above all the commandments of the Old

Testament. "But I say unto you which hear, love your enemies, do good to them which hate you". (Luke 6, 27.) But it is also important in other traditions. For example, as John Crook (1980) has pointed out in relation to Buddhism:

> In the Mahayana attitude, without a total dedication to the release of all sentient beings from suffering an understanding of Buddhism is not attained. This attitude of mind requires that all "merit" which accrues through any personal practice be deliberately dedicated to the task of personal enlightenment undertaken solely in the service of others (p. 378).

It can be seen then that the deep contentment of the completely religious state of mind derives not just from the pleasures of the telic and conformist states, but also from the satisfactions which religion makes possible in the sympathetic state through mergence and nurturance or, in more everyday Christian language, through feelings of oneness with God and through love.

Complications and implications

Obviously what has been presented so far is no more than the beginning of the argument, and a number of issues and themes are immediately raised. Although they cannot be developed in this paper, it might be useful to list some of these themes and to make one or two comments about them.

Relation to special religious states of mind

If one examines accounts of such states as those experienced during meditation, peak experiences and mystical communion, one is struck, even more forcibly than when examining the nature of more mundane religious states, by the way in which they involve the telic, conformist and, especially, the sympathy states, and the way in which the special feelings obtained in these states can be heightened beyond normal levels.

Dynamic aspects of religious experience

Reversal theory emphasizes the transience of metamotivational states, each state giving way to its opposite sooner or later, through the laws of an internal dynamic. This means that there is a continuing tendency for reversal between states, even during the course of the same action or while thinking about the same things. So religious content can continue to be experienced in a cognitively consistent way in the paratelic, negativistic and mastery states, producing at such times what one might call "paradoxical religious states". This theme has been examined in more detail in the chapter on religion in Apter (1982). For example, one can be negativistic on behalf of one's religious group by defying the requirements of a society that does not recognize the legitimacy of that group. Or one can attempt to master others in the service of God.

The relationship of religion to magic

It is, of course, possible to experience, or believe in, supernatural forces while in the paratelic, negativistic and mastery states and to do so in a way in which the cognitive content is in some sense opposite to that of people in religious states of mind. Thus, instead of being sympathetic with spiritual forces one can attempt to master and control them, using them for one's own selfish ends. This is the essence of magic in its various forms, including witchcraft, sorcery, shamanism, devil worship, and "the occult" in general. Indeed it can now be seen that the phenomenological distinctions which have been made here allow the difference between religion and magic to be expressed in a systematic and clear-cut way. The basic difference is that of whether the supernatural other is experienced in a sympathetic or mastery state. (It is notable in this respect that the very word "magic" appears to come from the root of the Latin word "magister" meaning "master".) Combined with this is a tendency in magic for the negativistic state to be experienced: thus black magic frequently involves flouting taboo and conventions, for example through blasphemy, sexual activity and violence of one kind or another. (Furthermore, particularly today, it tends to be carried out in a playful paratelic way, as a kind of game.)

Comparative aspects of religious states of mind

The approach which has been outlined here provides a new perspective on the ways in which different religious systems differ from each other. At the most obvious level they differ in terms of the relative emphasis given to the telic, conformist and sympathy states respectively. For example, in Islam the conformist aspect is particularly important, while in Christianity the central emphasis on love implies that in principle the sympathy aspect is predominant. However, religions also differ in more complex ways which have to do with the interplay between the noetic and noematic levels. For example, if God is seen as transcendent, then he becomes more than anything else the giver of rules (e.g. the Ten Commandments) and feelings of mergence therefore tend to be with something else, such as the religious group (e.g. the "Chosen People"). If, however, God is seen as potentially or actually immanent, then mergence can be with God and there is less need for identification with a particular group. This theme of the different patterns of relationship which are possible between metamotivational states and belief structures cannot be pursued further here; but it illustrates the way in which reversal theory leads to the possibility of new and important kinds of questions being asked about religion and fresh psychological insights gained about the nature of religious experience and behaviour.

References

APTER, M. J. Some data inconsistent with the optimal arousal theory of motivation. *Perceptual and Motor Skills*, 1976; **43**, 1209–1210.

APTER, M. J. *The experience of motivation: the theory of psychological reversals*. London and New York: Academic Press, 1982.

APTER, M. J. The possibility of a structural phenomenology: the case of reversal theory. *Journal of Phenomenological Psychology*, 1981; **12**(2), 173–187.

APTER, M. J. and SMITH, K. C. P. Psychological reversals: some new perspectives on the family and family communication. *Family Therapy*, 1979a; **6**(2), 89–100.

APTER, M. J. and SMITH, K. C. P. Sexual behaviour and the theory of psychological reversals. In *Love and Attraction – an International Conference*, Ed. M. COOK and G. WILSON, Oxford: Pergamon Press, 1979b; pp. 405–408.

APTER, M. J. and SMITH, K. C. P. Experiencing personal relationships. In *Reversal Theory: Applications and Developments*, Ed. M. J. APTER, D. FONTANA and S. MURGATROYD, Cardiff: University College Cardiff Press, in press; pp. 161–178.

BOWKER, J. *The sense of God*. Oxford: Clarendon Press, 1973.

BROWN, L. B. (Ed.) *Psychology and religion*. Harmondsworth: Penguin, 1973.

CROOK, J. H. *The evolution of human consciousness*. Oxford: Clarendon Press, 1980.

FONTANA, D. Obsessionality and reversal theory. *British Journal of Clinical Psychology*, 1981; **20**, 299–300.

HAPPOLD, F. C. *Mysticism*. Harmondsworth: Penguin, 1970.

HARDY, Sir A. *The spiritual nature of man*. Oxford: Clarendon Press, 1979.

HAY, D. *Exploring inner space*. Harmondsworth: Penguin, 1982.

HETHERINGTON, R. *The sense of glory: A psychological study of peak-experiences*. London: Friends Home Service Committee, 1975.

JAMES, W. *Talks to teachers of psychology: and to students on some of life's ideals*. London: Longmans, Green & Co., 1907.

JAMES, W. *The varieties of religious experience*. New York: Random House, 1960 (originally published 1902).

LOEWENTHAL, K. Psychology and religion: comments on Giles, Jones, Horton and Lay. *Bulletin of the British Psychological Society*, 1975; **28**, 349–350.

MULLEN, J. D. *Kierkegaard's philosophy*. New York: Mentor Books, 1981.

MURGATROYD, S. Reversal theory: a new perspective on crisis counselling. *British Journal of Guidance and Counselling*, 1981; **9**(2), 180–193.

MURGATROYD, S., RUSHTON, C., APTER, M. and RAY, C. The development of the Telic Dominance Scale. *Journal of Personality Assessment*, 1978; **42**(5), 519–528.

OTTO, R. *The idea of the holy* (trans. J. W. Harvey). Oxford: University Press, 1923 (first published in German in 1917).

SMART, N. *The religious experience of mankind*. Glasgow: Collins (Fontana Library), 1971.

STARBUCK, E. D. *The psychology of religion*. London: Walter Scott, 1901.

SVEBAK, S. and STOYVA, J. High arousal can be pleasant and exciting: the theory of psychological reversals. *Biofeedback and Self-Regulation*, 1980; **5**(4), 439–444.

SVEBAK, S., STORFJELL, O. and DALEN, K. The effect of a threatening context upon motivation and task-induced physiological changes. *British Journal of Psychology*, 1982; **73**(4), 505–512.

TYLOR, E. B. *Primitive culture*. London: John Murray, 1871.

7

Non-experimental and experimental methods in the psychology of religion: a few thoughts on their implications and limits

JEAN-PIERRE DECONCHY

IT IS naturally an impossible task to describe all the methods used or usable in the psychology of religion, or to do that in a manner which is both precise and innovative. A number of choices have to be made. In order to establish roughly what these pages propose I will start by specifying these choices, and giving a few preliminary details.

(1) I intend to focus on a number of methods, and on the current state of their use, but I do not propose to draw up a list of the objects to which these methods are applied. In this respect I am confronted with at least two difficulties: first the artificiality of considering methodological tools independently of the theories which have introduced them and independently of the theories which have emerged from the knowledge that these tools have helped to validate; secondly, in the absence of truly operational definitions of "religion", there is an unavoidable reliance on cultural labels, without recourse to the precise psycho-social mechanisms that define religion.

(2) Given the diversity of non-experimental methods, I will need to be selective and exclude some of them from consideration. Some exclusions are obvious, since I will not refer to theological approaches to religious attitudes and modes of behaviour, nor to studies which maintain some sort of correspondence between scientific and theological methodologies. I will thus leave out of account what has been termed "religiology" (for example, Kishimoto, 1967) and "psycho-theology" (as in Stern and Marino, 1970; McLemore, 1976, and in the regularly published proceedings of the Whitinsville Symposia), and I will omit the work of the so-called "integrative" school (for example, Carter and Narramore, 1979; Collins, 1977) despite the undoubted value of some of this work

(Koteskey, 1980). Other methods are excluded on practical grounds: not being well-versed in clinical psychology, I will leave out work which comes under this heading, even though some of it uses interesting information-gathering techniques (as in research on the relationships between the representations of God and parental figures by Godin and Hallez, 1964, and Vergote and Tamayo, 1981).

(3) It would, of course, be quite wrong to think that the sort of work I have been asked to comment on can be restricted to a catalogue and a mere inventory of available information. The choice of a method, particularly when it is to be applied to religious attitudes and modes of behaviour, is not epistemologically neutral, nor is it ideologically static. My study of this area of scientific work will necessarily be conditioned and filtered by a number of epistemological assumptions which I have discussed elsewhere (Deconchy, 1976, 1977, 1978b), and which can be summarized briefly. Firstly, I believe that religious modes of behaviour and religious functioning are social facts, like any others. Consequently, a scientific approach to them does not require methodological tools which are intrinsically different from those required to approach other social or psycho-social facts. Secondly, I believe that as things stand at present it makes sense, before attempting to establish the nature of any "specific differences", to relate religious modes of behaviour and religious functioning to the field on which they depend, and to link them with the ideological phenomena to which they logically and sociologically belong. Thirdly, I believe that these modes of behaviour and functioning are not totally beyond the scope of an experimental treatment, in the strict sense of that term, so long as this method is used with due care and circumspection, as in any other attempt to clarify complex social phenomena (Deconchy, 1981). The assumptions I have just summarized naturally reflect different options, open to discussion, criticism and revision.

Non-experimental methods*

In the first part of this section I will concentrate on studies based on more or less rigorous conceptualizations, which have sought to establish the "dimensions" of a religious attitude, using scales that enable subjects to be assessed in relation to their own group.

In the next part of this section I will concentrate on a number of studies, many of which are still incomplete, which seek to highlight some more or less fundamental mechanisms, of which the so-called "religious" modes of behaviour and functioning might be considered particular examples.

Studies are referred to here as illustrations of particular areas of research, as examples of an investigative process, or as symptoms of a global state of mind.

* Translated by Erik Pearse.

The chapter does not therefore contain an exhaustive bibliography, nor does it award prizes for merit.

The dimensions of religious attitudes or the religious dimensions of attitude?

There is no point in merely repeating others' inventories or plagiarizing analyses of particular fields. There is, for example, in an excellent manual edited by Malony (1977), Flakoll's (1977) list of the different information-gathering procedures used by the psychology of religion from 1900 to 1960 (these cover "questionnaires, interview, biographical, content analysis, recreative, diary, documentary, psycho-historical, introspection, observation, orders of merit, scales, tests, statistics, experiments, surveys, personal documents, projective techniques, clinical studies, timed-cross examination"), and Neil Warren's (1977) critical analysis of the primary methodologies in use from 1960 to 1970.

In the past few years there does not, technically speaking, appear to have been any radical new development of methodological tools. It is true that studies on the "dimensions" of the religious attitude have increased and spawned a rich harvest of specific scales and indices. Equally, there have been many comparisons between scores obtained on these scales and those obtained for other attitudes and modes of social behaviour. While statistical methods have become increasingly sophisticated and diversified, in the past few years the methodology in this research into the psychology of religion has remained relatively traditional, both in its tools and areas of application.

The area of operation and the conceptual framework of traditional tools in the psychology of religion

To evaluate a methodology solely on the basis of its technology is doubtless, in the field of research we are exploring, somewhat artificial. I will therefore spend no further time on it. Beyond the technology (which generally reduces to linguistic material), what really animates and supports the methodology is the set of concepts with which the research begins and around which it organizes its inquiry. In this respect the conceptual universe in which the psychology of religion takes root, and the parts on which it focuses, remain somewhat blurred, ambiguous, and confused. Roof's strictures (1979) are perceptive and hardly pessimistic:

> [This] tradition of research has been, and continues to be, plagued by alternative and inconsistent conceptual schemes, often making it difficult to replicate findings from one study to another. All too often in religious research, investigators proceed in an ad hoc fashion, looking at any and all "dimensions" that are presumed to exist without serious concern for their theoretical meanings, logical interrelations, or substantive significance. This results in a good deal of confusion over whether dimensions are of central or only of peripheral significance, and exactly how the many dimensions add up to a comprehensive

conception of religion. And the lack of a good analytic scheme often results in a potpourri of empirical findings, difficult to interpret in any meaningful sense (p. 35).

A harsh assessment, but probably well-founded. Rather than dwell on this, I will seek to highlight, within this field of research itself and independently of any particular deficiencies, some of the elements which, being integral to the field, may play a part in inducing some imprecision in our conceptual tools.

1. The formal ambiguity of this type of research

This research has abandoned the idea of using the "religious" variable as one which is univocal and coherent and has sought to separate different "dimensions" which would refract its complexity. In so doing, it has undoubtedly avoided a naive and artificial approach, even though doubts have been expressed about the relevance of such an initiative (Clayton and Gladden, 1974). This has led to the construction of an interesting set of methods which proceed almost exclusively by means of questionnaires and scales.

Such a procedure is, however, not devoid of ambiguities, since it is only infrequently related to the mechanisms which come into play in the religious attitude. Most of the time the basis for the choice of items for a questionnaire oscillates between a number of nebulous and poorly controlled criteria. Some of these criteria reflect a latent but immediate phenomenology of what constitutes the religious experience; others are related to patterns of social behaviour which are more or less directly controlled by the institutional systems within which the "religious" subject is found; others emerge purely and simply (whether instinctively or via "experts") from statements of belief which are judged to be characteristic of the ideological package which binds a particular religious group together. This constant oscillation between subjective, social, and institutional approaches, based on the juxtaposition and an unmeasurable weighting of different "components" of what might be a "religious" attitude, yet devoid of a real analysis of their interrelationships, leads to the construction of tools which are heterogeneous and difficult to correlate or compare one with another.[1]

The best of these tools aim to construct a multidimensional analysis of the religious attitude and partly succeed in avoiding vacillation and uncertainties. The conceptual base they stand on, and use, is at least in part constructive. In this respect our attention if naturally drawn to the conceptual categories in the work of Lenski (1961) (who contrasted the associational against the communal, and doctrinal orthodoxy against devotionalism); Fukuyama (1961) (with cognitive, cultic, creedal, devotional) or of Glock and Stark (Glock, 1959; Glock and Stark, 1965; Stark and Glock, 1968) (ideological, ritualistic, experiential, intellectual, consequential).[2] Sets of tools and concepts like these have undoubtedly helped to establish some order in an area of research characterized by the extremely varied nature of its

[1]The notes for this chapter are on pages 111–2.

phenomenology. It is nevertheless true, even when it is carefully controlled, that the formal ambiguity of this type of research is only partly overcome.

It is inevitable that, in order to cover the whole field, analyses which combine, without clearly defining how they are interrelated, both subjective and social approaches,[3] occasionally have recourse to a particular set of tools to organize one of those two approaches. The social approach sometimes goes as far as being ethnologically specific, as in Greeley (1963), where the tools vary ingeniously for the different religious contexts to which they are applied, whether for Protestants, Catholics or Jews. The subjective approach incorporates taxonomies and typologies suggesting that religious experience is a distinct entity, not specifically related to the social context which underpins and defines it (Stark and Glock, 1968).[4] Apart from tending to opposite extremes, such an undefined juxtaposition of the subjective and the social may also lead to a virtual disintegration of the object under study, as, for example, in the 176 final propositions in the work by Maranell (1974). Their organization around a series of unobjectionable concepts (church orientation, ritualism, altruism, fundamentalism, theism, idealism, superstition, and mysticism) makes an *a priori* assumption that certain combinations "are not expected to occur". Yet, in such a field and in the network of cognitive strategies which lie within it, can *any* combination realistically be excluded?[5]

2. A continuing distinction: the "two" religions

In speaking of the sets of tools used in any area of the psychology of religion, we have stressed the conceptual confusion which arises as a result of the undefined nature of the personal/social interface which organizes the religious attitude. There may be another unspoken element running through the psychology of religion which disrupts its conceptual base and could impede its development because of a common tendency in our field of research to distinguish two types of religion. It is epistemologically essential to axiomatize this tendency, part of which derives from a scientifically based analysis and part of which is possibly moulded by the acceptance, whether it is instinctive or apologetic, of the same evaluative criteria that are used by those holding the religious beliefs under study.

The most obvious example of such an analytical strategy, and also the one which provides the most elaborate scientific basis, is probably Allport's extrinsic/intrinsic distinction. Although it is sometimes considered as itself a "dimension" of the religious attitude which can be set in parallel or in juxtaposition to those already mentioned, this combination is surely different from them in nature and value. Step by step, Allport succeeded in transforming his initial personal religion/institutional religion dichotomy (Allport, 1955, pp. 451–456) into a more subtle "extrinsic–intrinsic" continuum. Whereas it was at first perceived in its own right as reflecting a religion associated with ethnic prejudice (Allport, 1960), extrinsicness (in which religion only plays an instrumental role) became one end of a continuum reflecting religious affiliation bounded at the other end by intrinsicness (in which religion is coextensive with life and personal commitment) (Allport, 1966; Allport and Ross, 1967). In the final analysis it is not religion itself which is being measured by this bi-polar scale, but the social motives associated with belief and religious practice.

Even though Allport's work is, in many respects, exemplary, and the model he has constructed has proved to be very fruitful, one cannot help noticing that, below the surface, it consists of a set of evaluations which are not underpinned and controlled by scientific analysis alone. Whatever might be said, and, indeed, whatever the intention, his research tools probably depend on an unformulated analytical grid which makes a distinction between a "good" religious attitude and a "less good" religious attitude, on the basis of criteria which are inevitably polysemic. This latent axiologization of the research tools is evident, though often less clearly than in Allport's work, in other typologies, especially in distinctions between the "committed" and the "consensual" (Allen and Spilka, 1967), the "mythological" and the "symbolic" (Hunt, 1972), the "behavioural" and the "ideational" (Himmelfarb, 1975), and an "acted out" and "internalized" religion (Roof, 1979; Himmelfarb, 1975). It can also be found in analyses of the relationship between locus of control and various religious indicators.

Little research has been done to assess interrelationships between the subjective and the social in the religious attitude, or the mechanisms which underlie this interrelationship, because they are generally considered to be self-evident. That judgement is in turn probably due to analyses which are close, and even internal to religious options and institutions, and which reflect such widespread social anthropologies as Bergson's closed/open religion or Tönnies' *Gemeinschaft/Gesellschaft*. These useful distinctions are, however, of limited value in terms of any empirical gathering of information. We are thus faced with tacitly adopting evaluative criteria or "definitions" of religion which religious groups themselves use to identify themselves and which, in a certain type of society, they have effectively succeeded in transmitting to other disciplines (including scientific approaches) as ones on which they should base their analyses. This may be a sensitive point in the potentially conflicted encounter between scientific knowledge and the analysis which religious groups make of their own functioning for inevitably "religious" purposes.

It is worth asking whether the latent distinction between a "good" and a "less good" religious attitude, between the "authentic" and the "less authentic", does not itself lead to accepting a distinction between types of psychology of religion (Sullivan, 1962), research strategies (Havens, 1961) and even in the techniques of measurement (Dittes, 1971) (cf. Wuthnow's, 1981, recent contribution on this subject). It remains to be seen whether, at the intersection of these distinctions, a psychology of religion concerned with patterns of behaviour and interaction bounded and controlled by a complex and more or less institutionalized social field, is not sometimes considered second-rate. Even though that type of psychology cannot realistically succeed in mastering the subject single-handed, it is difficult to see the scientific criteria for such an evaluation.

Roof's (1979) stern judgement does not need to be elaborated with further illustrations of our weaknesses. It may be more useful to show briefly, without the benefit of extensive argument, that the area we are exploring is bedevilled with great patches of uncertainty, some of a theoretical and epistemological nature, others of an ideological nature. We need to stress again the well-established fact of the weak theoretical base which supports attempts by the psychology of religion to establish itself as a scientific sub-discipline; especially the absence, or virtual absence, of specific theories concerning religious attitudes, religious functioning and religious mechanisms, and a reluctance in practice to make use of theoretical tools developed by and for other areas of research.

Towards a revised approach

It must be said, however, that despite the above assessment, several attempts have been made to renew this field of research with a new conceptual framework, and as a consequence, our research tools and methods have been adjusted. Wuthnow (1979) is right to point out that, in the past few years, the concept of religion, as an integral part of scientific research, is in the process of being re-examined and has undergone a number of transformations. This research has led us to "re-examine many of the relationships between religion and other social factors", to move more decisively "toward an investigation of religious change and the relationships between religion and other forms of social change" and to envisage "a more extensive application of quantitative methods to comparative and historical studies of religion". Eister (1974) makes similar points, albeit less forcefully.

1. Renewal and expansion of concepts

The religious attitude has traditionally, even when organized around a number of internal "dimensions", been a phenomenon relatively isolated from attitudes that have not been labelled "religious" by the culture, despite later attempts at integration, and from its sociological roots and social objectives.

Several strands of research have converged to see the religious attitude incorporating a more extensive set of attitudes that attempt to place it within wider sociological fields, already explored in other contexts. These developments naturally make it necessary to establish links with the other networks in which the religious attitude falls. The general tenor of these initiatives, though not yet integrated are underpinned by similar social developments that point to such links being readily found within different social environments.

Roof (1979) highlights three separate strands in this research and we shall consider each of them briefly.

(a) The "civil religious commitment"

The concept of "civil religion" is so closely interwoven with the American consciousness that it is sometimes difficult for us Europeans to understand it entirely. Based in particular on the work of Bellah (1967) and a few good analytical studies, such as those of Wimberley et al. (1976), the concept refers, according to Whitney (1968), to "the civil profession of faith . . . without which a man cannot be a good citizen or a faithful subject". Over and above specifically institutional and denominational features, there thus appears to be in the United States an all-embracing religious dimension which informs, in the Aristotelian sense and as a consequence of a more or less general, yet seldom critical, consensus, the whole of the social field, including the political dimension. If that is indeed the case, there is no point in trying to separate the attitude labelled "religious" from the social context of which it is a visible extrusion, like the tip of an iceberg. In the light of recent analyses (such as Hammond, 1981), one may wonder whether this concept of "civil religion" can survive its historical context.

(b) Interest in "ultimate concerns"

The "religious" attitude is in this instance seen to specify, through its own models, a whole set of values, interests and questions peculiar to human nature. Both institutional religion and the religion exercised by particular individuals through religious attitudes and behaviour, are responsible for bringing to the surface and making "visible" an "invisible" substratum (Luckmann, 1967) and a set of permanent and fundamental problems peculiar to the human predicament (Yinger, 1970, 1977).

It follows that such a "religion", which is explicitly lived by individuals and takes root in institutional or ritual phenomena which can be empirically identified, can only be effectively studied with reference to the deeply embedded substratum on which it depends. This is a very interesting approach, insofar as it reinstates the religious attitude within a totally subjective but still social situation, and provides a stronger base for the conceptual field established by the psychology of religion. Within our own field it presents operational and measurement problems which, although stimulating and probably fruitful, are still unsolved.

(c) Alternative systems of meaning

Wuthnow (1976) considers that the systems of meanings supported and carried by religions are taken from the "stock" of socially and anthropologically available systems from which choices are made selectively, simultaneously, or alternatively. These systems of meaning draw strands from theism, individualism, mysticism and social science itself, and reflect, amongst other things, methods of interpreting events and experiences known and lived by individuals, and the causal explanations they attribute to these events and experiences. Within such a conceptual framework (which is, surprisingly, seldom related to that which the theory of attribution has itself helped to establish), the "religious" label that is given to particular displays, attitudes and behaviour by the surrounding dominant culture is merely an historically dated and socially based specification of some general pattern of behaviour to which it must be grafted, and which is then to be explained and understood.

It would clearly take too long to assess the empirical work that has resulted from the widened scope of these concepts, even were we to concentrate simply on studies directly related to the psychology or the psycho-sociology of religion (cf. Klausner's (1964) analyses of an earlier period). It is nevertheless possible to say that recent empirical work has helped to enlarge and strengthen the conceptual field of our sub-discipline and has contributed to creating a climate for the partial reappraisal of our traditional tools.

2. The reappraisal of traditional concepts and dimensions

It may indeed be, as a result of this new epistemological sensitivity, that a critical reappraisal of the traditional conceptual tools has already taken place.

Formal examples can be found in the repeated attempts to enlarge and adjust the extrinsic/intrinsic distinctions which has had such fruitful implications that it has become a "popular psychological concept" (See the issue of the *Journal for the Scientific Study of Religion*, 1971; **10**(2).) This development can also be found in the reviews by Bagley (1970), Gorsuch and Aleshire (1974) and Payette (1981), where the "nomenclature" approach still leaves room for further analysis, and other examples can be found in the assessments by King and Hunt (1972), Tate and Miller (1971), Strickland and Shaffer (1971) and Hood (1971).

The readjustment and enlargement of these concepts also appear to have produced a strand of research in which epistemological reasoning seems to have a far-reaching impact, as for example with the use of religious orientations in understanding other psycho-social phenomena (Batson, Naifeh and Pate, 1978), with the contrast between psychological and sociological categorizations of the religious field itself (Dittes, 1971), and in formulating newer concepts, logically necessary for the proper functioning of the initial conceptual tools, like the concept of "salience" (Roof and Perkins, 1975).

3. The de-institutionalization of "religious" as a concept

At the interface of an emphasis that seeks religion within a broader sociological field and in more extended anthropological settings, and the attempt to formulate an analytic language distinct from the language (itself "religious" or "theological") accepted by the groups which are surveyed, another sphere of research has arisen, of which we shall mention three arbitrarily selected aspects.

De-institutionalization in relation to the "Church". Beyond the church/sect typology, with its obvious significance for the sociology of religion and its limited impact on research into the psychology and the psycho-sociology of religion (Carrier, 1960, being an exception), the study of the effervescent forms which may characterize religion is now central to many problems. Glossolalia, for example, severed from an area of practice and language traditionally and "doctrinally" occupied by ecclesiastical institutions, has been, and continues to be, responsible for some stimulating research work (see, for example, Bryant and O'Connell, 1971; Godin, 1975; Goodman, 1969, 1972, 1973; Hutch, 1980; Kildahl, 1972; Laffal, Monaham and Richman, 1974; Lovekin and Malony, 1977; Niesz and Kronenberg, 1978; Osser *et al.*, 1973; Richardson, 1973; Ryan, 1978; Samarin, 1972a,b, 1973; Spanos and Hewitt, 1979; Stanley, Bartlett and Moyle, 1978).

De-institutionalization of an institutional or theological language. This includes Embree's (1973) attempt to distance himself in part from the language controlled by institutions with recourse to free associations, Brown and Forgas' (1980) desire to use a "free collection of religious concepts", and Shuter's (1979) tentative correlations between religious affiliation and the characteristics of non-verbal communication.

De-institutionalization of the traditional concepts of affiliation. Beyond typologies specific to religious groupings (Filsinger, Faulkner and Warland, 1979), there have been repeated attempts to give a conceptual framework for the "non-religious" or the religious "nones", who have traditionally been considered unidimensional, and even ideologically void (Bender, 1968; Hadaway and Roof, 1979; Perry *et al.*, 1980; Tomka, 1979; Vernon, 1968), using tools geared to exploring the religious attitude (Wiebe and Fleck, 1980). From an epistemological point of view this area of research could have far-reaching consequences, insofar as it seeks to escape from the socio-cognitive controls established by religious institutions.

4. A critique of some traditional concepts

Studies which highlight the heterogeneous nature of some systems of belief (as in Hertel, 1980), or the extraordinary plasticity of the religious attitude, traditionally defined (as in the religion–astrology dialectic (Brink, 1978), or in the religion–paranormal belief shift of Emmons and Sobal, 1981), may be responsible for a reappraisal of conceptual tools that have been considered self-evident.

The operational significance of these concepts must be reappraised, whether they are all-embracing, like religious commitment (Stark and Bainbridge, 1980; Finney, 1978) and religious membership (Kelly, 1970), or restricted, like religiosity, religious affiliation and religious belief, (Campbell and Coles, 1973) or religious thinking and religious attitudes (Baither and Saltzberg, 1978). There has also been a critical evaluation of the methodology of information-gathering, itself dependent on the conceptual field which it explores, including self-designating behaviour (McPhail, 1972), the bipolarity of scales of religious attitudes (Hood, 1978), the ambiguity of concepts like "affiliation" (McCourt and Taylor, 1976) and measurement biases in the psychology of religion (Demerath and Levinson, 1971), even when they relate to declarations of intent (Brinberg, 1979).

Though they have not necessarily explained or alluded to this fact, several projects have operated at an epistemological level with consequences that are not fully appreciated, as, for example, in studies which first differentiate on relatively unformulated criteria between research on "religion" as an independent variable (Ploch, 1974; Davidson, 1972b), as a dependent variable (Davidson, 1972a) or as an interdependent factor (Clements, 1971). Over and above the value of inventories of a heuristic nature (Buhler, Hesser and Weigert, 1972), this work raises the problem of establishing an epistemology for the science of religion and attempting to give an account of the current state of this research. It does indeed seem likely that research where the "religious" species is classed as a dependent variable (religion is caused by . . .) is detached from the epistemology which the religious system would themselves favour, and is more ideologically divorced from those systems, than are studies where these "religious" species appear as independent variables (religion is the cause of . . .). Such a situation is likely to be conducive to a host of rhetorical, logical and epistemological strategies. Other works of a more theoretical nature question whether, now that a strictly rationalist approach has apparently been discarded, the time has come to reintroduce, at an empirical level, categories which had previously been set aside, including the concept of "transcendence" (Garrett, 1974), perhaps related to the work of Prola (1972), and the concept of the "supernatural" (as in Hodges, 1974). Work like this raises the problem of treating them in the same way as other socio-cultural objects or concepts to which religious systems give a significance based on a specific, and meta-empirical ontology. This as yet uncharted territory is full of promise. The first studies to venture there may not yet have assembled the requisite tools, nor have they been checked sufficiently to show if they measure up to the task.

We are thus faced with a field of research which, despite the survival of conceptual traditions which are quite fruitful but of uncertain epistemological status, can be organized by a renewed and increasingly complex set of tools which do not call into question cultural factors that have traditionally marked out this area of research and in which it has been considered technically, and possibly doctrinally, acceptable to use material of a scientific nature.

Paradoxically, any increased sophistication in these tools leads, even more than has been the case previously, to a fragmentation of the object. Such a scattering process is only partly overcome by the wide-ranging initiatives we have mentioned through civil religion, ultimate concerns, and alternative systems of meaning, which tend to concentrate more on the sociological aspects of the religious attitude or on its psychological aspects than on the interface of the psychological and the social. Evidence of fragmentation, however fruitful the analysis and the findings, accentuates a desire to highlight a number of fairly straightforward mechanisms which are more "fundamental" and thus, by experimenting in the epistemological field in the way described in an earlier paper (Deconchy, 1981), less dependent on specific cultural labels. These mechanisms, whether they are explanatory or have their roots confined to a particular sector, nevertheless require a fundamental reappraisal of the traditional tools, and a reassessment of the time-honoured methodological limitations. The time is ripe, especially in the field of social psychology, for a research project that is specifically directed at a clarification of such mechanisms.

I propose now to give a few examples of this approach, embryonic though they are. In doing so I will consider studies in which the methodology overlaps non-experimental and experimental methods, and which have logical relationships to the latter methods.

Attempts to elucidate a number of psycho-social mechanisms

The areas of research I propose to discuss are only formal examples, and no attempt is made to evaluate the quality of specific results. This selection covers cases which differ widely in their areas of application, research strategy and latent or explicit epistemology. I will first show how the concepts which underpin a particular scale create a better theoretical environment than that which emerges by contrasting attitudes with a "religious" mode of behaviour. I will then describe two types of research where religious functioning is merely an instance of more general mechanisms. Finally I will assess the possibility of deducing the precise function of a belief, whether religious or not, from a carefully controlled analysis of a particular psycho-social mode of behaviour.

Locus of control, religious attitudes and modes of behaviour

It is common practice in the psychology of religion to correlate "religious" variable with variables related to more general or different attitudes. It is worth considering whether, in a search for relatively fundamental processes, it might not be better to step back from those studies to examine the roots of the theoretical system which has produced particular sets of tools. This would not make any results valueless, although they could be seen as a symptom of that theoretical system. An example can be found in the "locus of control".

1. Several studies have contrasted locus of control with a diversity of beliefs (Lanskey and Pihl, 1976; Russel and Jorgenson, 1978), belief in an after-life (Berman and Hays, 1973), a general "religious" attitude (Kahoe, 1974; Kivett, Watson and Bush, 1977), or with various activities that refer to unverifiable objects (Martin, McDonald and Shepel, 1976). It is not always easy to make the results from these studies coincide. In relation to a belief in internal control, links are established with, for example, general religiosity (Rohrbaugh and Jessor, 1975 and to some extent, Piersma, 1974), ritual practice (Benson and Spilka, 1973), the "intrinsic" dimension (Kahoe, 1974; Strickland and Shaffer, 1971; Sturgeon and Hamley, 1979), and scores on a Protestant Ethic Scale (Mirels and Garrett, 1971; Lied and Pritchard, 1976; Waters, Batlis and Waters, 1975 and, to some extent, Singer and Alker, 1972). The belief in external control is less frequently linked to beliefs which are "supernatural" (Jahoda, 1970 and, to some extent, Munro, 1979), superstitious (Scheidt, 1973 and, to some extent, Peterson, 1978) astrological (Sosis, Strickland and Haley, 1980) and possibly "irrational" (Martin, McDonald and Schepel, 1976). This may depend on the latent similarities noted previously between the concept of a "truly religious" attitude and the enlightened, coherent and responsible attitude of an "internal" subject that is generally endorsed by contemporary society (Lefcourt, 1976). In this respect, Benson and Spilka's study (1973) seems less Manichaean and although they do not establish a clear link between belief in external control and belief in a controlling God, they found a correlation between belief in external control and recourse to an "avenging God" and to an "impersonal All", and a negative correlation between belief in external control and belief in a "loving God".

2. The confrontation between religious attitudes and locus of control (illustrated by the different scales which measure it) has given rise to a number of studies that suggest illuminating parallels. A more thorough analysis may show that the theoretical framework which underpins the parameters of any locus of control is based on mechanisms characteristic of those who are the likely subjects of a study of religion. Although Rotter's (1966) concepts, for example, are based on the notion of reinforcement, they depart appreciably from a traditional S–R theory and incorporate more dynamic elements.

Although these theoretical problems require further analysis, it seems clear that any intrinsically "religious" attitudes and behaviour take root within a subtle compound of the two formal types of belief illustrated by locus of control theory. With external control, the reference by Rotter and his successors to "chance" and even more to "fate" approximate very closely to certain strategies (cognitive or otherwise) inherent in a fundamental assessment of religious belief. More integral to such strategies are processes which project a "being" (who may be personalized) as the instrument of this external control. In accepting the existence of gods or of a God, the religious conscience makes a reference to beings or forces which cannot be found empirically (and are therefore beyond cognitive control) but which exercise control on human behaviour, either directly through visible intervention (good luck or misfortune), by a supposed intervention (grace), indirectly by the discrete organization of an ecology which the subject cannot entirely master, or eschatologically through the establishment of a place and a time (which cannot be controlled now) for a final and conclusive reward. The idea that man is subject to external control is thus an essential ingredient of the religious attitude, since a central belief and one of the social norms which sustain it requires a recognition of this "externality". Internal control of a religious attitude sustains a whole gamut of psychological and psycho-social processes which can overcome this externality. External control may also be subsumed within a purely subjective setting (as in the mysticism of contemplation where closeness to the external object reduces the externality of that object), within an axiological setting (as in the search for models of action which the beings or the Being who exercise external control might have left in the natural environment as "reflections", "signs", or "symbols"), or within social rituals of adoration, entreaty, negotiation and reconciliation which, in the final analysis, place under the control of the individual some of the control exercised by external forces and beings.

In terms of cognitive operations as well as social practice, the religious field is thus extended between two poles. It could be said that it exists *only* in this way and that the function of "religious" institutional forms is to make the distension "credible", and their interconnection "possible" cognitively, emotionally, socially and historically.

3. The theoretical universe within which the locus of control concept is embedded thus appears to be more directly characteristic of processes which might concern us, than as an inevitable set of tools which measure the culturally labelled symptoms of these processes. The very quality of the area of research we have been touching on can act as a spur to return to this theoretical universe. It would, for example, bring attribution theory to the fore, so seldom utilized, paradoxically, within our subdiscipline, despite interesting references to it (Proudfoot and Shaver, 1975). The epistemology which underpins attributional theory could offer a firm basis for the analysis of processes, curiously left out of account, which do not simply manage and organize representations of a primarily external locus of control (the gods), seen as an irritating "elsewhere", but creates an original representation and identifies its meta-empirical and ontological status. By standing aside from the bipolarity of the concepts which underpin measures of locus of control, it may be possible to find a necessary though not sufficient condition to focus on the interconnecting mechanisms (in this instance, between internal and external control) which seem to form an integral part of the religious field. This inevitably places religious processes in a wider framework, and makes a reappraisal of our methodological traditions even more pressing.

Other constructs to integrate religious processes

Attempts have already been made to integrate particular forms (whether cognitive or social) of religious processes into wider structures and into a framework of ideological systems. The nature of these attempts varies widely, and only two of them will be considered here.

1. Rokeach's "dogmatism"

In Rokeach's analysis, the structure of the belief–disbelief system that explains the "nature and significance of dogmatism" does not rely, as such, on any particular ideological field or system (see Rokeach, 1954, 1960). The "religious" field is only one of a number of fields of application of this construct, and Rokeach's treatment of religious attitudes and behaviour is purely illustrative. The research which relates the concept of "dogmatism" to particular aspects of religious attitudes and behaviour is too extensive to list here (see Deconchy and Cosnefroy, 1977), but Rokeach's undertaking not only appears to reflect a type of research I believe to be fruitful, but specifies conditions for producing a particular set of conceptual tools, as well as some problems and pitfalls which arise from an attempt to establish any concept of general significance for religion.

(a) By not concentrating specifically on the content of systems of belief in order to analyse their structure, Rokeach throws open what had previously been a closed field. The operation of these concepts is not directed at the cultural labels which underpin their contents and which, for the most part, cannot be empirically validated. Displacing the focus from this set of tools lessens, without altogether removing, the danger of reducing this research to analyses of a purely monographic kind.

(b) An analysis of the conditions which surround the establishment of this conceptual framework throws light on the types of question we are asking. The concept of "mental rigidity" which Rokeach first used sought to integrate into a broad structure the psycho-social rigidity of the "ethnocentric" dimension of Adorno's *Authoritarian Personality* depended on the specific contents and representations which underpin this dimension. While "mental rigidity" successfully accounted for a number of psychological processes, it showed its limitations when Rokeach approached complex socio-ideological subjects, probably because it was still over-influenced by its alignment with Adorno's "ethnocentrism" and the associated cultural labelling. The concept of "dogmatism", which accounts for one part of the function of complex socio-ideological systems, was elaborated beyond the sphere of any particular content or label (whether religious or not) and draws on more general mechanisms. This development may be symptomatic of the fact that, in terms of ideological processes (of which religious processes form a part), the psychological and the social can only be detected in relation to mechanisms not directly related to a specific cultural content.

Since we are raising this type of problem in relation to systems of belief with a specific content, it is worth noting that Rokeach highlights a number of social paradoxes that relate to religious beliefs. Although these do not make him question his concept, they lead him to recognize the importance and the urgency of being specific (Rokeach, 1965, 1968). Why is it, he wonders, that systems of religious belief which, more than any other proclaim the respect due to man, the equality of all and the wonders of love, are also those which have set up the most rigid systems of repression, the most inflexible hierarchical systems and the most effective forms of social control? In a way, and from a different viewpoint, this leads again to the independence of the content of a belief system from laws about the processes which make social systems viable. It also raises the question as to what is specific in religious beliefs. This is a question which the stream of research I will allude to shortly has partially sought to resolve in relation to studies of ideological orthodoxy.

(c) Before that, however, there is a further question concerning what is exemplary in Rokeach's undertaking. He put different systems of belief and ideological representation into a broad framework, which accounts for one type of functioning. As has already been said, this is necessary to direct the psychology of religion towards more theoretical areas than those they usually occupy. However, although the construct of dogmatism successfully accounts for a number of individual and social processes, the interaction of these two sets of processes is hardly ever considered in its own right. Yet that is where explanatory mechanisms could be most effectively found. One wonders whether a methodological choice may not have pushed Rokeach to make these processes work in parallel, rather than bringing out there interconnection. By choosing to use an attitude scale to measure dogmatism instead of attempting, even experimentally, to employ other methods which the quality of his concept would have made possible, he probably closed the door on the connections and mechanisms which function there.

2. The concept of "orthodoxy"

Attempts to highlight other fundamental psycho-social processes, of which religious processes are a specific manifestation, include the work on ideological orthodoxy. There is no time to deal with them extensively here, but I will do so briefly.

(a) Frequently used in the psychology of religion, the concept of "orthodoxy" is seldom related to psycho-social mechanisms that give it an operational status. "Orthodoxy" is used for the most part as if its meaning were self-evident and adequately covered conditions for the allegiance to a set of beliefs, and integration in a social group which has established and provided this set of beliefs for itself. To be considered "orthodox", a subject has to consent to a set of doctrinal items thought to be characteristic of a group (either *a priori*, as in Gregory, 1957 and Stewart and Webster, 1970, or by an expert jury as in Brown, 1962). That is the case in the most famous of the indices of "orthodoxy" (Glock and Stark, 1966; Stark and Glock, 1968). While the term generally refers to the purely "intellectual" dimensions of religious allegiance and integration, and has been explicitly distinguished from ritual conformism (Allport, 1955), it is occasionally extended to include a number of ethical practices (see for example Greeley and Rossi, 1968; Danesimo and Laxman, 1971). Both in the context of social psychology and sociology (Davidson and Quinn, 1976) the concept of "orthodoxy" has failed, over a long period of time, to be a subject of any theoretical analysis (but cf. Gaede, 1976). The way it is actually used in social psychology makes one wonder whether any analysis along these lines might not be narrowly dependent on conformity models.

(b) Attempts made recently to relate the concept of ideological orthodoxy to particular psycho-social mechanisms, without immersing it in a conformist-type model (Deconchy, 1971, 1980), seek to avoid being distracted by the specific content of systems of religious representations by working with a set of definitions, a central hypothesis and a more integral model.

In this set of definitions, a subject is termed "orthodox" insofar as he accepts and indeed requests that his thoughts, his language and his behaviour be controlled by the ideological group to which he belongs and by the power structure of such a group. A group is termed "orthodox" insofar as this type of control is sustained therein, and the axiological and technological validity of these controls is itself part of the "doctrine" attested by the group. An orthodox system is therefore made up of the whole dynamic range of social and psycho-social processes which regulate the activity of an orthodox subject within an orthodox group. As a central hypothesis, in an orthodox system the rational fragility of information is functionally counterbalanced by the strictness of social control. As a model and from an intra-ideological point of view, ideological "orthodoxy" is connected to that of ideological "effervescence". From an extra-ideological point of view, it is connected to ideological creativity.

It can be seen that these definitions, the model and the central hypothesis circumscribe a theoretical field which does not, as such, depend on religious forms and contents.

(c) It is only for convenience that experimental research which aims to bring into operation this set of conceptual tools has been implanted in the Catholic Church as a particular religious system, for reasons it would take too long to explain here. In the first generation of research, it has been demonstrated that, in this type of system, the perception of the divergence which the ideological proposition (which in this instance is "religious") imposes on the norms of what is customarily termed "rationality", is in practice effectively obliterated by the strictness of social control. The more this divergence is perceived by a subject, the stricter the control becomes; on the other hand if the divergence is effectively obscured social control is loosened. The looser it becomes, the more apparent becomes the rational fragility of the belief. In a second generation of research, an attempt has been made to show how an "orthodox" ideological system neutralizes empirical research and scientific analyses of its own operations. This is achieved by discharging, as a protective device, some of the ideological effervescence and hold which permeates it and which, in times of cognitive quiescence, are maintained under its control. In a third generation of research, which is still in progress, the aim is to establish the means whereby the orthodox system selects from different fields of knowledge, whether scientific or not, in such a way as to be confronted only by what does not seriously call into question the epistemology which underpins its ideological and social legitimacy.

This work on orthodoxy, whose significance is naturally open to review, tends to invert processes which have been fairly traditional in the psychology of religion, putting systems of religious representation into the wide framework of ideological systems. It seeks to establish mechanisms which are relatively independent of the specific contents for which they provide social support. This inevitably leads to examining more critically the so-called "impossibility" of applying to such objects some of the methods of experimental social psychology.

I will now turn, finally, to another area of research in which this type of methodology has been used in a very different epistemological context, following a research strategy which is both original and full of promise.

Behavioural analysis and inferences of a system of belief

Lerner's (1980) recent synthesis of his research on the "just world" may encourage psychologists of religion to direct their thoughts, if not their own research, in a relatively new direction. The research strategy, even more than the results obtained by Lerner's work, appears to be relevant to our context.

(a) From a formal point of view, Lerner's undertaking is original. To account for a paradoxical psycho-social pattern of behaviour, revealed in a controlled experiment, he postulated the "existence" of a particular belief – namely, that the world is just. His research started with the premise that experience of evil, suffering and injustice in human society is combined with an extraordinary capacity of the society, and mankind, to continue to do their daily chores. This fundamental paradox leads to complex cognitive and argumentative strategies which, whilst acknowledging the presence of evil, suffering and injustice, excel in finding reasons and explanations for things which discourage any sort of preventive action. Cause or effect? Whatever the answer, Lerner postulates that man (the human species?) deciphers the social interactions they observe by filtering them with the idea that what happens to someone must have a cause, and that this cause is related to their own merit if the event is happy and to their guilt if it is unhappy. When it is clear, in the latter case, that the victim is in no way "guilty", guilt and responsibility are sought and found at a symbolic level. The point of departure for Lerner's thought and his fundamental hypothesis are thus closely allied to questions (or ultimate concerns) of a philosophical or religious kind. It is nevertheless Lerner's research strategy which is of special interest.

(b) In the context of our analysis, Lerner's early work appears fundamental (cf. Chalot, 1980) insofar as it established in relatively well-controlled situations several complementary aspects of a paradoxical psycho-social mode of behaviour. In one case, although one person does not undertake a greater amount of work than his partner, one of them, without knowing it, is selected by chance to be the only one to be paid, and is believed by a spectator to have carried out a larger volume of work (Lerner, 1965). In another case, a "victim" undergoing a painful and iniquitous treatment who, objectively speaking, has done nothing to deserve it, is systematically derogated by a spectator, both in terms of his physical and his symbolic attributes (Lerner and Simmons, 1966). Finally, the victim recovers certain advantages if he can be seen as a substitute for the spectator in this painful situation (Lerner and Matthews, 1967). In each case it is as if the subject filters his reading of the social field by something unspoken; it remains to be said whether this depends on specific historical conditions or partly reflects a characteristic of our species. Lerner attributed it to a "belief" which is transcultural and even "natural".

This approach is, I think, stimulating in its own right. Work which compares indicators of "religious" attitudes and scores on the "Belief in a just world scale" of Rubin and Peplau (1973, 1975), using Lerner's model, is perhaps less stimulating.[6] In the context of a reassessment of Lerner and Simmon's experiments (1966) relating to the derogation of an innocent victim, it is worth noting that Sorrentino and Hardy (1970) "complete" the methodological triangle of cultural labelling (through self-rated religiosity), measurement of attitudes through the belief in a just world, and the evaluation of a fundamental mechanism, as in Lerner and Simmons' paradigm.

(c) Lerner's approach thus breaks a dominant tradition of research into beliefs with the controlled study of a pattern of behaviour (a man facing an apparently innocent victim) which leads him to infer the "existence", so to speak, of some sort of cognitive filter by means of which the man perceives, analyses and evaluates a particular situation without clear reference to empirical data and/or to data which can be rationally assessed or introduced by that situation. This filter, as a mediator of the perception, analysis and evaluation of situations (especially involving interaction) is operationally akin to a "belief", and is not restricted to straightforward interactions, to provisional situations, or to evanescent problems, but bears on the state and reality of the world, and on events and interactions which occur there.

To contribute to the elaboration of a theory of beliefs, our research needs to concentrate its efforts in two directions. At a heuristic level there is a need to make an inventory of situations wherein human behaviour, both cognitive and technological, cannot be explained without reference to the "existence" of a cognitive filter which is relatively transcultural, even if it is of limited application. At a methodological level independent of the previous level there is a need to locate situations which reinforce, as far as possible, obligatory references to a particular "ontology" of the world and our species.

This brief examination of the current state of some of the non-experimental methods in the psychology of religion has led us in two directions. First, following a demonstration to show how, in the approach to religious attitudes, traditional methods have been characterized by an inherent ambiguity, we analysed attempts to revise and adjust this methodology and the conceptual tools which underpin it. Secondly, we tried to show that a number of epistemological developments have introduced some new fields of reflection. Because systems of religious representation have influenced the wider social environment and refer to more or less fundamental mechanisms we need to ask whether experimentation can be used in an area which is often thought recalcitrant to that control. We deal with this issue next.

Experimental methods

Some classifications

Because debate about the place of experiments in the psychology of religion has recently increased (Batson, 1977, 1979; Deconchy, 1978b; Yeatts and Asher, 1979), it is worth considering the scientific problems involved there. The criticism that any controlled procedure must destroy religion will, however, be disregarded. Bibliographies of work in the psychology of religion rarely list "experiments" separately. To produce an inventory of the experimental work that has been done, it is easiest to start with others' classifications. While the contents of these classifications overlap slightly, they agree that well-controlled experimental studies are rare in the psychology of religion. The main groupings are:

A highly selective classification (Batson, 1977)

The use of strict criteria allowed Daniel Batson to identify only two studies as truly experimental. One concerned the effects of psilocybin on mystical experience (Pahnke, 1966) and the other was Dittes' (1961) study of the effects of ego-involving failure on the need for cognitive closure among divinity students.

A broader classification including quasi-experimental work (Deconchy, 1978b)

Table 1 shows studies that depend on laboratory procedures and quasi-experimental designs.

TABLE 1   *Experimental studies in religion, with their independent and dependent variables*

Author	Independent variable	Dependent variable
Magni (1972)	death stimulus	avoidance reflex
Darley and Batson (1973)	reading an evangelical text	helping behaviour
Long and Long (1976)	wearing religious or secular clothes	length of an interview
Osarchuk and Tatz (1973)	artifically induced anxiety	belief in life after death
Kelley (1955)	reading adapted texts	salience of belonging to the church
Batson (1975)	emitting dissonant information	intensity of belief
Carey (1971)	influence of peers	frequency of attendance at daily mass
Chadwick (1976)	gestures and attitudes of a preacher	deciphering information
Pelletier (1974)	transcendental meditation	auto-kinetic effect
Augustin, Miller and Kirchenbaum (1979)	wearing religious or lay clothes	obedience not to touch an enticing object
Elkins *et al.* (1979)	style of prayer	electromyograph
Lilliston and Brown (1981)	character of a problem	religious or non-religious solution
Ungar (1980)	anonymity of information	religious attitudes

Studies related to altruism and religion (Daniel, 1978)

Assuming that positive religious belief would involve helping behaviour, Marie-Paule Daniel (1978) found relevant experimental and quasi-experimental studies by Annis (1975, 1976); Batson (1976); Darley and Batson (1973); Forbes, Tevaut and Gromoll (1971); Greenwald (1975); Harris, Benson and Hall (1975); Maranell (1974, Chapter 8); McKenna

(1976); Nelson and Dynes (1976) and Smith, Wheeler and Diener (1975). (Batson and Gray (1981) might also have been included.)

A "typical" list (Brown, 1973)

In the sixth section of his collection of readings, and under the heading "Experimental studies", Brown (1973) refers to studies by Brown and Pallant (1962); Deconchy (1973); Dittes (1959); Feather (1964); Kelley (1955); Magni (1972); Morlan (1950); Pahnke (1966); Siegman (1961); Wallace (1970) and Welford (1947). In the introduction to that book Brown also acknowledged that these are not all strictly experimental studies, and says that for reasons we will return to, strict experiments do not seem possible in the field of religion.

These separate lists (which are not necessarily comprehensive) agree that there have been comparatively few experimental studies in the psychology of religion. That is why in 1958 Argyle said that experimentation is "almost unknown" in studies of religion, while Flakoll (1977) said it "has not fared well". Klausner (1964) found only two examples of this type of research in the period between 1950 and 1960, and Warren (1977) estimated that "only two or three studies employed a design that allowed for manipulation of the dependent variable[s]". There has been some progress since then, although many authors are still vague about the place of experimentation. Clark (1958) said that while it "is particularly difficult in the field of religion, it has been used" and Scobie (1975), having included the experiments as a method that is available, simply offered an imaginary example.

The classifications that have been referred to are not consistent in the criteria they use to identify an experiment, which reflects the methodological and epistemological confusion that typifies this field of research. Yet they all (except for some items in Daniel's list) agree in rejecting any research in which the independent or dependent variables are assessed from an attitude scale. Studies set out in Table 2 would have been included with that broadened definition.

Four other studies that have employed planned factorial designs with two independent variables, one invoked through an attitude scale or other measure and the other provoked or manipulated, are set out in Table 3.

While distinctions between experiments and quasi-experiments are not always clearly drawn even within social psychology, they are usually neglected by the majority of psychologists of religion, who rely on correlational analyses. Nevertheless, Batson's (1977) estimate that only 150 studies in the psychology of religion "involve empirical research" could be an underestimate (Deconchy, 1978b). Although Warren (1977), Batson (1977) and Deconchy (1977) have carefully distinguished experimental from correlational studies, there is still such methodological confusion about procedure that Gorsuch (1976), as the retiring editor of the *Journal of the Scientific Study*

TABLE 2   *Studies in which the dependent variable is defined by a psychological test*

Author	Independent variable	Dependent variable
Maranell (1974)	social deception and social gratification	scores for ritualism, idealism and altruism
Francis (1979)	religious or lay experimenter	scores for religiosity and dissimulation
Burtt and Falkenberg (1941)	following stance of majority or an expert	scores for religiosity
Walker and Firetto (1965)	religious or lay psychologist	score on the Taylor Anxiety Scale and the MMPI
Yabrudi and Diab (1978)	religious or non-religious investigator	scores on an inter-personal judgement test

TABLE 3   *Studies in which two independent variables have been used*

Reference	Independent variables		Dependent (variable)
	Invoked (measured)	Provoked (manipulated)	
Greenberg (1977)	protestant ethic scores	evaluations of performance	change in performance
Dor Shav, Friedman, and Tcherbonogura (1978)	self-rated religiosity	interaction with subjects identified as religious or not	intensity of shock administered to subjects
Sorrentino and Hardy (1974)	self-rated religiosity	presence of a more or less severely reprimanded confederate	evaluation of the confederate
Hood and Morris (1981)	intrinsic or extrinsic religious orientation	religious or non-religious imagery	reported imagery

of Religion, set out detailed methodological advice to future authors, of a kind that we have not found in other scientific journals.

Granted this uncertainty about the use of experimental methods in religion, perhaps we should regard *any* study which systematically varies "religious" characteristics (however they are defined) as belonging to an experimental psychology of religion (Deconchy and Cosnefroy, 1977). According to that definition, a study like that of Bryan and Test (1967), who found that whether a person belong to the Salvation Army has no effect on helping behaviour, hardly seems relevant to an experimental psychology of religion. Nor is the study of Campbell and Lancioni (1979), where the religious content of the experiment is described but not manipulated, or the Burdick and Burnes (1958) study which used "Life after death" as a subject for a "religious" discussion to establish strained or balanced situations in which the GSR could be measured. Studies by Commins and Lockwood (1978), Darmon and Paicheler (1978) and Saigh (1979), which used religious categories, do not relate specifically to religion.

The vague distinction between "experimentation in social psychology" and "social experimentation" (Boruch and Riecken, 1975) similarly introduces conceptual ambiguity. In a debate between Yeatts and Asher (1979) and Batson (1979), the argument was blocked when Yeatts and Asher asserted that "religion" is a value that should always be promoted. Theoretical analyses which do not explicitly recognize that position usually interpret "experimentation" as if it were a form of "social practice" (Deconchy, 1978b).

Evaluating experimental work in the psychology of religion

Theoretical problems

It is agreed by those with a positive attitude to experimentation that the lack of a clear theory or paradigm in the psychology of religion is an important reason for the shortage of experiments in this field and the preference for anecdotal evidence (cf. Warren, 1977; Batson, 1977; Deconchy, 1977, 1978b) or for correlational studies. But why should researchers be reticent in applying theoretical models to religion that are widely accepted in other areas? Batson (1977) see this as a problem that was overcome by Dittes (1969), and by Proudfoot and Shaver's (1975) paper on attribution theory. The theory of cognitive dissonance (Guthrie and Marshall, 1966; Lee and Doran, 1973; Batson, 1975; Adam, 1974; Hsieh, 1976; Dunford and Kunz, 1973; Brock, 1962; Carroll, 1979 and Festinger, Riecken and Schachter, 1956), games theory (Brams and Zagare, 1977), and risk-taking (McDonald, 1976) have all been applied to religion, and each could offer a paradigm for further work. Unger's (1978) use of the S–R model to decide if religion is a system of adaptation offers an incentive solution. We should also note that religion itself has been used as a model in more general work with concepts like schism (Gustafson, 1978), superstition (Reberg et al., 1979) and "conversion" (Moscovici, 1980). Despite that, social psychologists have made little theoretical use of religion, although Doise (1978), Mugny and Doise (1979), Lemaine (1975) and Touzard (1977) are exceptions to that generalization.

Epistemological censorship

Perhaps theorizing is believed to be foreign to a religious epistemology, competing against or contradicting the religious attitude itself. Furthermore, when the focus of a study comes close to confessional strategies, some disapproval or functional censorship may be invoked against it. In a recent series of experiments, Deconchy (1980) showed how "scientific" information coexists with the latent epistemology of theological students and whether they believed this information could be validated by descriptive or correlational methods. When the information was shown to be supported by the results of an experimental study its consistency with their established cognitive system was lost. On the basis of such findings the rejection of an experimental method could reflect an immunization against any approach that is formally irreconcilable with religious beliefs, or with their implicit religious epistemology. Thus Clark observed that "Prejudices and attitudes about religion being what they are, the religious psychologist needs to be either a great diplomat or a courageous investigator if he is to risk the criticism that may fall to his lot if, in cold blood, he uses religious stimuli for experimental purposes" (1958, p. 39). The beliefs of psychologists may similarly determine their choice of a particular methodology (cf. Beit-Hallahmi, 1977 and Ragan, Malony and Beit-Hallahmi, 1980). Hence the general pessimism about the possibility of building a psychology of religion from an experimental base. Thouless argued that "it is true that religion will not be able to make much use of *experiment*, that is, of the observation of the changes which are produced in phenomena by intentionally produced changes in the conditions under which they develop" (1956, p. 9), and Clark (1958, p. 51) even argued that it is impossible to build a psychology of religion from experimental methods. Such conclusions may also reflect a view of experimentation that contrasts with a vaguely "religious anthropology" which is simply descriptive and phenomenological. So Brown claimed that "the nature of religious commitment, its recognised importance and the ways in which it develops, all prohibit studies in which religious variables can be independently manipulated" (1973, p. 14). Koteskey (1980) similarly considered that experimental methods are perfectly adapted to the study of the "animal-like" aspects of human psychology but can not handle the "god-like" aspects, which are more directly accessible by other methods.

Batson (1977), who argued that while "an experimental psychology of religion is not likely to be developed", considered the practical difficulties to be less important than the ethical obstacles, which he feels are almost insurmountable. As he says, "most researchers would consider it unethical to manipulate the intensity or character of an individual's religion. Similarly, most would consider it unethical to manipulate variables thought to affect religiosity, such as family nurturance, or exposure to religious thought and practice." Argyle (1958) had similarly argued earlier that experiments are "not pertinent" because of their "artificial conditions". While Vergote (1972) considered that "experimental methods . . . in our domain, could only furnish artifacts. . . . At a time when even natural sciences have liberated themselves from several positivist dogmas, such as that of laws . . . [it seems preferable not] to submit to an outmoded ideal of scientificity".

Legrand (1975) argued against the use of experimentation to study religion because of the situational, historical and socio-political factors that are involved in the production of this knowledge. Similarly Vaillancourt (1979), when considering the possibility of using experimental methods in the sociology of religion says that "experimentation, even if it takes place in a natural setting rather than in the laboratory, seems to me to be one of the least interesting and fruitful techniques in the sociology of religion".

Ethical objections

As we have seen, Batson's (1977, 1979) balanced assessment stressed the ethical problems that make experimental control difficult for the psychology of religion. But that is a damaging conclusion. If the aim of science is to explain when causal relationships between events (or realities) can be identified, an experiment offers the best method for that, even if it must caricature reality to be able to understand it. This is why Batson (1977) pressed for quasi-experiments, despite his obvious preference for proper experimental control, not because experimentation is seen as the best method for finding proof, or that "a researcher is naive enough to think that, *as it is*, the experimental method permits taking into account such complex social phenomena as religion" (Deconchy, 1978b). In the one case we are encouraged to let the "dream" of experimental rigour animate research, the results of which will necessarily be approximate, while on the other it is believed that a challenge can be taken up which has implications for experimental social psychology in general and not just for the psychology of religion. Furthermore, since descriptive studies appear more interesting scientifically than are the results of a virtuoso experiment (Batson, 1979), we must ask whether the scientific spirit primarily involves applying particular methods rather than producing evidence (Deconchy, 1978a).

The ethical objections to religiously relevant experiments are, however, the most potent, because they are assumed to involve the systematic manipulation for scientific purposes of social or religious variables. Thus Argyle (1958) said that while it is "undesirable to change people's attitudes or beliefs on such fundamental matters, . . . the effects would be minimised under the artificial condition of experiments" (p. 13). (That view was not, however, repeated in Argyle and Beit-Hallahmi (1975).) Beyond a fear that people may be artificially "manipulated" is an implicit refusal to run the risk of influencing religious belief. As a solution to this problem it has been proposed that in "taking the risk of altering and endangering religious beliefs" an experimenter should begin by "respecting the same precautions which must be respected by all who have as their goal, or who give themselves the task of producing or reinforcing those beliefs" (Deconchy, 1978a).

On the other hand, Yeatts and Asher (1979) have argued by analogy from medical ethics that it is the *refusal* to carry out experiments that is unethical, since religious education must resort to rigorously validated methods if it is to escape from superficiality, and respect for later generations involves taking some risks with those who are the research subjects now. While Batson (1979) contests this view, Yeatts and Asher, operating within a confessional framework, consider it self-evident that transmitting the "religious message" must be done more efficiently than at present. Yet in ethics we must distinguish "that which relates to a truly ethical evaluation founded upon a set of moral values" from that which relates to an inconsistent and functional desire not to run the risk of questioning the intrinsic relevance of a belief system and the religious representations which are still a part, in different ways, of the consciousness and dominant ideology and which remains a powerful integrating social apparatus (Deconchy, 1978b).

A few suggestions

Rather than identifying what *might* work, Warren (1977) suggested that we should promote the use of experiments and not be overwhelmed by the difficulties of sampling (which have also been examined by Yeatts and Asher, 1979 and by Batson, 1979) or of volunteer subjects, but ensure a careful control of variables. He advocated using sophisticated designs (which can be quite simple, granted the availability of computers), the convergent replication of studies and avoiding any over-enthusiastic generalization of the findings. Batson's advocacy of quasi-experimental designs is more cautious (Batson, 1975, 1976; Darley and Batson, 1973; Brannon, 1970). He argues for the appropriateness in religious studies of time-series analyses and pre-test–post-test non-equivalent comparison group designs, and is against correlational studies because they can never identify causal chains. Deconchy (1977), who examined problems of the control of variables, and especially the consistency of "religion" as an independent variable (following Dittes, 1969), stressed the need to distinguish clearly between measured or invoked, and provoked independent variables and between studies in which religion is an independent variable and those where it is a dependent variable.

Theoretical models and the hypotheses to be tested must relate to prevailing theoretical systems, and do not depend entirely on any method that is to be used, especially since religion aligns with other ideological systems and social processes. We also need an acceptable definition of religion, which would add nuances to, for example, Zuckerman's (1975) use of the concept of "appeasing the gods" to describe the way subjects waiting for the results of an exam paper appear to take fate into their hands by adopting altruistic behaviour (cited by Lerner, 1980).

The problems of experimental methodology are not, however, specific to the psychology of religion. As with the rest of social psychology, questions relate to the historicity of religious and other belief systems and institutions (Pagès, 1979), and the conditions that form any social group, identity, or set of beliefs. Practical considerations therefore favour an experimental design that does not deny the historicity, whether it is individual or social, of the phenomena being studied, and makes proper use of tradition and of natural social groups.

References

ADAM, J. P. La culture religieuse au secondaire. Esquisse d'un cadre d'analyse psycho-sociale. *Cahiers de pastorale Scolaire* (Sherbrooke), 1974; **5**, 105–115.

ALLEN, R. O. and SPILKA, B. Committed and consensual religion: a specification of religion-prejudice relationships. *Journal for the Scientific Study of Religion*, 1967; **6**(2), 191–206.

ALLPORT, G. W. *The nature of prejudice.* Cambridge: Addison-Wesley, 1955.

ALLPORT, G. W. *Personality and social encounter.* Boston: Beacon Press, 1960.

ALLPORT, G. W. The religious context of prejudice. *Journal for the Scientific Study of Religion*, 1966; **5**(3), 447–457.

ALLPORT, G. W. and ROSS, J. M. Personal religious orientation and prejudice. *Journal of Personality and Social Psychology*, 1967; **5**(4), 432–443.

ANNIS, L. V. Study of values as a predictor of helping behavior. *Psychological Reports*, 1975; **37**(3), 717–718.

ANNIS, L. V. Emergency helping and religious behavior. *Psychological Reports*, 1976; **39**(1), 151–158.

ARGYLE, M. *Religious behaviour.* London: Routledge & Kegan Paul, 1958.

ARGYLE, M. and BEIT-HALLAHMI, B. *The social psychology of religion.* London: Routledge & Kegan Paul, 1975.

AUGUSTIN, J. W., MILLER, A. L. and KIRSCHENBAUM, D. S. Factors affecting generalized suppression of overt behavior during resistance to temptation: the priest effect. *Psychological Reports*, 1979; **45**(1), 259–262.

BAGLEY, C. Relation of religion and racial prejudice in Europe. *Journal for the Scientific Study of Religion*, 1970; **9**(3), 219–225.

BAITHER, R. C. and SALTZBERG, L. Relationships between religious attitudes and religious thinking. *Psychological Reports*, 1978; **43**(3), 853–854.

BASSETT, R. L. *et al.* The shepherd scale: separating the sheep from the goats. *Journal of Psychology and Theology*, 1981; **9**(4), 335–351.

BATSON, C. D. Rational processing or rationalization? The effect of disconfirming information on a stated religion belief. *Journal of Personality and Social Psychology*, 1975; **32**(1), 176–184.

BATSON, C. D. Religion as prosocial: agent or double agent? *Journal for the Scientific Study of Religion*, 1976; **15**(1), 29–45.

BATSON, C. D. Experimentation in psychology of religion. An impossible dream. *Journal for the Scientific Study of Religion*, 1977; **16**(4), 413–418.

BATSON, C. D. Experimentation in psychology of religion: living with or in a dream? *Journal for the Scientific Study of Religion*, 1979; **18**(1), 90–93.

BATSON, C. D. and GRAY, R. A. Religious orientation and helping behavior: Responding to one's own or to the victim's needs? *Journal of Personality and Social Psychology*, 1981; **40**(3), 511–520.

BATSON, C. D., NAIFEH, S. J. and PATE, S. Social desirability, religious orientation, and racial prejudice. *Journal for the Scientific Study of Religion*, 1978; **17**(1), 31–41.

BEIT-HALLAHMI, B. Curiosity, doubt and devotion. The beliefs of psychologists and the psychology of religion. In H. N. MALONY (ed.), *Current perspectives in the psychology of religion.* Grand Rapids: Eerdsmans, 1977.

BELLAH, R. Civil religion in America. *Daedalus*, 1967; **96**, 1–11.

BELLAH, R. *Beyond Belief,* New York: Harper and Row, 1970.

BENDER, I. E. A longitudinal study of church attenders and nonattenders. *Journal for the Scientific Study of Religion*, 1968; **7**(2), 230–237.

BENSON, P. and SPILKA, B. God image as a function of self-esteem and locus of control. *Journal for the Scientific Study of Religion*, 1973; **12**(8), 297–310.

BERMAN, A. L. and HAYS, J. E. Relation between death anxiety, belief in after-life, and locus of control. *Journal of Consulting and Clinical Psychology*, 1973; **41**(2), 318.

BORUCH, R. F. and RIECKEN, H. W. *Experimental listing of public policy: the Proceedings of the 1974 Social Science Research Council on Social Experiments.* Boulder: Westview, 1975.

BRAMS, S. J. and ZAGARE, F. C. Deception in simple rating games. *Social Science Research,* 1977; **6**(3), 257–272.

BRANNON, R. C. L. Gimme that oldtime racism. *Psychology Today,* 1970; **3,** 42–44.

BRINBERG, D. An examination of the determinants of intention and behaviour. A comparison of two modes. *Journal of Applied Social Psychology,* 1979; **9**(6), 560–575.

BRINK, T. L. Inconsistency of belief among Roman Catholic girls: concerning religion, astrology, reincarnation. *Review of Religious Research,* 1978; **20**(1), 82–85.

BROCK, T. C. Implications of conversion and magnitude of cognitive dissonance. *Journal for the Scientific Study of Religion,* 1962; **1**(2), 199–203.

BROWN, L. B. A study of religious belief. *British Journal of Psychology,* 1962; **53**(3), 259–272.

BROWN, L. B. Classifications of religious orientation. *Journal for the Scientific Study of Religion,* 1964; **4,** 91–99.

BROWN, L. B. (ed.) *Psychology and religion.* Harmondsworth: Penguin Books, 1973.

BROWN, L. B. and FORGAS, J. P. The structure of religion: a multidimensional scaling of informal elements. *Journal for the Scientific Study of Religions,* 1980; **19**(4), 423–431.

BROWN, L. B. and PALLANT, D. J. Religious belief and social pressure. *Psychological Reports,* 1972; **10**(3), 813–814.

BRYAN, J. H. and TEST, M. A. Models and helping. Naturalistic studies in aiding behavior. *Journal of Personality and Social Psychology,* 1978; **6**(4), 400–407.

BRYANT, E. and O'CONNELL, D. A phonemic analysis of nine samples of glossolalic speech. *Psychonomic Speech,* 1971; **22**(2), 81–83.

BUHLER, C., HESSER, G. and WEIGERT, A. A study of articles on religion in a major sociology journal. Some preliminary findings. *Journal for the Scientific Study of Religion,* 1972; **11**(2), 165–170.

BURDICK, H. A. and BURNES, A. J. A test of "strain toward symmetry" theories. *The Journal of Abnormal and Social Psychology,* 1958; **57**(3), 367–370.

BURTT, H. E. and FALKENBERG, D. R. The influence of majority and expert opinion on religious attitudes. *Journal of Social Psychology,* 1941; **14**(2), 269–278.

CAMPBELL, C. C. and COLES, R. W. Religiosity, religious affiliation and religious belief: the exploration of a typology. *Review of Religious Research,* 1973; **14**(3), 151–158.

CAMPBELL, D. E. and LANCIONI, G. E. The effects of staring and pew invasion in church settings. *The Journal of Social Psychology,* 1979; **108**(1), 19–24.

CAPPS, D. E. Contemporary psychology of religion. The task of theoretical reconstruction. *Social Research,* 1974; **41**(2), 362–383.

CAPPS, D. E., RAMBO, L. and RANSOHOFF, P. *Psychology of religion: a guide to information sources.* Detroit: Gale Research Co., 1976.

CAREY, R. G. Influence of peers in shaping religious behaviour. *Journal for the Scientific Study of Religion,* 1971; **10**(2), 157–159.

CARRIER, M. *Psycho-sociologie de l'appartenance religieuse.* Rome: Université Grégorienne, 1960.

CARROLL, R. P. *When prophecy failed. Cognitive dissonance in the prophetic tradition of the old testament.* New York: Seabury Press, 1979.

CARTER, J. D. and NARRAMORE, B. *The integration of psychology and theology.* Grand Rapids: Zondervan, 1979.

CHADWICK, T. W. *A study to determine what a pastor is communicating non-verbally from the pulpit.* Philadelphia, Pa.: The Eastern Baptist Theological Seminary, 1976.

CHALOT, C. La croyance en un monde juste comme variable intermédiaire des réactions au sort d'autrui et à son propre sort. *Psychologie Française,* 1980; **25**(1), 51–57.

CLARK, W. H. *The psychology of religion. An introduction to religious experience and behavior.* New York: Macmillan, 1958.

CLAYTON, R. L. and GLADDEN, J. W. The five dimensions of religiosity. Toward demythologizing a sacred artefact. *Journal for the Scientific Study of Religion,* 1974; **13**(2), 135–143.

CLEMENTS, K. The religious variable, Dependent, independent or interdependent? *A Sociological Yearbook of Religion in Britain,* 1971; **4,** 36–46.

COLLINS, G. R. *The rebuilding of psychology. An integration of psychology and theology.* Eastbourne: Coverdale, 1977.

COMMINS, B. and LOCKWOOD, T. The effects of mixing Roman Catholics and Protestants. An experimental investigation. *European Journal of Social psychology*, 1978; **8**(3), 383–386.

DANESIMO, A. and LAXMAN, W. A. Catholic attitudes and beliefs in transition. A decade study of a Jesuit college. *Psychological Reports*, 1971; **28**(1), 247–250.

DANIEL, M. P. Etudes expérimentales de l'effet de la croyance religieuse sur les comportements d'assistance. *Archives de Sciences Sociales des Religions*, 1978; **46**, 161–164.

DARLEY, J. and BATSON, C. D. From Jerusalem to Jericho: A study of situational and dispositional variables in helping behaviour. *Journal of Personality and Social Psychology*, 1973; **27**(1), 100–108.

DARMON, G. and PAICHELER, H. Modèle de l'équilibre: structures logiques et relations sociales réelles. *Bulletin de Psychologie*, 1978; **32**(338), 9–20.

DAVIDSON, J. Religious belief as a dependent variable. *Sociological Analysis*, 1972a; **33**(2), 81–94.

DAVIDSON, J. Religious belief as an independent variable. *Journal for the Scientific Study of Religion*, 1972b; **11**(1), 65–75.

DAVIDSON, J. D. and QUINN, G. J. Theological and sociological uses of the concept "Orthodoxy". *Review of Religious Research*, 1976; **18**(1), 74–80.

DECONCHY, J. P. La psychologie des faits religieux. In H. DESROCHE and J. SEGUY (eds), *Introduction aux sciences humaines des religions.* Paris: Cujas, 1970, pp. 145–174.

DECONCHY, J. P. *L'orthodoxie religieuse. Essai de logique psycho-sociale.* Paris: Editions Ouvrieres, 1971.

DECONCHY, J. P. Boys' and girls' choices for a religious group. In L. B. BROWN (ed.), *Psychology and religion.* Harmondsworth: Penguin Books, 1973.

DECONCHY, J. P. Expérimentation et processus d'influence idéologique dans les groupes réels. *Psychologie Française*, 1976; **21**(4), 281–286.

DECONCHY, J. P. La psychologie sociale expérimentale et les comportements religieux. *The Annual Review of the Social Sciences of Religion*, 1977; **1**, 103–132.

DECONCHY, J. P. La théorie du "locus of control" et l'étude des attitudes et des comportements religieux. *Archives de Sciences Sociales des Religions*, 1978a; **46**, 153–160.

DECONCHY, J. P. L'expérimentation en psychologie de la religion. Pourquoi ne pas rêver? *Archives de Sciences Sociales des Religions*, 1978b; **46**, 176–192.

DECONCHY, J. P. *Orthodoxie religieuse et sciences humaines*, suivi de (*Religious*) *orthodoxy, rationality and scientific knowledge.* Paris-La Haye: Mouton, 1980.

DECONCHY, J. P. Laboratory experimentation and social field experimentation. An ambiguous distinction. *European Journal of Social Psychology*, 1981; **11**(4), 323–347.

DECONCHY, J. P. and COSNEFROY, L. Dogmatisme et religion. Etudes empiriques utilisant le concept de Milton Rokeache. *Archives de Sciences Sociales des Religions*, 1977; **44**, 139–145.

DEMERATH, N. J. and LEVINSON, R. M. Baiting the dissident hook: some effects of bias on measuring religious beliefs. *Sociometry*, 1971; **34**(3), 346–369.

DITTES, J. E. Justification by faith and experimental psychologist. *Religion in Life*, 1959; **58**(4), 567–576.

DITTES, J. E. Impulsive closure as a reaction to failure-induced threat. *Journal of Abnormal and Social Psychology*, 1961; **63**(3), 562–569.

DITTES, J. E. Psychology of religion. In G. LINDZEY and E. ARONSON, *The handbook of social psychology* (V), 2nd edn. Reading and London: Addison Wesley, 1969, pp. 602–659.

DITTES, J. E. Two issues in measuring religion. In M. P. STROMMEN (ed.), *Research on religious development.* New York: Hawthorn, 1971, pp. 78–106.

DITTES, J. E. Typing the typologies. Some parallels in the career of church-sect and extrinsic-intrinsic. *Journal for the Scientific Study of Religion*, 1971; **10**(4), 375–383.

DOISE, W. Images, représentations, idéologies et expérimentation psycho-sociologique. *Informations sur les Sciences Sociales*, 1978; **17**(1), 41–69.

DOR-SHAV, N. K., FRIEDMAN, B. and TCHERBONOGURA, R. Identification, prejudice and aggression. *The Journal of Social Psychology*, 1978; **104**(1), 217–222.

DUNFORD, F. W. and KUNZ, P. R. The neutralization of religious dissonance. *Review of Religious Research*, 1973; **15**(1), 2–9.

EISTER, A. W. (ed.) *Changing perspectives in the scientific study of religion.* New York: Wiley & Sons, 1974.

ELKINS, D., ANCHOR, K. N. and HOWARD, M. Relaxation training and prayer behavior as tension reduction techniques. *Behavioral Engineering,* 1979; **5**(3), 81–87.

EMBREE, R. A. The religious association scale. A preliminary validation study. *Journal for the Scientific Study of Religion,* 1973; **12**(2), 223–226.

EMMONS, C. F. and SOBAL, J. Paranormal beliefs: functional alternatives to mainstream religion? *Review of Religious Research,* 1981; **22**(4), 301–312.

FEATHER, N. T. Acceptance and rejection of arguments in relation to attitude strength, critical ability and intolerance of inconsistency. *Journal of Abnormal and Social Psychology,* 1964; **69**(2), 127–136.

FESTINGER, L., RIECKEN, H. W., and SCHACHTER, S. *When prophecy fails. A social and psychological study of a modern group that predicted the destruction of the world.* New York: Harper, 1956.

FILSINGER, E. E., FAULKNER, J. E. and WARLAND, R. H. Empirical taxonomy of religious individuals. An investigation among college students. *Sociological Analysis,* 1979; **40**(2), 136–146.

FINNEY, J. M. A theory of religious commitment. *Sociological Analysis. A Journal in the Sociology of Religion,* 1978; **39**(1), 19–35.

FLAKOLL, D. A. A history of method in the psychology of religion. In H. N. MALONY (ed.), *Current perspectives in the psychology of religion.* Grand Rapids: Eerdsmans, 1977, pp. 77–92.

FORBES, G. B., TEVAULT, R. K. and GROMOLL, H. F. Willingness to help strangers as a function of liberal, conservative or catholic church membership: a field study with the lost letter technique. *Psychological Reports,* 1971; **28**(3), 947–949.

FRANCIS, L. The priest as test administrator in attitude research. *Journal for the Scientific Study of Religion,* 1979; **18**(1), 78–81.

FUKUYAMA, Y. The major dimensions of church membership. *Review of Religious Research,* 1961; **2**(4), 154–161.

GAEDE, S. A causal model of belief-orthodoxy: proposal and empirical test. *Sociological Analysis,* 1976; **37**(3), 205–217.

GARRETT, W. R. Troublesome transcendence: the supernatural in the scientific study of religion. *Sociological Analysis,* 1974; **35**(3), 167–180.

GLOCK, C. Y. The sociology of religion. In R. MERTON, L. BROOM and L. COTTRELL (eds.), *Sociology today.* New York: Basic Books, 1959, pp. 153–177.

GLOCK, C. Y. and STARK, R. *Religion and society in tension.* Chicago: Rank McNally, 1965.

GLOCK, C. Y. and STARK, R. *Christian beliefs and anti-semitism.* New York: Harper and Row, 1966.

GODIN, A. Moi perdu ou moi retrouvé dans l'expérience charismatique: perplexité des psychologues. *Archives de Sciences Sociales des Religions,* 1975; **20**(40), 31–52.

GODIN, A. and HALLEZ, M. Images parentales et paternité divine. In A. GODIN, *De l'expérience à l'attitude religieuse.* Bruxelles: Lumen Vitae, 1964, pp. 81–114.

GOLDMAN, R. *Religious thinking from childhood to adolescence.* London: Routledge & Kegan Paul, 1964.

GOODMAN, F. D. Phonetic analysis of glossolalia in four cultural settings. *Journal for the Scientific Study of Religion,* 1969; **8**(2), 227–239.

GOODMAN, F. D. *Speaking in tongues: a cross-cultural study of glossolalia.* Chicago: University of Chicago Press, 1972.

GOODMAN, F. D. Glossolalia and hallucination in Pentecostal congregation. *Psychiatria Clinica,* 1973; **6**(2), 97–103.

GORSUCH, R. L. Editor's reflections. *Journal for the Scientific Study of Religion,* 1976; **15**(1), 95–98.

GORSUCH, R. L. and ALESHIRE, D. Christian faith and ethnic prejudice: a review and interpretation of research. *Journal for the Scientific Study of Religion,* 1974; **13**(3), 281–307.

GREELEY, A. M. A note on the origins of religious differences. *Journal for the Scientific Study of Religion,* 1963; **3**(1), 21–31.

GREELEY, A. M. and ROSSI, P. H. *The education of Catholic Americans.* New York: Doubleday, 1968.

GREENBERG, J. The protestant work ethic and reactions to negative performance evaluations on a laboratory task. *Journal of Applied Psychology*, 1977; **62**(6), 682–690.

GREENWALD, A. Does the Good Samaritan parable increase helping? A comment on Darley and Batson's no-effect conclusion. *Journal of Personality and Social Psychology*, 1975; **32**(4), 578–583.

GREGORY, W. E. The orthodoxy of the authoritarian personality. *Journal of Social Psychology*, 1957; **45**(1), 217–232.

GUSTAFSON, J. P. Schismatic groups. *Human Relations*, 1978; **31**(2), 199.

GUTHRIE, G. M. and MARSHALL, J. F. Cognitive dissonance among Protestant fundamentalists. *Pennsylvania Psychiatric Quarterly*, 1966; **6**(2), 11–25.

HADAWAY, C. K. and ROOF, W. C. Those who stay religious "nones" and those who don't: a research note. *Journal for the Scientific Study of Religion*, 1979; **18**(2), 194–200.

HAMMOND, P. E. The shifting meaning of a Wall of separation. Some notes on Church, state and conscience. *Sociological Analysis*, 1981; **42**(3), 227–232.

HARRIS, M. B., BENSON, S. M. and HALL, C. L. The effects of confession on altruism. *Journal of Social Psychology*, 1975; **96**(2), 187–192.

HAVENS, J. The participant's vs. the observer's frame of reference in the psychological study of religion. *Journal for the Scientific Study of Religion*, 1961; **1**, 79–87.

HERTEL, B. R. Inconsistency of beliefs in the existence of heaven and after-life. *Review of Religious Research*, 1980; **21**(2), 171–183.

HIMMELFARB, H. Measuring religious involvement. *Social Forces*, 1975; **53**, 606–618.

HODGES, D. L. Breaking a scientific taboo: putting assumptions about the supranatural into scientific theories of religion. *Journal for the Scientific Study of Religion*, 1974; **13**(4), 393–408.

HOOD, R. W. A comparison of the Allport and Feagin scoring procedure for intrinsic/extrinsic religious orientation. *Journal for the Scientific Study of Religion*, 1971; **10**(4), 370–374.

HOOD, R. W. The usefulness of the indiscriminately pro and anti categories of religious orientation. *Journal for the Scientific Study of Religion*, 1978; **17**(4), 419–431.

HOOD, R. W. and MORRIS, R. J. Sensory isolation and the differential elicitation of religious imagery in intrinsic and extrinsic persons. *Journal for the Scientific Study of Religion*, 1981; **20**(3), 261–273.

HSIEH, T. Missionary family behavior, dissonance and children's career decision. *Journal of Psychology and Theology*, 1976; **4**(3), 221–226.

HUNSBERGER, B. Sources of "psychology of religion". Journal articles: 1950–1974. *Journal for the Scientific Study of Religion*, 1979; **18**(1), 82–85.

HUNT, R. A. The intrinsic-extrinsic concept: a review and evaluation. *Journal for the Scientific Study of Religion*, 1971; **10**(4), 339–356.

HUNT, R. A. Mythological-symbolic religious commitment. The LAM Scales. *Journal for the Scientific Study of Religion*, 1972; **11**(1), 45–52.

HUTCH, R. A. The personal ritual of glossolalia. *Journal for the Scientific Study of Religion*, 1980; **19**(3), 255–266.

JAHODA, G. Supernatural beliefs and changing cognitive structures among Ghanaian university students. *Journal of Cross-Cultural Psychology*, 1970; **1**(2), 115–130.

KAHOE, R. D. Personality and achievement correlates of intrinsic and extrinsic religious orientations. *Journal of Personality and Social Psychology*, 1974; **29**(3), 812–813.

KAHOE, R. D. Religious conservatism in a quasi-longitudinal perspective. *Journal of Psychology and Theology*, 1977; **5**(1), 40–47.

KELLEY, H. H. Salience of membership and resistance to change of group-anchored attitudes. *Human Relations*, 1955; **8**(1), 275–289.

KELLY, J. R. Religious membership and religious preference. Equal indicators of preferences? *Journal for the Scientific Study of Religion*, 1970; **9**(4), 273–279.

KILDAHL, J. P. *The psychology of speaking in tongues.* New York: Harper & Row, 1972.

KING, M. B. and HUNT, R. A. *Measuring religious dimensions.* Dallas: Southern Methodist University, 1972.

KISHIMOTO, H. Religiology. The scope of religiology. *Numen*, 1967; **14**(2), 82–86.

KIVETT, V. R., WATSON, J. A. and BUSH, J. C. The relative importance of physical, psychological, and social variables to locus of control orientation in Middle Age. *Journal of Gerontology*, 1977; **32**(2), 203–210.

KLAUSNER, Q. Z. Methods of data collection in studies of religion. *Journal for the Scientific Study of Religion*, 1964; **3**(2), 193–203.

KOTESKEY, R. L. *Psychology from a Christian perspective*. Nashville: Abingdon Press, 1980.

LAFFAL, J., MONAHAM, J. and RICHMAN, P. Communication of meaning in glossolalia. *Journal of Social Psychology*, 1974; **92**(2), 277–291.

LANSKEY, D. and PIHL, R. O. Personality correlates to placebo responsivity and religiosity. *Psychological Reports*, 1976; **39**(3), 975–982.

LEE, J. L. and DORAN, W. J. Vocational persistence. An exploration of self-concept and dissonance theories. *Journal of Vocational Behavior*, 1973; **3**(2), 129–136.

LEFCOURT, H. M. *Locus of control. Current trends in theory and research*. New York: John Wiley & Sons, 1976.

LEGRAND, M. E. Réflexions épistémologiques d'un psychologue. *Social Compass*, 1975; **22**(3/4), 397–400.

LEMAINE, G. Dissimilation and differential assimilation in social influence (Situations of 'normalization'). *European Journal of Social Psychology*, 1975; **5**(1), 93–120.

LENSKI, G. *The religious factor. A sociologist's inquiry*. New York: Doubleday, 1961.

LERNER, M. J. Evaluation of performance as a function of performer's reward and attractiveness. *Journal of Personality and Social Psychology*, 1965; **1**(2), 355–360.

LERNER, M. J. Belief in a just world versus authoritarianism syndrome . . . but nobody liked the Indians. *Ethnicity*, 1978; **5**, 229–237.

LERNER, M. J. *The belief in a just world. A fundamental delusion*. New York: Plenum Press, 1980.

LERNER, M. J. and MATTHEWS, P. Reactions to suffering of others under conditions of indirect responsibility. *Journal of Personality and Social Psychology*, 1965; **5**(2), 319–325.

LERNER, M. J. and SIMMONS, C. H. The observer's reaction to the innocent victim: compassion or rejection. *Journal of Personality and Social Psychology*, 1966; **4**(2), 203–210.

LIED, T. R. and PRITCHARD, R. D. Relationships between personality variables and components of the expectancy-valence model. *Journal of Applied Psychology*, 1976; **61**(4), 463–467.

LILLISTON, L. and BROWN, P. M. Perceived effectiveness solutions to personal problems. *Journal of Clinical Psychology*, 1981; **37**(1), 118–122.

LONG, L. and LONG, T. J. Influence of religious status and religious attire on interviewees. *Psychological Reports*, 1976; **39**(1), 25–27.

LOVEKIN, A. and MALONY, H. N. Religious glossolalia: a longitudinal study of personality changes. *Journal for the Scientific Study of Religion*, 1977; **16**(4), 383–393.

LUCKMANN, Z. *The invisible religion. The transformation of symbols in industrial society*. New York: Macmillan, 1967.

MAGNI, K. The fear of death. An exploratory study of its nature and its correlates. In A. GODIN (ed.), *Death and presence. The psychology of death and the after-life*. Bruxelles: Lumen Vitae Press, 1972.

MALONY, H. N. (ed.). *Current perspectives in the psychology of religion*. Grand Rapids: Eerdsmans, 1977.

MARANELL, G. M. *Responses to religion. Studies in the psychology of religious belief*. Lawrence: The University Press of Kansas, 1974.

MARTIN, R. D., MCDONALD, C. and SHEPEL, L. F. Locus of control and two measures of irrational beliefs. *Psychological Reports*, 1976; **39**(1), 307–310.

MCCOURT, K. and TAYLOR, D. G. Determining religious affiliation through survey research. A methodological research. *Public Opinion Quarterly*, 1976; **40**(1), 124–127.

MCDONALD, G. W. Sex, religion and risk taking behavior as correlates of death anxiety. *Omega. Journal of Death and Dying*, 1976; **15**(4), 311–321.

MCKENNA, R. Good Samaritanism in rural and urban settings: a non-reactive comparison of helping behavior of clergy and control subjects. *Representative Research in Social Psychology*, 1976; **7**(1), 58–65.

MCLEMORE, C. The nature of psychotheology. Varieties of conceptual integration. *Journal of Psychology and Theology*, 1976; **4**(3), 217–220.

MCPHAIL, C. Religious self-designating behaviors. *Journal for the Scientific Study of Religion*, 1972; **11**(3), 262–270.

MIRELS, H. L. and GARRETT, J. B. The Protestant ethic as a personality variable. *Journal of Consulting and Clinical Psychology*, 1971; **36**(1), 40–44.

MORLAN, G. K. An experiment on the recall of religious material. *Religion in Life*, 1950; **19**(4), 589–594.

MOSCOVICI, S. Toward a theory of conversion behavior. In L. BERKOWITZ (ed.), *Advances in experimental social psychology* (XIII). New York–London: Academic Press, 1980.

MUGNY, G. and DOISE, W. *Niveaux d'analyse dans l'étude expérimentale des processus d'influence sociale.* Genève: Faculté de Psychologie et des Sciences de l'Education, 1979.

MUNRO, D. Locus of control attribution. Factors among Blacks and Whites in Africa. *Journal of Cross-Cultural Psychology*, 1979; **10**(2), 157–172.

NELSON, L. D. and DYNES, R. The impact of devotionalism and attendance on ordinary and emergency helping behavior. *Journal for the Scientific Study of Religion*, 1976; **15**(1), 47–59.

NIESZ, N. L. and KRONENBERG, E. J. Self-actualization in glossolalic and non-glossolalic Pentecostals. *Sociological Anlysis*, 1978; **39**(3), 250–256.

OSARCHUCK, M. and TATZ, S. J. Effect of induced fear of death on belief in after-life. *Journal of Personality and Social Psychology*, 1973; **27**(2), 256–260.

OSSER, H. A., OSTWALD, R. F., MCWHINEY, B. and CASEY, R. L. Glossolalic speech from a psycholinguistic perspective. *Journal of Psycholinguistic Research*, 1973: **2**(1), 9–19.

PAGES, R. L'élaboration de la preuve et le fonctionnement de la psychologie, notamment sociale. *Psychologie Française*, 1979; **24**(1), 17–29.

PAHNKE, W. N. Drugs and mysticism. *International Journal of Parapsychology*, 1966; **8**(2), 295–324.

PAYETTE, M. Ethnocentrisme et religion. *Archives de Sciences Sociales des Religions*, 1981; **5**, 133–138.

PELLETIER, K. R. Influence of transcendental meditation upon autokinetic perception. *Perceptual and Motor Skills*, 1974; **39**(3), 1031–1034.

PERRY, E. L., DAVIS, J. H., DOYLE, R. T. and DYBLE, J. E. Toward a typology of unchurched Protestants. *Review of Religious Research*, 1980; **21**(4), 388–404.

PETERSON, C. Locus of control and belief in self-oriented superstitions. *The Journal of Social Psychology*, 1978; **105**(2), 165–173.

PIERSMA, H. L. The relationship between locus of control and religiosity. *Dissertation Abstracts International*, 1974; **35**(6-B), 3031.

PLOCH, D. R. Religion as an independent variable. A critique of some major research. In A. W. EISTER (ed.), *Changing perspectives in the scientific study of religion.* New York: Wiley & Sons, 1974, pp. 275–294.

PROLA, M. A review of the transcendence index. *Journal of Personality Assessment*, 1972; **36**(1), 8–12.

PROUDFOOT, W. and SHAVER, P. Attribution theory and the psychology of religion. *Journal for the Scientific Study of Religion*, 1975; **14**(4), 317–330.

RAGAN, C., MALONY, H. N. and BEIT-HALLAHMI, B. Psychologists and religion: professional factors and personal belief. *Review of Religious Research*, 1980; **21**(2), 208–217.

REBERG, D. INNIS, N. D., MANN, B. and EIZENGA, C. Superstitious behavior resulting from periodic-independent presentations of food or water. *Animal Behavior*, 1979; **109**, 167–174.

RICHARDSON, J. T. Psychological interpretations of glossolalia, a reexamination of research. *Journal for the Scientific Study of Religion*, 1973; **12**(2), 199–207.

ROHRBAUGH, J. and JESSOR, R. Religiosity in Touth. A personal control against deviant behaviour? *Journal of Personality*, 1975; **43**(1), 136–155.

ROKEACH, M. The nature and meaning of dogmatism. *Psychological Review*, 1954; **61**(3), 194–204.

ROKEACH, M. *The open and closed mind. Investigations into the nature of belief systems and personality systems.* New York: Basic Books, 1960.

ROKEACH, M. Paradoxes of religious belief. The golden rule versus the role of exclusion. *Trans-action*, 1965; **2**, 9–12.

ROKEACH, M. The paradox of religious belief. *Proceedings of the Christian Association for Psychological Studies*, 1968, pp. 51–58.

ROOF, W. C. Concepts and indicators of religious commitment. A critical review. In R. WUTHNOW (ed.), *The religious dimension. New directions in quantitative research.* New York: Academic Press, 1979.

ROOF, W. C. and PERKINS, R. B. On conceptualizing salience in religious commitment. *Journal for the Scientific Study of Religion*, 1975; **14**(2), 111–128.

ROTTER, J. B. Generalized expectancies for internal vs external control of reinforcement. *Psychological Monographs*, 1966, **80**, Whole No. 609.

RUBIN, Z. and PEPLAU, L. Belief in a just world and reaction to another's lot. A study of participants with national draft lottery. *Journal of Social Issues*, 1973; **29**(1), 73–93.

RUBIN, Z. and PEPLAU, L. Who believes in a just world? *Journal of Social Issues*, 1975; **31**(1), 65–90.

RUSSELL, G. M. and JORGENSON, D. C. Religious group membership, locus of control and dogmatism. *Psychological Reports*, 1978; **42**(3), 1099–1102.

RYAN, J. M. Ethnoscience and problems of method in the social scientific study of religion. *Sociological Analysis*, 1978; **39**(3), 241–249.

SAIGH, P. A. The effect of perceived examiner religion on the digit span performance of Lebanese elementary school children. *The Journal of Social Psychology*, 1979; **109**, 167–174.

SAMARIN, W. J. Sociolinguistic vs neurophysiological explanations for glossolalia: comment on Goodman's paper. *Journal for the Scientific Study of Religion*, 1972a; **11**(3), 293–296.

SAMARIN, W. J. Variation and variables in religious glossolalia. *Language in Society*, 1972b; **1**(1), 121–130.

SAMARIN, W. J. Glossolalia as repressive speech. *Language and Speech*, 1973; **16**(2), 77–89.

SCHEIDT, R. J. Belief in supernatural phenomena and locus of control. *Psychological Reports*, 1973; **32**(4), 1159–1162.

SCOBIE, G. E. W. *Psychology of religion*. London: Batsford, 1975.

SHUTER, R. A study of non-verbal communication among Jews and Protestants. *The Journal of Social Psychology*, 1979; **102**(2), 31–42.

SIEGMAN, A. An empirical investigation of the psycho-analytic theory of religious behavior. *Journal for the Scientific Study of Religion*, 1961; **1**(1), 74–78.

SINGER, S. P. and ALKER, H. A. Dimensions of locus of control and the Women's Liberation Movement. *Journal of Social Issues*, 1972; **28**(4), 115–129.

SMITH, R., WHEELER, G. and DIENER, E. Faith without works: Jesus people, resistance to temptation and altruism. *Journal of Applied Social Psychology*, 1975; **5**(4), 320–330.

SORRENTINO, R. M. and HARDY, J. Religiousness and derogation of an innocent victim. *Journal of Personality*, 1970; **42**(5), 372–382.

SOSIS, R. H., STRICKLAND, B. R. and HALEY, W. E. Perceived locus of control and beliefs about astrology. *The Journal of Social Psychology*, 1980; **110**(1), 65–71.

SOUTHARD, S. *Religious Inquiry*. Nashville: Abingdon, 1976.

SPANOS, N. P. and HEWITT, E. R. Glossolalia. A test of the "trance" and psychopathology hypotheses. *Journal of Abnormal Psychology*, 1979; **88**(4), 427–434.

STANLEY, G., BARTLETT, W. K. and MOYLE, T. Some characteristics of charismatic experience: glossolalia in Australia. *Journal for the Scientific Study of Religion*, 1978; **17**(3), 269–277.

STARK, R. A taxonomy of religious experience. *Journal for the Scientific Study of Religion*, 1965; **5**(1), 97–116.

STARK, R. and BAINBRIDGE, W. S. Towards a theory of religion: religious commitment. *Journal for the Scientific Study of Religion*, 1980; **19**(2), 114–128.

STARK, R. and GLOCK, C. Y. *American piety. The nature of religious commitment*. Berkeley: University of California Press, 1968.

STERN, E. M. and MARINO, B. G. *Psychotheology*. New York: Newman Press, 1970.

STEWART, R. R. and WEBSTER, A. C. Scale for theological conservatism and its personality correlates. *Perceptual and Motor Skills*, 1970; **30**(3), 867–870.

STRICKLAND, B. R. and SHAFFER, S. I–E, I–E and F. *Journal for the Scientific Study of Religion*, 1971; **10**(4), 366–369.

STURGEON, R. S. and HAMLEY, R. W. Religiosity and anxiety. *The Journal of Social Psychology*, 1979; **108**(1), 137–138.

SULLIVAN, J. E. Two psychologies and the study of religion. *Journal for the Scientific Study of Religion*, 1962; **1**(2), 155–164.

TATE, E. D. and MILLER, G. R. Differences in value systems of persons with varying religious orientations. *Journal for the Scientific Study of Religion*, 1971; **10**(4), 357–365.

THOULESS, R. H. *An introduction to the psychology of religion.* Cambridge: University Press, 1956.

TOMKA, M. The religious/non-religious dichotomy as a social problem. *The Annual Review of the Social Sciences of Religion,* 1979; **3,** 105–134.

TOUZARD, H. *La médiation et la négociation des conflits.* Paris: Presses Universitaires de France, 1977.

UNGAR, S. Attitude inferences from behavior performed under public and private conditions. *Social Psychology Quarterly,* 1980; **43**(1), 81–89.

UNGER, J. Is religion a system of adaptation?. In J. KALLSTAD (ed.), *Psychological studies of religious man.* Stockholm: Almqvist & Wiksell, 1978.

VAILLANCOURT, J. G. Review of the Annual Review of the Social Sciences of Religion, 19771–1. *Sociological Analysis,* 1979; **40**(3), 277–278.

VERGOTE, A. Psychologie de la religion. Propos préliminaire et justificatif. *Social Compass,* 1972; **19**(3), 329–345.

VERGOTE, A. and TAMAYO, A. *The parental figures and the representations of God. A cross-cultural study.* Paris-La Haye: Mouton, 1981.

VERNON, G. M. The religious "nones": a neglected category. *Journal for the Scientific Study of Religion,* 1968; **7**(2), 219–229.

WALKER, R. E. and FIRETTO, A. The clergyman as a variable in psychological testing. *Journal for the Scientific Study of Religion,* 1965; **4**(2), 233–236.

WALLACE, R. K. Physiological effects of transcendental meditation. *Science,* 1970; No. 167, pp. 1751–1754.

WARREN, N. C. Empirical studies in the psychology of religion. An assessment of the period 1960–1970. In H. N. MALONY (ed.), *Current perspectives in the psychology of religion.* Grand Rapids: Eerdsmans, 1977.

WATERS, L. K., BATLIS, N. and WATERS, C. W. Protestant ethic attitudes among college students. *Educational and Psychological Measurements,* 1975; **35**(2), 447–450.

WELFORD, A. T. An attempt at an experimental approach to the psychology of religion. *British Journal of Psychology,* 1947; **36**(1), 55–73.

WHITNEY, J. R. Commentary on civil religion in America. In D. R. CUTLER (ed.), *The religious situation.* Boston: Beacon Press, 1968.

WIEBE, K. F. and FLECK, J. R. Personality correlates of intrinsic, extrinsic and non-religious orientations. *The Journal of Psychiatry,* 1980; **105**(2), 181–188.

WIMBERLEY, R. *et al.* The civil religious dimension. Is it there? *Social Forces,* 1976; **54,** 890–900.

WUTHNOW, R. *The consciousness reformation.* Berkeley: University of California Press, 1976.

WUTHNOW, R. (ed.). *The religious dimension. New directions in quantitative research.* New York: Academic Press, 1979.

WUTHNOW, R. Two traditions in the study of religion. *Journal for the Scientific Study of Religion,* 1981; **20**(1), 16–32.

YABRUDI, P. and DIAB, L. N. The effects of attitude similarity-dissimilarity religion and topic importance on interpersonal attraction among Lebanese university students. *The Journal of Social Psychology,* 1978; **106**(1), 167–171.

YEATTS, J. R. and ASHER, W. Can we afford not to do true experiments in psychology of religion? *Journal for the Scientific Study of Religion,* 1979; **18**(1), 86–89.

YINGER, J. M. *The scientific study of religion.* New York: Macmillan, 1970.

YINGER, J. M. A comparative study of the substructures of religion. *Journal for the Scientific Study of Religion,* 1977; **16**(1), 67–86.

ZUCKERMAN, M. Belief in a just world and altruistic behavior. *Journal of Personality and Social Psychology,* 1975; **31**(1), 272–276.

Notes

1. See in this respect the partial but very useful schedule recently drawn up by Basset *et al.* (1981). To build an original scale to "differentiate Christians from Non-Christians", they examined 135 scales of religious attitudes, and analysed their components (belief, behaviour, knowledge,

affiliation, validity of religion, religiosity, the Church, attitudes, religious orientation, autobiographical).

2. Capps's work (1974) is also worth noting in this context; its significance is probably not simply documentary. In referring in particular to Ninian Smart's historic work, he proposes "a six dimensional scheme which, taken in toto, addresses virtually all of the current research concerns of both Freudian and Jamesian psychologists of religion" (through mythological ritual, dispositional, social, experiential, and directional dimensions). This classification has in any case shown its heuristic effectiveness (Capps, Rambo and Ransohoff, 1976; Hunsberger, 1979).

3. King and Hunt (1972) have created a composite set of scales and sub-scales which in their 1968 study involved creedal assent, devotionalism, congregational involvement (through church attendance, organizational activity, financial support), religious knowledge, orientation to religion (as growth and striving or extrinsically), the salience of behaviour or cognition, tolerance or prejudice, intolerance of ambiguity, purpose in life (positive or negative, having a proreligious response set).

4. Stark (1965) identified a confirming responsive experience: with salvational, miraculous and sanctionings sub-types, ecstatic and revelational experiences (being confirming or responsive).

5. As a counterpoint to the questions raised by the sorts of concepts from which scales of religious attitudes are derived, the same problem would arise in attempting to "name" the factors selected by factorial analysis. The quality and prudence of a number of these undertakings (Brown, 1964) is all the more praiseworthy.

6. Rubin and Peplau (1975) themselves establish a correlation between positive scores on the BJW Scale, religious practice (Christians and Jews), the degree of allegiance to the belief in an "active God". Sorrentino and Hardy (1974) obtained comparable results. Lerner (1978) himself established a link between this score and those obtained on Mirels and Garrett's Protestant Ethic Scale (1971).

Editor's note: Copies of these original texts are available from Professor Deconchy.

8

An S–O–R model of religious experience

H. NEWTON MALONY

IN A recent article entitled "Religious experiencing: a phenomenological analysis of a unique behavioral event" (Malony, 1981), I suggested that religious experience could be subsumed under an S–O–R (or stimulus–response) paradigm. Although some may feel this model somewhat outdated, I feel that it captures the essence of religion as a behavioural response to a perceived stimulus and it both permits a focus on the uniqueness of that of which persons say they are aware, that is on the transcendent or the divine, and allows for interdisciplinary communication in that it corresponds to the terms theologians use to describe these events, i.e. revelation (stimulus), faith (organism) and work (response). This essay, therefore, uses this S–O–R paradigm as a foundation and attempts to relate it to several theories of religious motivation and demonstrate its utility in empirical research.

An expanded S–O–R model

In the earlier essay, I suggested that the term "religious EXPERIENCE" encompasses all three components (stimulus, organism and response), not just one or two of them. By this, I did not mean to discount those moments in which persons sense they are in the presence of a transcendent reality, as did William James in his library that fateful evening. Nor did I intend to disparage thoughtful philosophizing about religion or action on behalf of social justice. What I did mean to do was to distinguish any and all of these isolated events from "religious EXPERIENCE" and to restrict the use of that term to those times when all three components were present. I think this aligns the model with the Judeo-Christian understanding of God/human interaction plus it avoids the danger of separating reality into small unrelated bits, as has been done in the past. The classical Hebrew–Christian model for religion has included a meeting between humans and God followed by a call to obedience and a response of commitment. Further, the psychological understanding of experience always includes elements of perception, conception and response blended into a unity or gestalt.

The experience of the prophet in Isaiah 6:1–9 is illustrative. Isaiah was in the temple and "saw the Lord sitting upon a throne, high and lifted up" (v. 1). This is the initial sensation/perception response to the stimulus of the divine. The next several verses describe the event in terms of visual and auditory events. There are seraphims with wings; voices calling out "Holy, holy, holy is the Lord of hosts . . ."; shaking resembling an earthquake; and smoke that fills the whole house. All this Isaiah sees, smells, hears and feels. Then he expresses his dismay. "Woe is me! For I am lost . . . for my eyes have seen the King, the Lord of hosts" (v. 5). Next, there is an interaction between Isaiah and God. One of the seraphim touches his lips with a burning coal and declares that Isaiah's sins are forgiven. At this point God speaks and asks, "Whom shall I send, and who will go for us?". Isaiah responds with conviction, "Here I am! Send me". And God says, "Go!". This series of events includes all the parts of the S–O–R paradigm. God is the stimulus. Isaiah sees, perceives and reacts. This is the O or organism. God asks for help and Isaiah volunteers. This is the response. Religious experience is all of these put together and no one of them by itself.

This does not mean that an analysis of the several components (the S, the O and the R) is unimportant. It is to say that sensation, perception and behaviour go together and form a unity. To this unity we shall give the term EXPERIENCE. To the several components we shall give the term EVENT and suggest that several "events" go into an "experience". It is to a further consideration of these religious "events" that I now turn.

Table 1 illustrates the viewpoint expressed above, and depicts the several events from behavioural, theological and phenomenological perspectives. Keeping this paradigm in mind, I would next like to consider the several events one at a time.

TABLE 1   *Perspectives on the three events in religious experience*

	Event 1	Event 2	Event 3
Behavioural perspective	Stimulus	Organism	Response
Theological perspective	Revelation	Faith	Work
Phenomenological perspective	Need	Perception/conception	Action

Event 1 in religious experience

Event 1 has been labelled Stimulus, Revelation or Need. The underlying presumption of this event is that people are motionless unless prodded into action by some force from without or some impulse from within. The former, some force from without, was the thesis of Newtonian physics while the latter, some impulse from within, was the thesis of Thomistic philosophy. In both cases a somewhat passive organism is "stimulated" (cf. Stimulus) into action.

Although theologians following the Platonic/Aristotelian synthesis of insight and discovery proposed by Thomas Aquinas have defined Stimulus largely as "an inner impulse", a significant trend in Reform theology has defined it as a revelatory force from outside, namely God visiting or disclosing himself to persons. Theological differences in this regard have been complex and subtle and have even included combinations of these two emphases as can be seen in the concept of "prevenient grace" wherein what appears to be a search for God on the part of the individual was perceived as an example of power instilled in the individual by God. Augustine implied this in his famous prayer, "Thou hast made us for thyself, and our hearts are restless till they find their rest in thee."

A twentieth century illustration of these differences can be seen in the debate between Emil Brunner and Karl Barth in the volume *Nature and grace* (1946). Although both theologians agreed that there was a God who revealed himself to people, they disagreed as to how and when this occurred. The phrase "point of contact" became the point of contention between them. Brunner felt that God revealed himself by establishing a point of contact with persons' anxieties and that persons would not recognize God apart from His being an answer to the concerns they were experiencing. Barth, in contrast, felt that God needed no point of contact and that if God had to wait on persons to ask for His help He would be limited and, thus, the transformation which He worked in human life would never be radical. Barth felt that God revealed himself in a manner that revolutionized life rather than simply resolved it.

In developing a model for understanding Event 1, we shall call the first theological position "Revelation – Overwhelming" (cf. Reform point of view and Barth) and we shall call the second theological position "Revelation – Answering" (cf. Thomistic point of view and Brunner).

Since the issues in this essay are largely those of the psychology of religion, not theology, these subtleties will not be belaboured. Suffice it to say that these differences have important implications for both the design and interpretation of studies in this area, and while the psychology of religion cannot settle the validity question of whether there is a God or not, it should be well-informed regarding the assumptions that theologians have about the divine and the unique interpretations individuals make about the event.

Turning to the phenomenological perspective it can be seen that there are clear parallels to the theological positions noted above even though this perspective makes no presumptions about a transcendent reality and confines itself to a description of religious experience from within the confines of human psychological processes. For example, Wilber (1980) is one among many transpersonal psychologists who postulate a higher dimension to life than the mundane, and who perceive altered states of consciousness as indicative of this "religious" possibility. Although many such theorists take a passive or benign view regarding the induction of such events in the sense that they encourage persons to acknowledge them when they occur, others, such as Clark (1969), take a more active position and recommend the actual perpetration of them. He shares the view of many that western society militates against such events with its overemphasis on the pragmatic and the positivistic.

The NEED which could be posited in this case would be a need to actualize one's potential for experience which goes beyond mundane sensationism. As a further construct in our development of Event 1, we shall call this "Need – Potential".

Custom refers to the manner in which persons are conditioned by culture to interpret events and to perceive the Gods via a given world view through certain types of language. Weber (1963) and others have commented on the tendency over time for religions to routinize religious events into rituals and theologies so that members of church-type groups come to envision reality in fairly common ways. Oden (1972) noted that there have been periodic attempts to break out of these traditions throughout religious history via pietistic revivals which have attempted to restore pristine religious experience. Nevertheless, most people continue to sense a need to repeat the type of religious event which has been handed down to them by their particular tradition. We shall label this "Need – Custom" and recognize that it functions as a stimulus towards perceiving reality in a given manner.

Comprehension is somewhat related to Custom. It refers to an impulse postulated by Proudfoot and Shaver (1975) wherein persons attempt to make sense of ambiguous situations in which they are hyper- or hypo-aroused. In such states persons interpret the meaning of events by referring to the environment and the actions of those around them. Proudfoot and Shaver suggested that religion should be no exception to this rule, and called for research to determine whether or not such aroused persons would interpret and experience a religious event more in the presence of religious, as opposed to neutral, cues. Imhoff and Malony (1979) attempted to test these hypotheses with only limited success. The study to be described later in this chapter is an extension of that research. Suffice it to say at this juncture that an impulse to make sense of the environment is postulated as a need and, thus, we label this aspect of the stimulus component of religious experience "Need – Comprehension". Although "Need – Custom" also functions to assist persons in making sense of reality, the emphasis in Comprehension is more on the current environment than on an ideological tradition.

The next alternative for defining the need component of religious experience is termed Resolution. Resolution refers to the "point of contact" assertion made by the theologian Emil Brunner. Religion has long been understood to be the answer to the enigmas, tragedies, mysteries and injustices of life (cf. Yinger, 1970). In a volume entitled *Understanding your faith* (1978), I affirmed this position and suggested, along with the theologian

Paul Tillich, that "life poses the questions to which faith is the answer". I noted several basic anxieties that seem to be common to all human existence and concluded that religion provides resolutions to such concerns as suffering, death, tragedy, survival, and injustice. As noted, this point of view has a long tradition (cf. religion as the opiate of the people, Karl Marx) and it accords with the root meaning of religion as "binding things together". The label for this alternative is "Need – Resolution".

Relationship is yet another possible definition of the need which impels persons into religious experience. In an essay entitled "The therapeutic ingredients of religious and political philosophies" (1982), Edith Weisskopf-Joelson makes the point that there is a continuing nostalgia throughout life to re-establish the intimate and symbiotic relationships of childhood. Freud (1927/1961) felt this to be the essence of religion. Numerous theoreticians (e.g. Erik Berne, 1965) have posited this need for intimacy in human relationships. Religion could be conceived of as this urge on a transcendent scale. Sunden (1974), the Swedish psychologist of religion, has constructed a total model of religious experience on this foundation. Persons are impelled to relate personally to their God and then adopt a style similar to the heroes of their faith. In a dramatic manner they take on one of these traditional roles and imagine themselves to be in communication with the divine. This aspect of the religious event will be labelled "Need – Relationship" and will refer to this basic human impulse which relates so integrally to religion.

The last alternative in this phenomenological perspective of Event 1 is termed "meaning". This refers to the search for values or for understanding the purpose of life. Gordon Allport (1961) termed this the impulse to find a unifying philosophy of life, while Daniel Batson called it the "quest" dimension of religion (cf. Darley and Batson, 1973). Batson distinguished this from the traditional extrinsic (social comfort) and intrinsic (individual resolution) dimensions of religion. Herein one is compelled to seek religious events out of a need to find meaning in life and a purpose for living. The impulse is perennial, and changes in format and content as life goes on and new situations arise as Jung (1963) and Erikson (1958) have noted. In this endeavour, doubt is not avoided but embraced as inspiring one to further discovery. This led Edgar Brightman (1940) to define religion as the search for values in life. This sense of and response to value implies something which supersedes one's egotistic impulse to survive. It functions to integrate life into a whole and provides a sense of groundedness or connectedness. This alternative is labelled "Need – Meaning". It functions as a basic stimulus for many religious persons.

It should be noted that there is an affinity between the Theological and Phenomenological perspectives when Revelation is understood as "answering" and Need is understood either as "resolution" or "relationship". Here, the divine stimulus to which persons respond seems to be acknowledged to be that which answers a person's search for a purpose in life, for intimate companionship and for a rejoinder to the crises of existence. This could be thought of as a CONFLICT model for religion.

Similarly, there is an affinity between Theological and Phenomenological Perspectives when Revelation is understood as "overwhelming" or "meaning" and Need is understood as "potential". The divine stimulus to which persons respond in this case seems to be an unexpected discovery of a dimension to existence which one had not anticipated or known was there. This could be thought of as a CAPACITY model for religion.

With this elaboration of the first religious event in our model of religious experience, I will now turn to a similar elaboration of Event 2 – Organism, Faith, Perception/Conception. Hopefully, these elaborations will provide a basis for understanding the research to be reported later in this chapter. As an anticipation of that which is to come, let it be said at this juncture that the study to be reported was an attempt to ascertain which one of the several understandings of Need or Revelation best predicted the likelihood of persons having a religious experience.

Event 2 – organism in religious experience

Event 2 refers to those inner processes which occur in the mind of persons as they interpret Event 1. It is commonly assumed that most interactions with the environment by human beings involve thoughtful responses rather than the instinctual reactions characteristic of lower forms of life. Certainly this is true where the stimulus is trans-empirical, as is most often the case in religion. This is the rationale behind conceiving religious experience as Stimulus–ORGANISM–Response rather than Stimulus – Response. ORGANISM refers to those higher mental processes whereby humans take in sensations and interpret them. This is analogous to the Need – Comprehension alternative discussed under Event 1. The outworking of that need is the way the mind works. As Kelly (1955) and others have suggested, there seems to be a practical compulsion in humans to make sense of the world in order that they may order reality and determine how to act within it. The point being made here is that there is nothing automatic or instinctual about that process. It involves "inside the head" thinking – especially in religious experience.

Two Biblical examples illustrate this process. The first was the experience of Moses and the burning bush (Exodus 3). Here Moses saw a bush that burned without burning up. He heard a voice calling his name from within the bush. He answered "Here I am". The voice told him to take off his shoes because the ground was holy. It also told him that the voice was that of the God of Abraham. Then Moses hid his face because he was afraid to look at God. It is noteworthy that while Moses' leaving the path to look at a burning bush may have been instinctual, his perceiving the voice as that of his God, his taking off his shoes and his hiding his face all involved thoughtful responses.

The second experience was that of Thomas (John 20:24–29) who doubted that Jesus has risen because he had not seen "in his hands the print of the nails" or placed his "hand in his side". Jesus appeared to him and encouraged him to touch his body. Thomas did and then proclaimed "My Lord and my God". This is a clear distinction between sensation and interpretation. Although the feel of Jesus' hand and side was a physical sensation, the faith which Thomas stated was evidence of a higher mental process which involved a thoughtful response.

There are two basic steps involved in this cognitive event – perception and conception. Perception is the term applied to the labelling of those messages sent to the brain by nerves which lead from the basic sense of touch, sight, hearing, smell and taste. Perception is the process by which the brain interprets sensations in terms that make sense to the person. Conception is the term applied to the organizing of these perceptions in the light of a larger context or a system. The perceptions are hereby incorporated either into another dimension of reality or into a pattern of meaning which serves as an answer to questions which one was asking. With minimal reflection persons can recognize these processes going on within themselves. This is the "phenomenological" perspective on Event 2.

The "theological" perspective terms this response FAITH. The eleventh chapter of the book of Hebrews is often called the "faith chapter" and provides us a framework for understanding what theologians often mean by the term "faith". As will be seen, faith is very similar to what social psychologists term "attitude" and includes at least two components: belief and feeling (cf. Fishbein and Raven, 1962). Belief has to do with whether something is true or not, while feeling has to do with whether one is attracted to that something or not. In faith one believes that the stimulus with which one is interacting is divine, and one feels strongly attracted to that relationship.

The theological words for belief and feeling are "assurance" and "conviction". Hebrews 11:1 puts it thus: "Now faith is the assurance of things hoped for, the conviction of things not seen." Of course, this is a statement within the Judeo-Christian tradition, but the format probably applies to religious experience in general. "Assurance of things hoped for" refers to the needs in Event 1 in the sense that it suggests that faith is the belief that one has found what one was looking for – be it an answer to problems or a higher dimension of life. What one "hoped to find" one has found! This is assurance.

The "conviction of things not seen" goes beyond assent or belief, however. What the social psychologists call "feeling" and what the theologians term "conviction" implies an intuition that one can commit oneself to this relationship with the divine and that things will work out to the good. This is often referred to as "trust" – which is the meaning of the Greek word for faith "pistis", interestingly enough! The result of this aspect of faith is to provide the person with a positive stance or set towards acting in response to whatever it is that one feels the divine is asking one to do. This process can be seen in the example of Isaiah 6:1–9. In the course of that interaction he experienced forgiveness and said with great conviction, "Here I am – send me!". This is conviction. A fuller discussion of these theological meanings of faith can be found in the volume *Understanding your faith* (Malony, 1978).

To summarize, the processes under Event 2 have been discussed in terms of phenomenological and theological perspectives. Combining these two, the organismic processes going on within persons as they interact with a transcendent stimulus include:

(1) perception – the reception of the information from the senses and the labelling of these sensations as divine or supernatural;
(2) conception – relating these perceptions to an understanding of the divine with which one is familiar and in terms of which the event has meaning;
(3) belief – affirming the event as true and the self assurance that one is interacting with a person or a dimension that is real;
(4) feeling – the emotion of positive attraction wherein one wants to continue the relationship and in which one is ready to act in response to the event.

Event 3 – response in religious experience

The third and final event in religious experience is the response of the person. In the second event the individual has perceived that s/he is in the presence of some transcendent reality and has conceived this reality in terms that make sense. Thereafter, the individual has passed judgement on the event to the point where s/he believes it to be true and is positively disposed to respond to it. It is at this point that the person acts. S/he does something in response to this interaction with the supernatural. According to William James, this IS religion. He stated that religion was "The feelings, acts, and experiences of individual men in their solitude, so far as they apprehend themselves to stand in relation to whatever they may consider the divine" (1902, p. 31).

James's emphasis, and the import of this third event in religious experience, is on the observable responses people make rather than on the inner processes detailed in Events 1 and 2. Certainly "responses" are what can be seen and what most people mean when they talk about religion. Religion is church-going, alms-giving, public praying, Bible-reading, creed-saying, choir-singing, etc. These are the observable RESULTS.

Berger (1974) termed this "substantive" as opposed to "functional" religion in the sense that religion defined as observable behaviour had a SUBSTANCE to it which is missing in religion when it is understood as processes within an individual. In the present chapter the functional processes are those referred to in Events 1 and 2 while the substantive processes are those which can be observed in Event 3. No one of the events, be they substantive or functional, are to be preferred or emphasized over another. As has been said, they ALL go together to compose religious experience. However, "responses", such as are being discussed here, are best termed "substantive" religion.

There are several types of responses which can be made to the perception/conception of a transcendent reality or faith. These are termed "actions" from a phenomenological and "work" from a theological perspective.

"Action" is a term applied to all intentional and self-conscious behaviour. As noted in the discussion of Event 2, they are thoughtful responses, not instinctual reactions. Stark and Glock (1969, pp. 28–39) have identified five dimensions of religion which are only one of several taxonomies for delineating religious action (e.g. King and Hunt, 1975). These five dimensions are:

(1) ideological – referring to a religious response understood as the effort to work out and affirm doctrines or systematic beliefs;
(2) ritualistic – referring to religious response understood as participation in organized worship or individual devotional activities;
(3) experiential – referring to religious response understood as seeking out, entering into and labelling future events as interactions with transcendent reality;
(4) intellectual – referring to religious response understood as the attempt to acquire historical and theoretical knowledge about religion;
(5) consequential – referring to religious response understood as the moral or idealistic acts and attitudes in which one engages.

"Works" is the term theologians usually use to refer these responses to "faith" (the term they use to denote Event 2, as noted earlier). In fact these two, faith and works, are often paired together and the presumption is made that one cannot exist without the other. In the Judeo-Christian religion, at least, there is a deep-seated conviction that mature religious experience always involves a response to faith. It is not enough to believe. There MUST be action in response to the new knowledge that one has obtained through interaction with the divine, or religion is not complete.

The eighth-century prophets were most vocal about this connection between faith and work. Amos, for example, cautioned the ancient Hebrews, "Woe to those who are at ease in Zion . . ." (6:1, RSV). By this he meant to warn those who were satisfied with being God's chosen people without doing good. In another place, Amos has God say:

> I hate, I despise your feasts,
>   and I take no delight in your solemn assemblies . . .
> Take away from me the noise of your songs;
>   to the melody of your harps I will not listen.
> But let justice roll down like waters,
>   and righteousness like an everflowing stream
>   (Amos 5:21, 23–24, RSV)

Righteousness, justice, neighbourliness, kindness, love – these are just a few of the words used by the Biblical writers to refer to the "work" which those who have met God are supposed to undertake. The New Testament writer of the book of James spoke for the whole tradition in saying ". . . faith by itself, if it has no works, is dead" (2:17) and "Whoever knows what is right to do and fails to do it, for him it is sin" (4:17). All of this is to reassert how important this aspect has been to theologians and how much emphasis has been put on this dimension of religious experience.

Although the "consequential" dimension in the Glock and Stark taxonomy would seem most similar to "work" as understood by the theologians, "response" as understood herein is much broader than that, and includes all of the other dimensions in their paradigm. Although in the Judeo-Christian faith a concern for love and justice seems to take priority over the other responses (such as worship), these other behaviours are of equal concern to social scientists in their endeavours to understand the total panorama of religion.

There may well be a sense in which the type of response that is given to the interaction between the individual and the divine (Event 2) is determined by the type of need which provoked the experience in the first place. For example, the "intellectual" response may be related to the search for "meaning". A list of the possible relationships between the other Glock and Stark dimensions and the needs mentioned in Event 1 follows:

Need: Potential may be related to Consequential responses;
Need: Comprehension may be related to Experiential responses;
Need: Resolution may be related to Ideological responses; and,
Need: Relationship may be related to Experiential responses.

In summary, this section has considered Event 3 in the S–O–R paradigm of religious experience. The Stark and Glock (1968) model of dimensions of religion was used as a helpful paradigm for conceptualizing the intentional and self-conscious responses persons make to encounters with the divine. A possible paradigm for understanding responses as related to needs was offered. It was noted that such responses are termed "work" by the theologians who integrally relate such behaviours to the "faith" which precedes them.

An experimental investigation of some S–O–R issues

The above has been an extensive introduction to the following description of an experimental study. The discussion was intended to provide a paradigm in terms of which both the categories and the procedures would make sense. It was also hoped that such a foundation would provoke interpretations which would have meaning both for psychologists and for theologians. I am convinced that much work by both groups in the past has gone unnoticed because not enough attention has been paid to the ways in which their two disciplines interrelate.

In an effort to explore some of these S–O–R dimensions of religious experience we assessed the religious perceptions and behaviours of persons under conditions that controlled for the environmental setting and their predisposing states of mind (cf. Spradlin and Malony, 1981). This research was conceived as an attempt to investigate Events 1 and 2 in the S–O–R paradigm detailed above.

A voluntary sample of 64 women participated in a visit to a local art museum. Half had been judged to be religious and half non-religious on the basis of prior questioning. They listened to a guided fantasy of flying which included all the dimensions of a classical mystical experience as they walked through either a religious or non-religious gallery of the museum. In addition, half of the women were induced through suggestion into an excited state of physiological arousal and half were induced into a relaxed state.

After completing the gallery visit, participants rated the degree to which they had PERCEIVED the event to be religious and the degree to which they, personally, had had a religious EXPERIENCE. The data from this research are reported below. Table 1 reports the data on whether the event was religious while Table 2 includes the data on whether participants had a religious experience. We were interested in which of the three variables (religious environment of the setting, previous religiousness, and present mental state – excited/relaxed) would most influence these results. The results were controlled for each participant's ability to go into an altered state of arousal and to enter into the taped fantasy.

Analyses of variance of the data in both these tables revealed that only "religious background" was significantly related to the dependent variables. Neither being in an excited or relaxed mental state nor visiting a religious or non-religious art gallery had any effect. Only women who were previously religious perceived the event as religious and had a religious experience. Neither differences in setting nor state of mind influenced the results. It should also be noted that there was no relationship between the number or type of life crisis events over the last six months reported by the women and either of the dependent variables.

Returning to the S–O–R model previously discussed, these results seem to support the Custom Need alternative in Event 1. The women who were religious approached the situation with a history of involvement in organized religious activities. Their previous behaviour reflected an accommodation to culture although it should be noted that the questions asked did not assess their original motive for meeting their needs in such a manner. Nor did the research design provide for a comparison of all needs which were detailed in the discussion of Event 1.

At most the Comprehension Need and the Relationship Need alternatives could be inferred to be operative because in both cases the processes that occur

TABLE 1   *Answer to the question "Was the event religious?" (1–5 rating: religious to non-religious)*

		Religious background			
		Religious		Non-religious	
Gallery setting		Excited	Relaxed	Excited	Relaxed
Religious	$\bar{X}$	3.50	2.63	2.25	2.25
	SD	1.07	0.74	0.89	1.04
Non-religious	$\bar{X}$	2.88	2.63	1.63	2.00
	SD	1.64	0.92	0.74	1.07

Total $N = 64$, N in each sub group $= 8$.

TABLE 2   *Answer to the question "Did you have a religious experience?" (Religious Episode Experience Measure: Hood, 1975)*

		Religious background			
		Religious		Non-religious	
Gallery setting		Excited	Relaxed	Excited	Relaxed
Religious	$\bar{X}$	41.00	49.25	29.88	28.50
	SD	17.94	17.33	11.73	12.82
Non-religious	$\bar{X}$	41.88	33.25	29.63	37.50
	SD	20.80	16.80	12.66	16.71

Total $N = 64$, N in each sub group $= 8$.

in Event 2 are perceptual and experiential. In this regard, the two dependent variables of perceiving the event to be religious and having a religious experience could be said to be biased toward some but not other need alternatives. Certainly, the interaction between a mystical fantasy and the viewing of art would seem to be more compatible with such alternatives as Potential, Comprehension, Relationship and Meaning. The Resolution of conflict would not seem to fit this paradigm as was demonstrated by the lack of a relationship between life crisis events during the previous six months.

It should also be noted that the use of the term "experience" in this research was non-technical. It was not used in the way that the S–O–R model applies it to the composite processes of Events 1, 2 and 3. It referred to the more typical use of the term in which a person reports a momentary contact with the spiritual dimension of life.

Conclusion

In conclusion, this chapter has presented an S–O–R model for understanding religious experience and it has illustrated how components within this model can be subjected to empirical investigation. The research which was reported did not include investigation of Event 3, the consequences or results of religious events, but future studies could be designed to include this component. The model presented here, coupled with the demonstration experiment which was reported, are intended to communicate a complex set of events which can only be simplified to the detriment of the experience. Religious experience has been denuded of its true complexity in much past research and this S–O–R paradigm is offered for its heuristic value for future investigations.

References

ALLPORT, G. W. *The individual and his religion: A psychological interpretation.* New York: Macmillan, 1961.
BERGER, P. L. Second thoughts on defining religion. *Journal for the Scientific Study of Religion,* 1974; **13,** 125–133.
BERNE, E. *Games people play.* New York: Grove Press, 1965.
BRIGHTMAN, E. S. *The philosophy of religion.* New York: Prentice Hall, 1940.
BRUNNER, E. M. and BARTH, K. *Nature and grace.* Translated by Peter Frankel. London: G. Bles – The Centenary Press, 1946.
CLARK, W. H. *Chemical ecstasy: psychedelic drugs and religion.* New York: Sheed & Ward, 1969.
DARLEY, J. M. and BATSON, C. D. "From Jerusalem to Jericho": A study of situational variables in helping behavior. *Journal of Personality and Social Psychology,* 1973; **27,** 100–108.
ERIKSON, E. *Young man Luther: A study in psychoanalysis and history.* New York: W. W. Norton, 1958.
FISHBEIN, M. and RAVEN, B. H. The A–B scales: an operational definition of belief and attitude. *Human Relations,* 1962; **15**(1), 35–44.
FREUD, S. *The future of an illusion* (1927). In Standard edition of the complete works of Sigmund Freud, vol. 21, pp. 3–56. London: Hogarth Press, 1961.
HOOD, R. W., Jr. The construction and preliminary validation of a measure of reported mystical experience. *Journal for the Scientific Study of Religion,* 1975; **14,** 29–41.
IMHOFF, M. and MALONY, H. N. Physiological arousal, environmental cues and the report of religious experience: a test of attributional theory. Paper presented at the annual meeting of the Society for the Scientific Study of Religion, Hartford, Connecticut, October, 1979.
JAMES, W. *The varieties of religious experience: a study of human nature.* New York: Longmans, Green & Co., 1902.
JUNG, C. *Psychology and religion: West and East.* New York: Bollingen Foundation, 1963.
KELLY, G. A. *The psychology of personal constructs:* Volume 1 – *A theory of personality.* New York: W. W. Norton, 1955.
KING, M. B. and HUNT, R. A. Measuring the religious variable: national replication. *Journal for the Scientific Study of Religion,* 1975; **14,** 13–22.
MALONY, H. N. *Understanding your faith.* Nashville: Abingdon Press, 1978.
MALONY, H. N. Religious experiencing: a phenomenological analysis of a unique behavioral event. *Journal of Psychology and Theology,* 1981; **9**(4), 326–334.
ODEN, T. C. *The intensive group experience: The new pietism.* Philadelphia: Westminster Press, 1972.
PROUDFOOT, W. and SHAVER, P. Attribution theory and the psychology of religion. *Journal for the Scientific Study of Religion,* 1975; **14**(4), 317–330.
SPRADLIN, W. H. and MALONY, H. N. Physiological state deviation, personal religiosity, setting variation and the report of religious experience. Paper presented at the annual meeting of the Society for the Scientific Study of Religion, Baltimore, Maryland, October, 1981.
STARK, R. and GLOCK, C. Y. *American Piety.* Berkeley: University of California Press, 1968.
SUNDÉN, J. *Religion psykologi: problem och methoder.* Stockholm: Proprius, 1974.

WEBER, M. *The sociology of religion.* Translated by Ephraim Fischoff. Boston: Beacon, 1963.
WEISSKOPF-JOELSON, E. The therapeutic ingredients of religious and political philosophies. In PAUL W. SHARKEY (ed.), *Philosophy, religion and psychotherapy.* Washington, DC: University Press of America, 1982, pp. 187–210.
WILBER, K. A developmental model of consciousness. In R. N. WALSH and F. VAUGHAN (eds), *Beyond ego: Transpersonal dimensions in psychology.* Los Angeles: J. P. Tarcher, Inc., 1980.
YINGER, J. M. *The scientific study of religion.* New York: Macmillan, 1970.

9

Frame of reference as a prerequisite for the induction of religious experience through meditation: an experimental study

JAN VAN DER LANS

WHICH are the psychological antecedents of religious experience? Depending on one's theoretical perspective, this problem is approached in different ways. Researchers who are psychoanalytically oriented will primarily take into consideration biographical factors that have constituted the development of the psychodynamic structure of the individual or they will observe the religious experience from the perspective of the adaptive equilibrium the person attempts to achieve. From the viewpoint of cognitive psychology, however, human behaviour is not primarily seen as reactive or adaptive, but as a search for meaning and as a subjective construction of meaningful reality. Answering the question of the psychological antecedents, psychologists of religion, working with a cognitive psychological framework, look upon religious experience as a phenomenon of perceptual change and assume that cognitive factors are responsible for it.

In the first half of this chapter I will give an overview of three approaches in the cognitive psychology of religion that differ somewhat in the conceptual framework they use. In the second half I will report some findings of a laboratory experiment that I set up some years ago in order to test the theoretical assumption concerning the cognitive psychological basis of religious experience.

The first cognitive psychological approach in the study of religious experience to be mentioned is attribution theory. This name does not refer to a distinct theoretical school, but is applied as a common denominator for a rather loose collection of approaches, in which man is regarded as a cognitive being constantly prompted by the need to attribute external events as well as one's own bodily states to some causal process. The concept of "personal constructs" introduced by Kelly (1955) is a precursor of the attribution–theoretical approach that was developed by Heider (1958). Students of religious experience who can be considered as representatives of this school of thought are, for example, Malony (1973), Barbour (1974) and Bowker (1973), while Proudfoot and Shaver (1975) showed the usefulness of attribution research for understanding religious experience. With a lot of examples they demonstrate that attribution theory considers labelling and interpretation as the crucial factors in religious experience.

Another cognitive psychological approach to religious experience to be mentioned here is the Swedish school, founded by Hjalmar Sundén. Because of their explanatory model, Sundén and his disciples could very well be considered as belonging to the attribution–theoretical authors. However, the major reason to mention them separately is the conceptual uniformity of this school, a characteristic that is hardly to be found among the authors usually reduced to the denominator of attribution theory. In their explanation of religious experience Sundén (1959, 1964, 1965, 1967) and his coworkers (Källstadt, 1974; Unger, 1976; Holm, 1976; Pettersson, 1975; Holmberth, 1980; Geels, 1980) use the concept "religious reference frame". A subject has a religious reference frame when he is familiar with the symbols and myths of a religious tradition. This is considered to be a necessary precondition for religious experience. Characteristic for this Swedish school is, furthermore, that role-theoretical concepts are introduced in the definition of a religious reference frame. Every religious tradition is viewed by them as a description of role-patterns because the religious myths tell about the interaction between God and men. For everyone who knows the myths, it is possible to identify with a particular mythological figure according to the demands of his situation. Identifying with a figure from a myth involves taking the role of God. This implies that one anticipates how God will act again as he did in the situation described in the myth. In other words, identifying with a figure from the religious tradition implies a disposition to become aware of the presence of God. In Sundén's point of view religious experience is a perception resulting from role-playing and role-taking, made possible by a religious reference frame that is the product of having learned the role-patterns of the religious tradition. When this religious reference frame is active, there is a readiness to perceive reality in the same way as the persons described in the myths did.

Besides attribution theory and the Swedish school, a third way to study religious experience from a cognitive psychological viewpoint can be distinguished, which has not, however, been much elaborated so far. Salient for this view is that, in analysing the determining factors underlying religious experiences, the contemporary conceptual model of cognitive psychology is applied, where cognition is viewed as information-processing (Van der Lans, 1977, 1981). From the descriptions it becomes clear that religious experience always includes perceptual changes. Sometimes emphasis is laid on a changed self-perception. Mostly the environment is said to be perceived differently. New features are seen in familiar objects or attention is drawn to things that usually are not consciously perceived. According to the terminology of the psychology of perception this means that a different part of the sensory input is selected for attention than is usual, and that the cognitive process of the construction of an object is also enacted differently. The information of the senses is processed in such an unfamiliar way that it astonishes the subject himself, so that he cannot find words to describe it.

Let me briefly summarize the information-processing model (Neisser, 1967). According to the contemporary viewpoint, in which an analogy with computer programs is easily recognized, sensory information is processed in successive stages. On a first level the information picked up by the sensory receptors is coded and separated into units or recognizable patterns. This stage is called the preattentive process, and it is chiefly guided by an iconic memory. Following the preattentive mechanisms comes the second level of pattern analysis. Now features are recognized and a meaningful object is constructed under the influence of past experiences which have been stored in the long-term memory. Through the guiding function of the long-term memory, factors like personal and cultural values and also defence mechanisms will influence the information processing. The information can be structured at various levels of abstraction and meaning (Neisser, 1976, p. 21), and the level on which the meaning of an object will be specified depends on the particular memory scheme that is currently active. Anticipatory schemes or memory programs are the cognitive structures that play a crucial role in defining the final perceptual outcome of the information processing.

Applying this model to the phenomenon of religious experience, we must assume that in this case the information has been processed according to a very particular memory program. To be able to experience reality in a religious way, a subject, earlier in his life, must have obtained a specific knowledge that has been stored in his memory. As such it can be conceived as a particular potentiality that under certain circumstances can become an active cognitive scheme that directs perceptual activity.

All three cognitive approaches mentioned agree in relating religious experiences to the working of specific preexisting cognitive structures. In the attribution–theoretical approach they are conceptualized as "religious constructs" (Malony, 1973; Bowker, 1973), in the Swedish school as "religious reference frames" and in the information processing model as religious memory programs. But it is not enough to point at such cognitive structures. In order to be able to explain religious experience, another question must be answered: namely how these specific cognitive structures become active and dominant, replacing the usual schemes of interpretation that underlie everyday experiences. It seems to me that this problem has not yet been studied sufficiently among cognitive psychologists, except by those studying the domain of religious experience.

Some attribution theory authors who pay attention to this problem refer to the influence of the social environment in this respect. If the setting or context is religious, then religious attributions will be suggested (Proudfoot and Shaver, 1975). Representatives of the Swedish school speak about an "exchange of phases", comparable with the structural change in the perceptual field that is known from experiments with reversible figures. Everybody who has a religious reference frame at his disposal can switch from the profane reference frame to the religious reference frame, which means to restructure the perceptual field. An event, otherwise interpreted as accidental, can then be experienced as a sign given by God (Unger, 1976).

The problem remains, however, how it is possible to switch off the secular frame of reference, that is continually reinforced in our social interaction of everyday life. Merely suggesting religious attributions will not be sufficient, for this is done rather often, e.g. in a sermon. Only very rarely, if ever, do such suggestions occasion a religious experience. Usually the profane frame of reference retains its dominance.

What can we conclude from these cognitive-psychological considerations? For the moment we leave aside conclusions applicable to religious education or pastoral counselling, and limit ourselves to conclusions which seem to be relevant for experimental research. For the induction of religious experiences in a research setting it is not sufficient to activate religious cognitive structures or memory programs (cf. Pahnke, 1966). It is also necessary to use a technique that can suppress or inhibit the memory schemes that usually determine how information will be processed.

I will now report the results of a laboratory experiment that I carried out some years ago (Van der Lans, 1981) and criticize the design that I used. The experiment was announced as a practical course in Zen meditation. This was done not only in order to get subjects, but primarily to realize one of the just-mentioned preconditions for religious experience to come about. As has been known for centuries, this technique of meditation constitutes such a manipulation of attention as is required to produce an inhibition or suppression of the usual way of information processing (Deikman, 1966; Sundén, 1968).

Meditation by itself, however, does not lead to religious experience, as sometimes is wrongly assumed. One of the characteristic elements of the meditation procedures as they have been practised in every religious tradition is the activation, by reading and repetition, of religious memory schemes.

In my experiment I wanted to test the hypothesis that religious experiences will come about in meditating subjects only if they have a religious memory program at their disposal. The experimental variable of a "religious cognitive structure" was introduced by a combination of selection and intervention. This means that, using an intake interview as a selection procedure, the 45 subjects who wanted to participate in the meditation course were divided into two groups – one consisting of those with a religious cognitive structure and the other of those with a weak, or without a religious cognitive structure. The intervention was done by referring in the tape-recorded instructions for the religious group to the functions which have always been attributed to meditation in religious–mystical traditions, whereas the terminology in the instruction for the non-religious group referred to the therapeutic function meditation may have. According to Runkel and McGrath (1972), this combination of selection and intervention is the best procedure for manipulating the experimental variable, when the behaviour to be investigated is a product of interaction between an internal disposition and situational conditions; in other words, when the behaviour will not occur unless it is aroused. This exactly fits the case of religious experience. The meditation course took four weeks. During this period all subjects performed a Zen meditation exercise daily in the laboratory. They did it while sitting alone in a quiet room. The occurrence of religious experiences was measured in two ways. Firstly, by asking each person daily after his exercise to describe on a sheet all the unusual experiences which had occurred during the exercise. Secondly, by means of a questionnaire which the subjects had to fill up on the last day of the training and in which they were asked directly whether a religious experience had occurred during the meditation and, if so, to describe it. Unfortunately, no results were obtained with the first method. It often appeared that subjects returned blank sheets and did not report any unusual experience. On the direct question at the end of the meditation course, however, 14 subjects answered positively. The descriptions of their religious experiences were content-analysed critically by three independent raters. It appeared that only seven (50 per cent) described experiences that could be accepted as a religious experience according to the criteria adopted. These seven subjects all belonged to the religious cognitive structure group. Applying Fisher's exact probability test to the data it appears that the probability of the occurrence of the observed distribution under the null-hypothesis is less than 0.01.

Before we could conclude that the hypothesis has been varified we had to analyse whether the occurrence of religious experiences could be attributed to other differences between the two groups rather than to the experimental variable, "religious cognitive structure". A first possibility was that the difference in experimental results between the two groups had primarily been caused by the fact that the terminology of the meditation instruction was slightly different: religious symbols had been used for the experimental group and therapeutic concepts for the control group. To check whether the terminology of the instructions, apart from the cognitive structure of the subjects, might have had an independent influence, all the subjects were asked in the questionnaire whether there had been therapeutic experiences during or connected with the meditation exercises. From the fact that no more subjects in the control group answered positively than in the experimental group, it can be concluded that the kind of meditation instruction had not influenced the experimental result apart from the cognitive structure. Besides the independent variable, there were differences between the two groups in their belief in parapsychological phenomena and their experience with drugs, which might influence the occurrence of religious experiences.

An analysis of variance revealed that religious experiences had more frequently occurred to subjects with a religious cognitive structure who also believed in parapsychological phenomena ($p = 0.001$). The interaction between these two factors was also significant ($p = 0.01$). However, further analysis revealed that the factor "belief in parapsychological phenomena" had no significant effect by itself. In a separate analysis no correlation was found between the occurrence of religious experiences and experience with drugs.

Consequently we can conclude that, statistically, the hypothesis has been verified. The difference between the experimental group and the control groups in the occurrence of religious experiences cannot be related to any other variable than the selection variable "religious cognitive structure".

However, the fact must not be overlooked that half of the subjects in the experimental group did not report any religious experience. A first reason for this negative result could be that in these subjects the meditation process had not succeeded in bringing about a suppression of the ordinary way of processing information. The extent to which the subjects had been able to reach a certain depth of meditation was checked daily after the exercise by some specific questions. It appeared that in this respect subjects who had reported religious experiences did not significantly differ from those who had not. Secondly, from descriptions they gave of their experiences it became clear that the latter subjects had had unusual experiences. For instance, some felt the plausibility of their everyday world weakened; some had felt they faced a border situation. But these experiences had not been interpreted by them in a religious way. Probably it must be concluded that our experimental results demonstrate the limitations of a purely cognitive approach. Readiness for religious experience appears not to be only a matter of cognitive preconditions as is suggested in cognitive psychological approaches. On the basis of the cognitive models discussed one can predict that a religious experience will not occur if there is no religious cognitive structure. But on the basis of a cognitive model alone it cannot be predicted that religious experiences will occur when a religious cognitive structure is present and experimentally aroused. Such a cognitive structure is a necessary condition but not the only one. It appeared from the analysis of variance that the greater part of the total variance was not explained by the experimental variable. This means that more variables than those we have controlled must have influenced the differences between the subjects with regard to the dependent variable. We have to conclude that when one wants to investigate religious experiences experimentally, a research design in which one confines oneself to cognitive factors is inadequate. The variable of motivation must not be overlooked. There is some evidence that in our experiment motivational factors have played a crucial role. It appeared that those subjects of the religious group who had confirmed the occurrence of religious experiences had also obtained higher scores in the intake interview than those in the religious group who denied that religious experiences had occurred. The correlation between these two variables was highly significant (0.74; $p < 0.001$).

In the interview schedule used to constitute the group with a religious cognitive structure, some questions probed for the presence of religious motivation with regard to meditation (e.g. "What do you expect to be the result of this meditation exercise?"; "What use is it to you?"; "Why exactly do you judge meditation to be worthwhile?"; "What is the most basic value in your life?"). Those subjects who had a religious experience during the meditation experiment appear on average to have more frequently given answers that refer to religious motivation than those who had also been categorized as religious but who did not report religious experiences during meditation. This means that not only the presence or absence of a religious cognitive structure discriminates between subjects who had a religious experience and those who did not, but also the strength of religious motivation. Of course, this view is all but new and original. It reminds me of an interesting observation made by James Horne in his book on mysticism (1978). Whether unusual experiences are reported as mystical experiences depends on the degree to which one wants to take them seriously, Horne says. He refers to the difference between Huxley's and Zaehner's drug experiences. While Huxley thought that it was a profound mystical experience, Zaehner felt it was not significant.

So when I or someone else ever repeats this laboratory experiment (and it seems worthwhile to do so) a design should be used that will make it possible to control for motivation besides cognition, and a method should be devised in order to manipulate this variable.

References

BARBOUR, I. G. *Myths, models and paradigms*. London: SCM Press, 1974.

BOWKER, J. *The sense of God*. Oxford: Clarendon Press, 1973.

DEIKMAN, A. Deautomatization and the mystic experience. *Psychiatry*, 1966; **29**, 324–338.

FITZGERALD, E. G. *The measurement of openness to experience: a study of regression in the service of the ego*. (Doctoral dissertation, University of California, Berkeley.) *Dissertation Abstracts*, **27**, 1966 (University Micofilms no. 66–8311).

GEELS, A. *Mustikern Hjalmar Ekström*. Lund: Doxa, 1980.

HEIDER, F. *The psychology of interpersonal relations*. New York: Wiley, 1958.

HOLM, N. G. *Tungotal och andedop*. Stockholm: Almquist, 1976.

HOLMBERTH, N. G. *Innan för eller utanför*. Uppsala: Almquist, 1980.

HORNE, J. R. *Beyond Mysticism*. Waterloo, Ont.: Wilfrid Laurier University Press, 1978.

KÄLLSTADT, Th. *John Wesley and the Bible. A psychological study*. Stockholm: Nya Bokförlag, 1974.

KELLY, G. *The psychology of personal constructs*. New York: Norton, 1955.

NEISSER, U. *Cognitive psychology*. New York: Appleton-Century-Crofts, 1967.

NEISSER, U. *Cognition and reality*. San Francisco: W. H. Freeman, 1976.

MALONY, H. N. Religious experience: inclusive and exclusive. A psychologist's point of view. In: W. H. CLARK (ed.), *Religious experience: its nature and function in the human psyche.* Springfield, Ill.: C. C. Thomas, 1973.

PAHNKE, W. N. Drugs and mysticism. *International Journal of Parapsychology*, 1966; **8**(2), 295-314.

PETTERSSON, Th. *The retention of religious experiences.* Stockholm: Almqvist, 1975.

PROUDFOOT, W. and SHAVER, P. Attribution theory and the psychology of religion. *Journal for the Scientific Study of Religion*, 1975; **14**, 317-330.

RUNKEL, P. H. and MCGRATH, J. E. *Research on human behavior. A systematic Guide to Method.* New York: Rinehart & Winston, 1972.

SUNDÉN, H. *Religionen och rollerna. ett psykologisk studium av fromheten.* Stockholm: Svenska Kyrkana diskonistyrelses bokförlag, 1959.

SUNDÉN, H. Die Rollenpsychologie als heutige Aufgabe der Religionspsychologie. *Archiv. für Religionspsychologie*, 1964; **8**, 70-84.

SUNDÉN, H. What is the next step to be taken in the study of religious life? *The Harvard Theological Review*, 1965; **58**, 445-451.

SUNDÉN, H. Bedingungen religiöser Erfahrung. *Archiv für Religionspsychologie*, 1967; **9**, 41-49.

SUNDÉN, H. Meditation and Perception. Some notes on the psychology of religious mysticism. In: SVEN HARTMAN and C. EDSMAN (eds), *Mysticism*. Stockholm: Almqvist, 1968.

UNGER, J. *On religious experience. A psychological study.* Stockholm: Almqvist, 1976.

VAN DER LANS, J. Religious experience. An argument for a multidisciplinary approach. *The Annual Review of the Social Sciences of Religion*, 1977; **1**, 133-145.

VAN DER LANS, J. *Religieuze ervaring en meditatie. Een godsdienstpsychologische studie.* Deventer: van Loghum Slaterus, 1981.

Note

As a measure of the control-variable "cognitive flexibility" Fitzgerald's "Experience Inquiry" (1966) has been used. Analysis of the degree of difficulty showed that 20 of the 55 items were answered by our subjects in the same (flexible) way. An iterative cluster analysis on the remaining items results in three clusters. The first cluster was interpreted by us as a measure of "belief in parapsychological phenomena". With the second and third cluster an index was constructed to measure the degree of openness to experience.

10

Religious experience and its induction

DAVID HAY

Theology and science

The scientific study of reports of religious experience has tended to be a Western preoccupation, and more particularly an American and British one. Anyone attempting research in this context finds himself contending with two intractable problems. Firstly there is the debate in the academic community on the definition or prescriptive limits of religious experience; the conclusions reached seem to vary according to whether one is talking to students of comparative religion, philosophy or theology. Secondly there is the conception of religious experience which the ordinary person has inherited from his membership of Western society in all its historical complexity.

Frankly, I find disentangling that maze too daunting to be able to contemplate it for very long. However, if the object of the exercise is to get in touch with what is taken to be religious experience by ordinary people, it does seem important to be aware of the religious metaphors that have dominated our culture most thoroughly, and hence to take mystical theology seriously.

Most controversially (in view of the title of this chapter), according to Christian theology, mystical states cannot be induced. "We apply the word mystic to those supernatural acts or states which our own industry is powerless to produce, even in a low degree, even momentarily" (Poulain, 1912). They are thus a matter of God's grace, and whilst it is possible at times to become aware of the action of grace, self-deception is notoriously easy. Discernment, which is the task of a spiritual director, involves assessing "the fruitfulness of the experience in terms of personal religious growth and charitableness to others" (Fransen, 1969). Whilst the spontaneous occurrence of experiences like these takes place occasionally in the lives of many people, they are not a sign of merit in the eyes of God. On the other hand it is likely, though not necessary, that they will be granted by God from time to time to those following a disciplined course of asceticism, prayer and contemplation (Maréchal, 1927). Mystical experience seems typically to involve a quasi-perceptual awareness of the sacred, sometimes thought of as God, an aspect of God, an angel or one of the saints and theological differences of opinion normally set proscriptive

135

limits in this area. Experiences involving an apparently physical seeing or hearing of something are always felt to be less trustworthy than what St Teresa calls an "intellectual vision"; that is, an awareness of a presence which is not perceptible to the ordinary organs of sense.

The intuition of the sacred has unfortunately become seriously blurred as a concept, at least since the days of Schleiermacher, with his reference to the essence of religion as a feeling of absolute dependence. This understanding of religion, in particular its use of the ambiguous word "feeling", has led a number of eminent but non-believing students of religious experience to assume that it is primarily emotional rather than cognitive.

Theologians normally insist on the perceptual aspect of mystical experience, which in some ways resembles the kind of direct perceptual experience which forms the basis for empirical science. It differs, or so theologians claim (Moltmann, 1980), in requiring a passive receptivity, a participation, on the part of the experiencer. They sometimes offer a critique of scientific as opposed to religious ways of knowing, in that science, it is said, imposes its will upon the object from the outside, and takes possession of nature. "And then nature becomes mute" (Moltmann, 1980).

This evidence of a continuing suspicion between theologians and scientists may help to explain why much scientific speculation about religious experience pays the most minimal attention to orthodox theology. Yet to the extent that theologians are trying to make sense of the real experience of the members of a culture, they are offering a subtle phenomenology of that culture. Many other strands of tradition of course contribute to our notion of religious experience, some of them very ancient, like Judaism, or the folk or "common religion" discussed by Robert Towler (1974). Others are more recent, such as nature mysticism, Asiatic religion, the new religious movements and fringe religious ideologies like UFOlogy. All of them, I suspect, continue to be heavily influenced by orthodox Christian theology, though not always consciously, of course.

Investigating religious experience

It is in this complicated context that a number of attempts have been made, over the past 15 years or so, to estimate the frequency and nature of reports of religious experience in this country and in the United States. Because in a survey it is necessary to *ask* questions, all have had to grapple with the impossible problem of definition. Most attempts have tried to steer clear of anything directly orthodox, because of the feeling that the use of a too-specific religious metaphor may exclude responses from people who are unhappy with it. In our surveys we have used a question devised by Sir Alister Hardy (1979):

Have you ever been aware of or influenced by a presence or a power, whether you call it God or not, which is different from your everyday self?

There seems to be an assumption that practically any question directed in this area will tap a similar population of responses, though there is seldom direct evidence of this. However we do know that this is true for the question used by Greeley and McCready in their national survey of reports of ecstatic experiences in the United States (Greeley, 1975). That question, which asks, "Have you ever felt as though you were very close to a powerful spiritual force that seemed to lift you out of yourself?", we inserted into the same NOP omnibus package as Hardy's question in 1976. The coefficient of concordance between the two populations of positive replies was in the region of 0.9. It may be that people do recognize a more or less discrete universe of discourse which can be referred to by using a number of different questions.

In the United States the results of new surveys on religious experience are constantly being published, but the consensus of the ten or so of which I am aware suggests that between 30 and 40 per cent of British and American adults would certainly claim to have had an experience like this, at least once in their lives (Glock and Stark, 1965; Back and Bourque, 1970; Greeley, 1975; Wuthnow, 1976; Hay and Morisy, 1978; Hay, 1979; Hay, 1982; Hay and Morisy (forthcoming); American Institute of Public Opinion, 1978; Princeton Religion Research Center, 1978; Shaver, Lenauer and Sadd, 1980). The figures for Hay and Morisy's (1978) national survey in Great Britain are shown in Table 1. The close similarity in the proportions between Britain and the United States is noteworthy in view of the fact that proportionately three or four times as many Americans as Britons attend church regularly.

Apart from the national survey in Britain, I have directed two surveys of random samples of particular populations in the Nottingham area, employing lengthy structured interviews. One group was made up of 100 postgraduate students in my own department (Hay, 1979), the other was a random sample of 172 adults in the city of Nottingham (Hay and Morisy, forthcoming). In both cases the positive response rate was over 60 per cent (see Table 2). Now I can't of course exclude the possibility of bias causing an inflation of positive responses, but my guess is that it is probably something to do with the very strong taboo people have against admitting to these experiences. In the less threatening atmosphere of a lengthy structured interview it may be easier to speak of profound experience than in a brief conversation with an opinion pollster (Hay and Morisy, forthcoming). A quarter of those we interviewed had never spoken to anyone at all about their experience; a much higher proportion had only hinted at it. Their usual explanation for reticence was that they feared ridicule or that they would be thought insane.

The evidence from surveys does not support their fear. As measured by the Bradburn Balanced Affect Scale, both British and American mystics score significantly more highly on psychological well-being than do non-mystics (Greeley, 1975; Hay and Morisy, 1978) (British results are in Table 1). This agrees with an informal observation made some years ago by Abraham Maslow (1964) that people reporting peak experience (which includes

TABLE 1   *Percentages of people aware of or influenced by a presence or power compared with demographic and other data (British National Survey, adapted from Hay and Morisy, 1978)*

| | Report of being aware of or influenced by a presence or power | | | | | | |
| | Negative – "Never in my life" | Total positive response | Positive response by frequency | | | | Numbers (*n*) |
			"Once or twice"	"Several times"	"Often"	"All of the time"	
Total	63.6	36.4	18	10	6	2	(1865)
Social class							
Upper middle	54	47	28	11	6	2	(65)
Middle	50	49	22	16	9	2	(209)
Lower middle	59	41	20	13	5	3	(408)
Skilled working	68	31	16	9	5	1	(698)
Unskilled + subsistence	67	32	15	9	6	2	(485)
Terminal education age (years)							
13–14	63	37	17	13	5	2	(706)
15	71	29	17	8	3	1	(531)
16	64	37	15	9	10	3	(275)
17–19	56	44	23	9	8	4	(188)
20+	44	56	25	20	10	1	(113)
Psychological well-being*							
High	47	54					(830)
Low	53	46					(838)

Numbers vary due to availability of information. Slight numerical discrepancies occur due to rounding.

*$\chi^2 = 6.48$; $p < 0.02$.

TABLE 2   *Percentages of people reporting being aware of or influenced by a presence or power in two in-depth surveys in Nottingham (adapted from Hay, 1979 and Hay and Morisy, forthcoming)*

	Yes	No	Not sure
Random sample of adult population of Nottingham	62	28	10
Random sample of postgraduate students	65	29	6

religious experience) appear to be less neurotic and defensive than other people. Ralph Hood (1976) at the University of Tennessee claims to have demonstrated a positive statistical link between report of mystical experience and a number of measures of psychological competence.

All but one (Back and Bourque, 1970) of the surveys known to me report that mystics are more likely to be well educated and middle-class than other people (Hay and Morisy (1978) attempt an explanation of this anomaly). Other data suggest that they are somewhat more likely to be female than male (Princeton Religion Research Center, 1978) (Table 1); more likely to be church-goers (though in Britain 46 per cent of those reporting religious experience seldom or never go to church, whilst 45 per cent of those who go to church regularly, say they have never had such an experience (Hay, 1979)) (cf. Table 3). They are more likely to be optimistic (Greeley, 1975), feel life has

TABLE 3   *Proportions of total number of people reporting awareness of a presence or power who do/do not attend church (British National Survey, adapted from Hay, 1982)*

	Attend church at least occasionally	Never attend apart from weddings, funerals etc.
Percentage	54%	46%
(Numbers)	(367)	(311)

meaning (Wuthnow, 1976), be concerned with solving social problems and with helping people in need (Wuthnow, 1976). They are less likely than others to be materialistic (Wuthnow, 1976), racially prejudiced (Greeley, 1975) or status-conscious (Wuthnow, 1976).

The nature of the experience

Most of the accounts of experience collected by the Religious Experience Research Unit (RERU) in Oxford, or by us in Nottingham, give the appearance of occurring spontaneously, taking the person by surprise, even if they have been formally engaged in some religious activity:

> I had been half-listening to the 11.30 service on the radio (I can't remember a thing about it now) and was crossing our farmyard preparatory to feeding some of the stock; I also remember that I was humming the first verse of "There is a Green Hill Far Away", when suddenly I knew I was in the presence of God. I managed to walk twenty yards to one of the sheds, where I bowed down before One who was so much greater than I. I would not and could not open my eyes at this time, but I know that with me in that shed was the living presence of Christ. . . . For God, could be substituted the Spirit of Truth, The Almighty etc. . . . I felt that there was a great Light in front of me, and until that instant I did not know what humility meant . . . the whole experience was so unexpected.

About half of all experiences reported to us in the Nottingham city survey were associated with a time of distress. An example drawn from the RERU files illustrates this, and also the sense of recognition accompanying the experience:

> One night I was in great distress over a family situation and cried out to God to come to me if he existed. I suppose I was nearing the hysterical . . . suddenly God came. Not with a clap of thunder or a flash of light, but gently and slowly and imperceptibly he filled the room with his

presence until he was everywhere. The comfort and warmth were indescribable. The room was Love . . . and I said over and over again, "So *this* is what they mean, this is what they mean."

When initiated in a time of distress, such experiences invariably are followed by a change for the better in the person's feelings. This seems not to be simply a mechanical shift in affective state but a response to a perception. Very occasionally it is reported in association with recovery from psychosis, as in this report from a man recalling three years in a mental hospital during which he underwent numerous ECT treatments.

At one time I reached utter despair and wept and prayed God for mercy instinctively and without faith in reply. That night I stood with other patients in the grounds waiting to be let into our ward. It was a very cold night with many stars. Suddenly someone stood beside me in a dusty brown robe and a voice said "Mad or sane, you are one of my sheep." I never spoke to anyone of this, but ever since, 20 years, it has been the pivot of my life. I realise that the form of the vision and the words I heard were the result of my education and cultural background.

The pattern of distress followed by relief has been independently reported in a survey conducted by Margolis and Elifson (1978) in the United States, and of course corresponds with the expectations of religious orthodoxy. The other very common circumstance in which experience is reported is at times of solitude, 70 per cent of reports in the Nottingham city survey occurring in such circumstances. Marghanita Laski remarked on this also in her study of "ecstasy" in 1961.

Explaining the induction of religious experience

To ask for an empirical answer to the question, "What induces religious experience?" is already to circumscribe what is an acceptable way of understanding such experience. If one takes it in its full force, one may be creating a realm of meaningfulness which excludes theological interpretations as for ever unsatisfactory. Nevertheless, induction in a remote sense must be admitted, even by adherents to a doctrine of grace, if only because it is implied in the multitude of systems of prayer and contemplation which have developed within Christianity:

. . . the Christian mystics demand of the contemplative the assiduous practice of asceticism, renunciation, prayer, and they make of this not only a salutary exercise of moral perfection but also, and especially, a pre-requisite condition for the states of union (Maréchal, 1927).

Perhaps a better way of putting it from a theological point of view would be to talk of getting into a state of preparedness or of laying one's self open.

So what happens when we look at the numerous scientific conjectures that have been made about the induction of religious experience, in the light of the data I have been discussing? I'll arrange them in an order which moves approximately from a micro to a macro level.

Pharmacology

Psychedelic substances like LSD or psilocybin

There are two positive pieces of evidence here. Greeley's national survey of "ecstatic" experiences asked people to respond to a checklist of "triggers", including drugs. The drug category was ticked by no one (Greeley, 1975). In an analysis of 3000 accounts sent in to the RERU in Oxford, just over 0.5 per cent referred to psychedelic drugs, though 1 per cent spoke of the effect of anaesthetics (Hardy, 1979). No-one we have interviewed in Nottingham referred to any kind of drug.

Endogenous substances

Endorphins, endogenously produced morphine-like analgesics, are produced by the brain in response to stress or pain. Raymond Prince of McGill University has speculated that this might explain the resistance to pain of religious adepts in trance states (Prince, 1980). Correspondingly, endorphin release at times of stress might be interpreted by religiously inclined people as a religious experience, since it relieves their pain. As there appear to be diazepam-specific receptors in the brain it might also be the case that feelings of tranquillity in religious experience are induced by an endogenously produced tranquilliser. Whilst this might account for certain feelings during religious experiences which occurred in distressing circumstances, it doesn't explain the other 50 per cent in the Nottingham sample, including a substantial minority which were associated with times of great happiness. Nor of course does it explain the sense of presence.

Epilepsy

Psychiatric orthodoxy has it that temporal lobe epilepsy is associated with mystical experience (Dewhurst and Beard, 1970; Bear and Fedio, 1977). Dr Peter Fenwick at the Maudsley Hospital tells me that he comes across too many cases of epileptics with a right temporal lesion who describe mystical experience to doubt that there is something in this. Nevertheless a very recent survey by Fenwick and Sensky (Sensky, 1983) of epileptics treated at the Maudsley, shows that as a group, temporal lobe epileptics are far less likely to report religious experience than the general population (12 per cent compared with 36 per cent) whilst people with generalized epilepsy do not differ from the general population.

Physical techniques

Ludwig (1968) summarized techniques normally used by shamans and other religious adepts to produce altered states of consciousness which might be thought to be equivalent to or to induce religious experience.

Hypoventilation

Reduction of oxygen supply to the brain has been linked by Fenwick with near-death experiences of the type described by Raymond Moody (1978). The argument goes that partial heart failure leads to reduced blood pressure, retention of carbon dioxide and decreased oxygen, all causing changes in brain function. These, however, prove to be reversible in people recovering from near-death, so one is looking at changes in the activity of the temporal lobes, which are known to be particularly sensitive to a drop in oxygen level (Hopkins, 1981). As mentioned above, malfunction of the temporal lobes is thought to relate to the mystical experience of epileptics. About 1.5 per cent of those writing in to the RERU associate their experience with the "prospect of death", so this explanation may perhaps have validity for some of them, depending on what is meant by that rather ambiguous phrase.

Hyperventilation

We have no information about that. I don't know either, if there is much reason to suppose that many of those reporting religious experience in Nottingham have undertaken it.

Hypoglycaemia – due to prolonged fasting

Again there is no information on this point, though conceivably it might be a factor in people whose distress was in the form of a severe illness.

Sleep deprivation

Again this might be a factor associated with distress.

Exposure to extreme temperatures

No information, though again it seems relatively unlikely for the average Nottingham inhabitant.

Rhythmic sensory stimulation

This would include photic driving which is known to cause epileptic fits in certain people; also auditory driving, which Neher (1962) has demonstrated, can be evoked by prolonged drum-beating of the type which goes on at many tribal rituals around the world. Whether this kind of drumming is a factor in the lives of our Nottingham mystics it is hard to say, but it seems unlikely as an inducer of their experience, since the great majority were alone and in silence.

Increased exteroceptive stimulation and motor activity

As mentioned above this is unlikely to be a factor since most people were alone in silence. Only 1 per cent of the RERU sample (Hardy, 1979) and 1 per cent of Greeley's sample (Greeley, 1975) mentioned physical exertion as a factor.

Decreased exteroceptive stimulation and motor activity

This seems more promising, because of the reasons just mentioned, since 70 per cent of those we interviewed mentioned being alone, 42 per cent of Greeley's American national sample mentioned quiet reflection, and 30 per cent said they were alone in church (Greeley, 1975).

All the above practices are presented by Ludwig as means by which religious adepts attempt to induce altered states of consciousness. Whilst this may have some relevance for a minority of our Nottingham sample, I doubt if any of them were very significant for the majority, with the possible exception of the last category, to which I will return later.

Deprivation

Deprivation theories understand religion as a compensation for some kind of personal lack or loss. As such they have face validity in relation to some of the data cited earlier, since a large proportion of the reports of religious experience are associated with times of personal distress. Deprivation theories probably get their main impetus from Marxist and Freudian interpretations of religion. The very richness and diversity of thought arising in the wake of these contributions has led to a multitude of contradictory assertions about the nature of religion. Consequently the empirical testing of hypotheses generated from these positions is fraught with difficulty. Nevertheless it is possible to examine the plausibility of certain derived notions of religious experience, at least at the level of their naive face value.

Psychological deficits

It could be argued that people who think they have had a religious experience are simply too stupid or poorly educated to discriminate between reality and fantasy. In fact the more highly educated people are, the more likely they are to report religious experience.

Neurosis or mental illness has also been commonly associated with reports of religious experience. Most notably, J. H. Leuba (1929) claimed a direct relationship between sexual deprivation and neurotic or psychotic fantasies interpreted as religious experience. The evidence cited earlier appears to contradict this view, since people reporting religious experience appear to be significantly less likely than others to be psychologically disturbed. This fact was clear to Freud writing at the beginning of the century, presumably on the basis of his clinical experience. His interpretation saw religion as a kind of "crooked cure" for neurosis; religious people didn't suffer from individual neurosis as much as other people because they were already coping with repressions through the universal neurosis of religion (Freud, 1928). The cure is only crooked, of course, if you grant the basic assumption that religion is the product of neurotic fantasy. At this point the argument ceases to be scientific and enters the realm of philosophy.

Some neo-Freudians interpret religious experience in a more positive sense, seeing it as a form of "regression in the service of the ego" (Prince and Savage, 1972). There have been a number of objections made to this on the grounds that when the detailed phenomenology of religious experience and of regression is examined the correspondence between them is said to be only superficial (Owens, 1972; Hood, 1976). However, particularly in its emphasis on the retrieval in fantasy of experiences of being held by a loving parent, the regression explanation at least takes account of the sense of presence in religious experience (Rizzuto, 1980). This is something most other theories avoid. Perhaps associated with this type of explanation are those religious experiences preceded by a period of acute personal distress which is relieved by the experience itself. Raymond Prince (1979–80), among others, has suggested that it is indeed induced by stress, but is in the nature of a problem-solving activity which relieves the stress or the neurosis. Here he is drawing analogies with that school of psychiatry which interprets schizophrenia as an attempt to solve a painful personal problem (Laing and Esterson, 1965). This seems to me at least plausible for some of the reports we have come across; at any rate, on a variety of measures of psychological well-being "after the event", those reporting religious experience score more highly than others.

Social or physical deprivation

The most familiar strand of Marxist thinking about religion is that which sees it as an opiate enabling the alienated members of class society to bear the pain of their lot. An extrapolation of this might include reports of religious experience as an extreme form of fantasizing or false consciousness induced by severe injustice. Views of this kind appear to underlie certain anthropological studies of the religion of oppressed peoples.

On this basis one might expect reports of religious experience to be more frequent amongst the poor than amongst the comfortably off. In fact the reverse is the case; poverty is significantly associated with a lack of reports of religious experience.

Social effervescence

Durkheim's interpretation of religious experience (Durkheim, 1915) as being induced in an individual when he is swamped by the collective effervescence generated at a religious assembly, does take account of the feeling of presence. The force which an individual feels as greater than himself is said to derive from the group in which he finds himself. This is a view recently expounded by Finney (1978) to explain most of the religious experiences reported in a sample of the adult population in Washington State. But it certainly cannot be true in an unmodified form for our Nottingham sample, since the great majority of them were alone at the time of their experience. Very few indeed were in a religious assembly, or any kind of assembly, for that matter. Laski (1961) speaks in her book of the presence of other people as a "negative" trigger, which in my view is highly plausible.

Proudfoot and Shaver (1975) have proposed an emotional induction explanation of religious experience, based on attribution theory, which has some analogies with Durkheim's idea. They suggest that emotional arousal at an excited evangelical gathering, or occurring as an aftermath of such a meeting, might be given a religious attribution, in the absence of other explanations, because of the context in which it occurred. This interpretation suffers from the same weakness in relation to our data as Durkheim's. In addition it assumes that religious experience is primarily emotional, whereas normally in our culture it is described as the perception of a presence.

Meditation and prayer

Meditation or contemplation

In scientific literature meditation or contemplation is almost always understood as a means of inducing an altered state of electrical activity in the brain, and various other alterations in the physiology of the body. The number of studies in this area is beyond the ability of a single mortal to review but the general claim seems to be that people following standard meditation instructions in a variety of religious cultures (Zen, yoga, Catholic Carmelite, etc.) exhibit a slowing-down of the brain rhythms and the appearance of high-amplitude alpha rhythms on an EEG; some also claim the appearance of theta rhythms after a time, especially if the subjects are adepts (West, 1979). One interpretation of the effect of this physiological process is that it results in the suppression of the activity of the left (dominant) hemisphere of the brain (Prince, 1978). Very few if any of our interviewees in the city of Nottingham had been involved in a formal programme of meditation, though two members of the student sample had done some TM, so this explanation may have some validity for them.

Prayer

To my knowledge there has been one attempt to study brain rhythms during the activity of discursive prayer (Surwillo and Hobson, 1978). Surwillo and Hobson noticed an increase in the frequency of the brain rhythms of a group of people engaged in prayers of praise and adoration, when compared with a prior resting phase. The most parsimonious explanation of this is that the speeding up was due to an increase in cognitive activity during discursive prayer. Whether there is anything special about the physiology of prayer must remain an open question, which may or may not be unfortunate, since 48 per cent of McCready and Greeley's (1976) positive respondents reported their experience in a context of prayer, though only 5 per cent of our Nottingham sample did so (Hay and Morisy, forthcoming).

Conclusion

Several of these proposals for a mechanism of the induction of both major and minor forms of religious experience have *a priori* plausibility, though there is a permanent problem in tying inner states of consciousness to externally measurable phenomena on the basis of statistical correlations. Even if this is justified, it is clear that in the case of experiences which in Western society are taken to be in the religious mainstream, few of the alleged external correlates are statistically significant. From the point of view of scientific prediction they thus have poor validity.

Nevertheless there have been a number of attempts to measure how often people report religious experience, when intentionally placed in settings thought likely to induce it. For example, subjects have been asked to report on the extent to which they are able to generate religious imagery in a sensory isolation tank (Hood and Morris, 1981); on whether mystical experience turned up when they were sent on an Outward Bound course in the wilderness (Rosegrant, 1976); or what happens when they follow a set of simplified meditation instructions (Deikman, 1971). Many researchers, because of their adherence to a metaphor of mechanical induction, choose to cut their subjects off from the religious culture and language which, even for those who have broken their formal links with religious institutions, is the natural setting of religious experience. (An honourable exception is Pahnke's (1972) study of the effects of psilocybin on theology students attending a Good Friday service.) By avoiding this very obvious variable, these approaches at best have a Popperian function, in that certain conjectures may be refuted or at least made doubtful. That may be what science is all about; however, many of the speculations I have discussed above are at the level of extreme conjecture, extrapolations from prior theoretical positions which are themselves uncertain.

The use of the metaphor of induction, with its connotation of "forcing" or "dominating", perhaps derives from a scientific stance which finds theological interpretations of such experience intolerable or a threat to its competence in the area. Perhaps it would prove more fruitful to shift the investigative metaphor, so that instead of thinking of religious experience "as if" it were induced, we could consider it "as if" it were something of which people become aware.

I do, of course, admit the probability of an inductive aspect to this. Students of the realm of meditation or contemplation tend nowadays to accept that it induces an altered state of consciousness, different from, but at least as valid as, everyday consciousness. The achievement of such awareness can be seen as a mechanical skill (Overall, 1981) which can be worked at, more or less successfully, under the guidance of a teacher. Recent studies by Brown (1977), Goleman (1977) and others have illustrated the ordered nature of progression within meditation across many cultures, including of course our own. It is claimed to sensitize or de-automatize (Deikman, 1971) awareness, and if persevered with, to have a number of positive secular outcomes (Shapiro and Giber, 1978; Walsh, 1980).

As a zoologist, I take for granted the physiological unity of the species. I tend to trust the evidence purporting to show close similarities in the states achieved by adepts across widely differing cultures, even when at the conceptual level there appear to be profound contradictions (Fischer, 1977–78).

I would be prepared to go still further and accept a possible link with the spontaneous experience of Nottingham people. Meditative skills were quite likely developed over many thousands of years from observation of the circumstances in which spontaneous altered states of consciousness occurred. So although very few people indeed, of those we interviewed in Nottingham, were engaged in formal programmes of meditation, many were alone, perhaps in a state of inner stillness, or in that kind of distress which forces an intense awareness of the here-and-now. In a manipulative culture such as ours it may be on these occasions that meditative modes of awareness which are latent within people become available, at least briefly.

But what is then made of such an occasion must depend in a paramount degree, and not merely epiphenomenally, on the available cultural concepts and language, which I see as filtering and directing us to particular aspects of our awareness (Hay, 1982). Religious concepts and language provide us with an extremely rich set of metaphors, and I am beginning to understand those who see metaphor acting as a very powerful screen or opening, into our experience (Ortony, 1979). On the other hand, scientific language in its search for reality tries hard to abandon metaphor. Paradoxically, it may restrict access to experience.

In the field of psychotherapy novel areas of personal experience are often explored via the use of metaphor. For example in the case of someone in a state of depression who experiences the world "as if" it were a machine, it might lead to important personal discoveries to consider the world "as if" it were a person (Mair, 1977).

Religion is sometimes taken to be a kind of psychotherapy, though personally I take it to be more than that. It seems to me that one way forward in the study of religious experience would be to go beyond the metaphor of "induction" to consider religious language "as if" it uncovered novel areas of experience, including perhaps what Mircea Eliade calls hierophany, the awareness of the sacred, which in Western culture is found to be personal.

References

AMERICAN INSTITUTE OF PUBLIC OPINION. *Religion in America – the Gallup Opinion Index, 1977–78*, Princeton: The Gallup Organization, 1978.
BACK, KURT, and BOURQUE, LINDA BROOKOVER, Can feelings be enumerated? *Behavioural Science*, 1970; **15**, 487–496.
BEAR, DAVID M. and FEDIO, PAUL Quantitative analysis of interictal behaviour in temporal lobe epilepsy. *Archs. Neurol.* 1977: **34**, 454–467.
BROWN, DANIEL P. A model for the levels of concentrative meditation. *International Journal of Clinical and Experimental Hypnosis*, 1977; **25**, 236–273.
DEIKMAN, ARTHUR J. Bimodal consciousness. *Archives of General Psychiatry*, 1971; **25**, 481–489.
DEWHURST, KENNETH and BEARD, A. E. Sudden religious conversions in temporal lobe epilepsy. *British Journal of Psychiatry*, 1970; **117**, 497–507.
DURKHEIM, EMILE. *The Elementary Forms of the Religious Life*, (trans. J. W. Swain). London: Allen & Unwin, 1915.
FINNEY, JOHN M. A theory of religious commitment. *Sociological Analysis*, 1978; **39**, 19–35.
FISCHER, ROLAND. On images and pure light: integration of east and west. *Journal of Altered States of Consciousness*, 1977–78; **3**, 205–212.
FRANSEN, PETER, *The New Life of Grace*. New York: Seabury Press, 1969.
FREUD, SIGMUND *The Future of an Illusion*. London: Hogarth Press, 1928.
GLOCK, CHARLES Y. and STARK, RODNEY. *Religion and Society in Tension*. Chicago: Rand McNally, 1965.
GOLEMAN, DANIEL. *The Varieties of Meditative Experience*. New York: Dutton, Rider & Co., 1977.
GREELEY, ANDREW M. *The sociology of the paranormal: a reconnaissance*. Sage Research Papers in the Social Sciences (Studies in Religion and Ethnicity Series No. 90–023). Beverley Hills/London: Sage Publications, 1975.
HARDY, ALISTER C. *The Spiritual Nature of Man*. Oxford: Clarendon Press, 1979.
HAY, DAVID. Religious experience amongst a group of postgraduate students: a qualitative study. *Journal for the Scientific Study of Religion*, 1979; **18**(2), 164–182.
HAY, DAVID. It's all right Jack, I'm fireproof. *New Society*, 1981; **51**(982), 426–427.
HAY, DAVID. *Exploring Inner Space: Scientists and Religious Experience*. Harmondsworth: Penguin Books, 1982.
HAY, DAVID and MORISY, ANN. Reports of ecstatic, paranormal or religious experience in Great Britain and the United States: a comparison of trends. *Journal for the Scientific Study of Religion*, 1978; **17**(3), 255–238.
HAY, DAVID and MORISY, ANN. Secular society/religious meanings: a contemporary paradox. *Review of Religious Research* (forthcoming).
HOOD, RALPH. Conceptual criticisms of regressive explanations of mysticism. *Review of Religious Research*, 1976; **17**, 179–188.
HOOD, RALPH W. and MORRIS, RONALD J. Sensory isolation and the differential elicitation of religious imagery in intrinsic and extrinsic persons. *Journal for the Scientific Study of Religion*, 1981; **20**, 261–273.

HOPKINS, ANTHONY. *Epilepsy: the facts.* Oxford: University Press, 1981.

LAING, R. D. and ESTERSON, A. *Sanity, Madness and the Family,* Vol. 1: *Families of Schizophrenics.* London: Tavistock, 1965.

LASKI, MARGHANITA. *Ecstasy.* London: Cresset Press, 1961.

LEUBA, JAMES H. *The psychology of religious mysticism.* London: Kegan, Paul, Trench & Trubner, 1929.

LUDWIG, A. M. Altered states of consciousness, in R. H. PRINCE (ed.). *Trance and Possession States,* Montreal: R. M. Bucke Memorial Society, 1968.

MAIR, MILLER. Metaphors for living, in *Nebraska Symposium on Motivation, 1976.* University of Nebraska Press, 1977.

MARÉCHAL, JOSEPH. *Studies in the Psychology of the Mystics.* London: Burns Oates & Washbourne, 1927.

MARGOLIS, ROBERT D. and ELIFSON, KIRK W. Antecedent and consequent conditions of the religious experience. Paper read at the Annual Meeting of the Society for the Scientific Study of Religion, 1978.

MASLOW, ABRAHAM. *Religions, Values and Peak Experiences.* Columbus, Ohio: State University Press, 1964.

MOLTMANN, JURGEN. *Experiences of God.* London: SCM Press, 1980.

MOODY, RAYMOND. *Life After Life.* New York: Bantam Books, 1976; *Reflections on Life After Life.* New York: Bantam Books, 1978. See also OSIS, KARLIS and HARALDSSON, ERLENDUR, Deathbed observations by physicians and nurses: a cross-cultural survey. *Journal of the American Society for Psychical Research,* 1977; **71,** 237–259.

NEHER, ANDREW. A physiological explanation of unusual behaviour in ceremonies involving drums. *Human Biology,* 1962; **34,** 151–160.

ORTONY, ANDREW (ed.). *Metaphor and Thought.* Cambridge: Cambridge University Press, 1979.

OVERALL, CHRISTINE. The nature of mystical experience. *Religious Studies,* 1981; **18,** 47–54.

OWENS, CLAIR MYERS. The mystical experience: facts and values, in *The Highest State of Consciousness* (ed. JOHN H. WHITE). New York: Anchor Books/Doubleday, 1972.

PAHNKE, WALTER N. Drugs and mysticism, in *The Highest State of Consciousness* (ed. JOHN H. WHITE). New York: Anchor Books/Doubleday, 1972.

POULAIN, AUGUSTE. *The Graces of Interior Prayer.* London: Kegan Paul, Trench & Trubner, 1912.

PRINCE, RAYMOND. Meditation: some psychological speculations. *Psychiatric Journal of the University of Ottawa,* 1978; **3,** 202–209.

PRINCE, RAYMOND. Religious experience and psychosis. *Journal of Altered States of Consciousness,* 1979–80; **5**(2), 167–181.

PRINCE, RAYMOND. Shamans and endorphins: exogenous and endogenous factors in psychotherapy. Paper read at a conference in Honolulu, 1984.

PRINCE, RAYMOND and SAVAGE, CHARLES. Mystical states and the concept of regression, in *The Highest State of Consciousness* (ed. JOHN H. WHITE). New York: Anchor Books/Doubleday, 1972.

PRINCETON RELIGION RESEARCH CENTER. *The Unchurched American.* Princeton Religion Research Center and the Gallup Organisation, 1978.

PROUDFOOT, WAYNE and SHAVER, PHILLIP. Attribution theory and the psychology of religion. *Journal for the Scientific Study of Religion,* 1975; **14,** 317–330.

RIZZUTO, ANA-MARIA. The psychological foundations of belief in God, in *Toward Moral and Religious Maturity – First International Conference on Moral and Religious Development.* Morristown, NJ: Silver Burdett Co., 1980.

ROSEGRANT, JOHN. The impact of set and setting on religious experience in nature. *Journal for the Scientific Study of Religion,* 1976; **15,** 301–310.

SENSKY, TOM. Religiosity, mystical experience and epilepsy, in *Research Progress in Epilepsy* (ed. F. CLIFFORD ROSE). London: Pitman, 1983.

SHAVER, P., LENAUER, M. A. and SADD, S. Religiousness, conversion and subjective wellbeing: the "healthy-minded" religion of modern American women. *American Journal of Psychiatry,* 1980; **137**(12), 1563–1568.

SHAPIRO, DEAN H. and GIBER, DAVID. Meditation and psychotherapeutic effects. *Archives of General Psychiatry,* 1978; **35,** 294–302.

SURWILLO, W. W. and HOBSON, D. P. Brain electrical activity during prayer. *Psychological Reports*, 1978; **43,** 135–143.
TOWLER, ROBERT. *Homo Religiosus*. London: Constable, 1974.
WALSH, ROGER. The consciousness disciplines and the behavioral sciences: questions of comparison and assessment. *American Journal of Psychiatry*, 1980; **137,** 663–673.
WEST, MICHAEL. Meditation. *British Journal of Psychiatry*, 1979; **135,** 457–467.
WUTHNOW, ROBERT. *Peak Experiences: Some Empirical Tests.* Mimeographed Publication A161 of the Survey Research Center, University of California, Berkeley, 1976.

11
Social attitudes and religion

L. B. BROWN

THERE is no doubt that religious attitudes, or rather attitudes to religion and religious beliefs, have offered the most popular approach to a psychological study of religion. Thus Spilka *et al.* (1981) found that "religion" is most often referred to in social psychology textbooks under the headings "attitudes" and "attitude formation", and Gorsuch (1984) asserts that the continuing concern with attitude measurement shows that this, rather than any "school" or scientific sub-discipline, is the paradigm for progress in the psychology of religion. In line with that, Capps, Rambo and Ransohoff (1976) note in their survey of publications between 1950 and 1974 that studies of religious belief and attitudes were "overwhelmingly quantitative" then, and that their number increased over this period. That finding gains point in contrast to earlier conclusions that theoretical analyses of religion were more common than empirical studies of it: Michaels (1956, quoted by Cline and Richards, 1965), for example, estimated that only 12 per cent of studies on religion in the *Psychological Abstracts* between 1927 and 1953 were empirical. Furthermore, in a survey of work during 1950 and 1960, Klausner (1964) found that 44 per cent of the empirical studies in the psychology and sociology of religion involved "self-administered questionnaires, usually multiple choice", and that a further 26 per cent depended on "individual interviews". The widespread use of closed questionnaires has continued, and in recent numbers of the *Journal for the Scientific Study of Religion* between one-third and two-thirds of the papers are based on closed survey questionnaires. An important feature of this method is the way it keeps investigations of religion inside language, where meanings are agreed, but not fixed in the way that rules fix actual practice or behaviour, as F. H. Allport (1934) showed in his J-curve distributions of behaviour conforming with religious (and other) norms.

Not every study of religious attitudes is specifically focused on religion itself. Fishbein and Ajzen's (1975) general text on attitudes frequently used religious attitudes to exemplify the general properties of attitudes, and reference to current numbers of the *Psychological Abstracts* shows that religion is being widely used as an independent variable in studies of attitudes to sex, marriage and contraception, and with reference to anti-social behaviour, self-actualization, ego-identity, moral values and the purpose of life. The variables in these studies of attitudes and personality processes draw on issues that broadly identify what "religion" is expected to involve.

While William James (1902) said that religion concerns what a person does in solitude, it is impossible to neglect institutional and ideological constraints on what it is possible to do, even when one is alone. That religion is not simply aligned with its institutional forms is shown by Roof's (1979) distinction between church and non-church religions, and by Yinger's (1977) identification of a non-doctrinal religion which "rests upon the persistent experience of suffering, injustice and meaninglessness". Yinger developed a 20-item Likert measure of this non-doctrinal conception of religion, although in an analysis of Australian responses to it and to Martin and Westie's (1959) "religious fundamentalism scale", Brown (1981b) found that the first factor involved Christian fundamentalism, while the other factors contrasted Yinger's powerlessness and alienation items against his suffering and meaninglessness items, independently of fundamentalism.

Religionism

We can take it that the elements of a fundamentalist Christian position have a particular coherence. Brown (1962a) found a single religious factor involving orthodox Christian beliefs about God, Christ and evil, general religious beliefs about, for example, the existence of angels, and religious knowledge, in items like "Moses was the author of the first five books of the Bible". This religious factor was independent of anxiety and of Eysenck's personality traits, and independent of the belief certainty that formed the second factor. In another Australian study, with a carefully drawn sample of students at the University of Adelaide, Wearing and Brown (1972) used Poppleton and Pilkington's (1963) scale to measure the strength of religious belief, a set of religious items that had been found to discriminate between members of a theologically conservative student group and of a liberal religious group (Brown, 1962b) and the Allport–Vernon–Lindzey *Study of values* (1960), together with questions about religious practice, changes in religious belief, parents' religion, moral judgement and personality trait measures of dogmatism, authoritarianism and neuroticism. In the factor analysis of that material, a single factor covered religious fundamentalism, belief in a personal God, the frequency of prayer and Church attendance, religious values, and belief in an evil power and in a "supreme being". The second factor, independent of religion, was related to honesty and morality as determinants of one's career. The third factor was defined by the family's religious denomination and by the duration of Sunday School attendance. That, and the fourth factor's high loadings on the frequency of the mother's church attendance, entail socialization into a religious orthodoxy. The fifth factor was similar to Rokeach's (1960) anxious dogmatism, on which the strength of religious belief had a loading of $+0.16$. Finding a general religious belief factor, independent of dogmatism, and of a specific denominational training and alignment (with the denominational weights derived from a paired comparison procedure being similar to those reported by Rokeach, 1960, p. 305) suggests that accepting conventional or traditional statements of religious attitudes and beliefs defines a broadly Christian or theistic position.

Dittes (1969) stressed that the development of attitude scaling methods was "prompted in no small part by the search for ways to study religion" (p. 602). This concern with the systematic description and measurement of religion can be traced to Starbuck's (1897) questionnaire-based study of religious experience which William James used in his *Varieties of religious experience* (1902). Thurstone's method of attitude scaling, first applied to attitudes to the Church (Thurstone and Chave, 1929), was a most influential step forward. Although the items in that scale refer to "feelings" and "beliefs" about the Church, as in "I feel the need for religion . . .", "I think the Church is a parasite on society . . .", and "I believe in sincerity and goodness without any church ceremonies", they were directed to the Church as a specific attitude object. Others, including Sanai (1952), have treated religious "attitudes" and "beliefs" as roughly equivalent, with such Likert-type items as "There is no personal god", "Christ was not divine", and "One can lead a good life without religion", in their religious scales.

The questionnaire for Sanai's (1952) original British study of the structure of attitudes assessed political and moral attitudes as well as responses to religion. In Sanai's study, the first factor accounted for 25.4 per cent of the variance, with items that were "concerned mainly with religious topics or topics on which religious persons have strong views (e.g., sterilization)". He called it "religious and political conservatism". The second factor accounted for 8.3 per cent of the variance, and contrasted "political, social or ethical stability against change". When Sanai's items were presented to a comparable Australian sample in 1978 (Brown, 1981a) the same pattern of factors emerged, although "religionism" then accounted for 19.7 per cent of the variance and the second "personal morality" factor accounted for 7.6 per cent of the variance. The stability of this factor pattern suggests that it relates to a religious, or rather a Christian, ideology that aligns religion with social and sexual control. This general "religionism" factor does not entail sophisticated views about religiousness beyond the coherence of responses to statements or propositions for or against religion. Answers to single questions about a person's religion correlate around $+0.76$ with scores from such multiple item scales. Dittes (1969, p. 609 f.) has already emphasized that religious items involving "attitudes toward the Church, including reports of church attendance (and we might add, respect for the Bible) or consent to conventional theistic or Christocentric statements" contrast against items that assess social attitudes which are not directly related to religion. It could be that our typical measurement techniques, with their simplified items, are easily accepted or rejected and therefore produce a religious factor that aligns with conservatism.

Another important problem with those studies, and of the others reviewed by Dittes (1969) and Gorsuch (1984), is their reliance on what are, from the subjects' point of view "found" or prescribed items, with a content that covers what the investigator assumes is important, or can be derived from one of the Creeds. As Fullerton and Hunsberger (1982) say, "whatever other differences the various Christian denominations might have among themselves, the Creed [sic] comprises a 'rockbed' of doctrinal beliefs on which is virtually unanimous agreement by Catholics and Protestants alike". The scales that have been built in this way give what Gorsuch has identified as the measurement paradigm for religion. It may be a psychometrically sound approach, although, being based on received beliefs or "doxemes" (Deconchy, 1980) it may miss the essential features of a person's private religious beliefs and attitudes. While religious people have *some* alignment with creedal statements, there is a greater tendency to certainty about any religious statement than for directly factual statements about, for example, the natural world (Thouless, 1935). Thouless' finding, which was confirmed by Brown (1962a), aligns with Allport and Ross' (1967) conclusion that some people are inconsistently pro- or anti-religious and either agree or disagree with *any* religious statement. Personal beliefs about religion are not necessarily tapped by our conventional measures. In the same way, when Anglican clergy are asked to affirm that the doctrine of the Church of England, to be found in the Book of Common Prayer and in the 39 Articles (which have not been modified since 1571), is agreeable to the Word of God they are giving formal assent to a recognized position, and are not necessarily stating their own beliefs.

Religious identity

Common sense identifies an explicit religiousness that is based on some evidence of a person's commitment through church membership, with terms like nominal adherent, Sunday Christian and firm believer, which religious leaders (and others) also use to classify their people (cf. Fichter, 1954). Distinctions between those who belong to different traditions or denominations are more complicated, although psychological rather than historical and theological factors have often been assumed to account for them. Thus Ducker (1961) argued that Catholics are on the side of Jung's "collective unconscious" while Protestants are "for the individual", and Clark (1958), who distinguished "sacramental churches" from those with a "sterner theology", argued that those in the sacramental churches have less anxiety because of their access to auricular confession. There is, however, no good empirical evidence to support such theoretical generalizations.

Religious denominations are, however, a part of "objective religion" (Wach,

1951) and sanction the social groups to which individuals belong or with which they are identified (although a piece of graffiti in Sydney says, "Forget the Church, follow Jesus"). Recognizing differences between Catholics and Methodists, or between Jews and Buddhists, may reflect knowledge, or some prejudiced judgement about social representations, and allows religious groups to be scaled empirically along a single dimension which, like the Right–Left political continuum, may be curvilinear, but contrasts a closed or traditional orthodoxy against more open reactions. Rokeach (1960, p. 307) showed that the judged similarity of such denominational labels depends on the frame of reference within which they are understood, although people change their religious affiliation or identity by moving between adjacent groups along this continuum. Whether people alter their religious affiliation to gain social status because of some theological or liturgical preference, for psychological or for social reasons raises unexplored contextual questions about the personal and other contexts within which religion is cast.

Sociologists have not only distinguished Churches from sects but they often use a self-ascribed religious identification as an index of religion. That it is now illegal to ask about religious affiliation in some countries, especially in the context of a job interview, shows the potency of religion. Nevertheless an open-ended question about "religion" is still included in the population censuses in Australia, and in New Zealand. In the report of the 1976 Census in New Zealand (1980), 68.1 per cent of the population fell into the four groups of "Anglican (Church of England)" (29.2 per cent), Presbyterian (18.1 per cent), Roman Catholic ("including Catholic undefined") (15.3 per cent) and Methodist (5.5 per cent). Another 14 per cent exercised their statutory right "to 'object' when answering the question", 7.5 per cent were grouped as "others" and 3.2 per cent returned "no religion". The remainder were distributed among 73 "other religious professions". In the 1981 Census in Australia, 64.8 per cent of the population fell into the same four basic groups, while 10.9 per cent "did not state" their religion and 10.8 per cent returned "no religion". There were more males in those last two categories, and the numbers there have increased systematically over recent censuses.

Opinion polls, which typically involve closed questions, show a similar majority agreement about religious identity. In a recent British survey, while 60 per cent of the adult population claimed membership of a church or religious group, 72 per cent said they believed in a deity (NOP, 1982). Perhaps simple questions necessarily produce undifferentiated answers because they give little opportunity to express disagreements, or because elaborated or qualified answers must be disregarded in the analysis. In a Morgan Gallup Poll in Australia in early December, 1975, 77 per cent said they believed "there is a God", 58 per cent believed "in going to heaven after death" and 43 per cent believed "there is a Hell". (Benson, 1981, has summarized comparable data from the United States.)

To avoid the problems with direct or explicit questions, especially about religious identity, indirect measures have included the "Twenty questions test" in which repeated answers are collected to the question, "Who am I?". Classifications of these answers can detect the importance of a religious identification. Vernon (1962), for example, found that 72 per cent of a sample of 170 Michigan students gave such an identification, although there was no relationship between their use there and the answers to a direct question about the importance of religion "in your day-to-day living". Of the 28 per cent who did not give a religious identity, 78 per cent had checked that religion was of "great" or "moderate importance" to them. In another part of that study, Vernon found that although "the Bible continued to be a best seller, 53 per cent of our population, when asked to name the first four Gospels, could not even name one of them". He concluded that "appearing to be religious is the thing which is important to many Americans".

In research in Sydney in 1982 only 23 per cent of students there gave a religious identifier in a modified "Who are you?" task. Other data that have compared Australian and Canadian students show that religion seems to sit more lightly on the Australians (Hunsberger and Brown, 1984).

While a religious identity is important, it involves ready-made and coarse labels that capture only one of the elements or constructs that are involved with religion. The labels accepted by religious people themselves seldom express the subtlety embodied in religious descriptions as when, for example, Lutherans or Anglicans use terms like "evangelical" or "reformed", "Catholic" or "charismatic" to describe their position. Religious groups may share a vocabulary, but disagree about specific definitions and meanings, which are often implicit and might only be clarified by the context, or by more detailed enquiry. The assumed privacy of a person's religion also means that any questions about it must be tentative. Only when it is clear that religious questions will not be reacted to defensively can we gather detailed knowledge about reactions to it. This could be yet another explanation why religious enquiries sometimes seem to reach superficial conclusions, with inconsistent responses. Due attention is not always given to the context within which an enquiry is cast, or recognizes that those actively involved with religion can be expected to draw fine distinctions. Despite that, in an unpublished study, I have found that the structure of general religious items is similar for believers and disbelievers.

Conceptual and empirical analyses have, however, broken up the coherent uni-dimensional solutions to the structure of religion. Dittes (1969) argued that not only are the subjects in studies that have found a single factor heterogeneous with respect to religious commitment, but they are typically in "late adolescence, . . . [when] issues of autonomy versus institutional loyalty and conventional orthodoxy would seem to be especially keen". Furthermore, not only do "outside" views of religion and of attitudes to religious institutions and knowledge make it appear coherent, but religious insiders readily adopt outsiders' views when they might be under attack; in appropriate circumstances insiders alter their religious responses (cf. Deconchy, 1980), which itself breaks up the religious factor. Gorsuch (1984) argues, however, that second-order analyses of multiple-factor solutions to religious structure still produce a single, higher-order religion factor.

Religious orientations

Allport (1950) broke up a unitary view of religion by distinguishing religious orientations in terms of their functional implications. He first contrasted institutional and individual perspectives, which probably involve responses to orthodoxy, and later distinguished between extrinsic and intrinsic orientations of intentions. These latter concepts have proved to be a most useful analytic tool, to which Batson has added a "quest" orientation (see Chapter 13). The basic orientations, which Allen and Spilka (1967) have identified as "consensual" or "committed", focus on the meanings or implications of any religious beliefs, not so much in the sense of what should be done about them as how they can be used, which might resolve some of the ambiguities of intention.

Other attempts to move beyond a single religious factor have relied on contrasts between, for example, an emphasis on religious belief or on institutional membership (Maranell, 1968), or on complex maps of "religious space", like Glock's (1962) widely accepted proposal that religious variables refer to belief, practice, feelings or experience, knowledge, and the consequential effects of religion. That scheme was used by Clayton (1971) and Clayton and Gladden (1974) to form five separate measurement scales. King (1967, and King and Hunt, 1975) identified nine, and later more, religious dimensions, one of which, for example, contrasts "dogmatism against openness to growth and change" as an alternative to the general "conservative fundamentalism" (cf. Deconchy's analysis here in Chapter 7). Strommen *et al.* (1972) went further and used 78 separate religious scales in their study of Lutherans in the United States. Some others, like Keene (1967), and Cline and Richards (1965), who used a modified TAT, a "depth interview" and a religious belief questionnaire, have found that the general factors involve church attendance and belief, with other smaller factors that relate to socialization or social support, religious commitment and some form of attachment, which in Cline and Richards' study involves "loss of faith for the males and religious hypocrisy for the females".

While different terms have been advanced to identify these patterns of religious belief and attitudes, beneath them all is religion as a social phenomenon, with which those who carry or embody a religious perspective interact. While separate psychologically significant aspects of religion can be identified both theoretically and empirically, their importance has usually been established by correlating defined characteristics of a religious perspective against other psychological and social variables. Direct observation of religious behaviour has, however, proved to be relatively uninformative because it disregards behavioural intentions, which must be expressed indirectly or verbally.

Religious attitudes and religious behaviour

There has been less interest in the links between religious attitudes and religious behaviour than in other areas such as politics or ethnic prejudice (cf. Eiser, 1980). While ethnic attitudes were, from the beginning, externally validated against behaviour (La Piere, 1934), religious attitudes have typically been validated against the membership of known groups, or through their internal coherence. Furthermore, attitudes, behaviour and behavioural intentions are now seen either as facets of some single predisposition or dimension, or as separate traits. Ostrom (1969), however, found that when separate measures were used to assess the cognitive, affective or behavioural components of attitudes they were more highly correlated than were measures of these different components using the same method. We must also recognize that although generally low relationships between religious attitudes and actual behaviour have been found, in appropriate circumstances or situations people with positive religious attitudes are *expected* to do something about them. An important but under-explored problem therefore requires us to identify the base rates of religious responsiveness and the situations where such expected responses can be elicited. This covers a wide range of accepted behaviour, and the reasons that can support religious actions and duties which do not necessarily include regular church-going, since it is a relatively infrequent activity for most people. Only a close correspondence between action, and beliefs *about* actions allows good predictions to be made from one to the other, which Fishbein and Ajzen (1975) have argued is not easy to find since we have attitudes to specific objects, to specific behaviours that relate to those objects, and to the norms governing such behaviour.

Any solution to the attitude–behaviour controversy thus involves devising measures of religiousness with a behavioural reference, and recognizing that religious attitudes are often used to make our actions appear consistent.

Religion within personality

The essential coherence of religious responses has led some to regard religiousness as a component of personality, partly because it offers solutions to life's problems, and because of assumptions about the emotional basis of its appeal. To adopt this view usually involves a generalization about the restrictive or controlling functions of religion. Wilson's (1972) measure of "conservatism" was based on the personality "characteristics of the ideal conservative" which include "religious dogmatism" as well as "insistence on strict rules and punishments", intolerance, an "anti-hedonistic outlook", "superstition, and resistance to scientific progress" (p. 51). Wilson found that the religious items of his conservatism scale emerge as a separate factor, with samples from Britain, Holland and New Zealand. Ray (1982) has confirmed this with Australian data. Wilson's religious items are simply "Church authority", "Bible truth", "Birth control", "Sabbath observance", "Divine law", and "Horoscopes", which he argues relate "not so much to religion in general, as to the rather more fundamental [*sic*] and dogmatic religion which is associated with the Roman Catholic Church and the more puritan of Protestant denominations and sects" (p. 79). Ray (1979) found that while a "Protestant Ethic Scale" did not distinguish Catholics from Protestants, or even high from low achievers, it did distinguish religious from non-religious people, despite the fact that this Ethic has now lost most of its religious significance. Demerath and Roof (1976) concluded from a review of the Protestant Ethic literature that "if any single religious group represents it more than any other, it is the Jews" (p. 24); they also note that religious groups are no longer sociologically monolithic and homogeneous, and that ethnicity might be a more coherent social differentiator than religion. This suggestion could simply replace one general form of identification by another, and it neglects the extent to which among some groups (like the Greeks in Australia) a formal religious identity is closely linked to their nationalism. Wilson (1972, p. 124) used "known groups" to validate his measure of conservatism, and showed for instance that while those in the Salvation Army agreed with his religious items, humanists did not. That finding can be accounted for more simply by Deconchy's (1980) notion that an orthodox system itself regulates the way beliefs and attitudes are expressed; we need not assume that members of the Salvation Army have this conservatism as a personality characteristic, but rather that social processes help them express similar religious beliefs.

Heist and Yonge (1968) based their *Omnibus Personality Inventory* on "differences among college students with regard to their attitudes, opinions and feelings on a variety of subjects" (p. 4), and included among their 14 scales a 26-item religious orientation measure. Their "High scorers are skeptical about conventional religious beliefs and practices and tend to reject most of them, especially those that are orthodox or fundamentalistic in nature . . . low scorers are manifesting a strong commitment to Judaic–Christian beliefs and tend to be conservative in general and frequently rejecting of other viewpoints." The validity of this scale was established through a correlation of − 0.66 with "the *Study of Values* Religious score", by reference to the religious identity of parents and to the "frequency of religious service attendance" (p. 30). That the lowest standard deviation in these responses was for those attending church "more than once a week" and "never" (3.1 and 3.8 respectively), while those attending "once a month" have the highest standard deviation (4.6) further supports the coherence of religious responses (p. 44).

Heist and Yonge offer no specific justification for having included a religious orientation measure in a personality inventory which also assesses complexity, autonomy, social extroversion and impulse expression, beyond claiming an eclectic theory with dimensions that are relevant to academic activity and to understanding students in an educational context. They say, however, that their religious measure taps the "underlying concept of authoritarian vs. non-authoritarian thinking" (p. 3), which expresses the common psychological reaction to religion as a necessarily restrictive process in the context of personality. Although other evidence is not unequivocal, it may be that some form of conservatism or dogmatism offers the only direct link between religion and personality but one that is not necessarily attributable to the effects of religion on personality.

The elements of religion

Psychological study is not needed to persuade us that those who call themselves Christians, or who hold particular religious beliefs, can strenuously disagree among themselves about what others should believe, or about the "true path". Whether broad or detailed principles are at issue depends on who is being criticized. Yet only a few people have recently been formally charged with heresy for their public pronouncements, since most take the easy way and refuse religious arguments unless they are committed to evangelism or do not mind exposing their position. An important reason for developing psychometrically sound measurement procedures has been to control the openness of ordinary conversation, although these forced choice procedures do not tap the idiosyncratic emphases behind formally prescribed beliefs. Not only is it easy to conceal one's position, especially when answering the measures of religious belief that can be found, for example, in Robinson and Shaver (1973) or Shaw and Wright (1967), but these measures assume that they offer a neutral context, and that what a person agrees to or says reflects underlying states or predispositions, despite the extent to which what is said directly accomplishes explicit goals, which include self-presentation (Lalljee, Brown and Ginsburg, 1984).

In an early exploration of the direct meanings of religion that was linked to Allport's work on religious orientation, I asked students to complete the stems, "For me as an individual person, a set of religious beliefs . . ." and "In my everyday life, religious beliefs . . ." (Brown, 1964). A content analysis of these responses showed that they involved belief–disbelief, individual or institutional reference points, and contrasted an intrinsic or committed against an extrinsic or consensual perspective on religion. These continua emerged independently of questions about specific religious beliefs. The data suggest that reactions to religious disbelief parallel reactions to religious belief, and that both these reactions reflect some understanding of religious beliefs.

It is clear that the factorial structures underlying answers to conventional questionnaires depend on the item content, characteristics of the subjects and the technique of data analysis. A core problem here concerns what should be included as the elements in measures of religious belief and attitude. Most measures take their items from traditional Christian doctrines, as does Fullerton and Hunsberger's (1982) scale of "Christian orthodoxy", which has been validated in Canada and Australia. There is, however, an important place for new scales with items drawing on Pentecostal interests, a concern with "Christian action", or the content of new hymns.

To explore what is now recognized to be religiously relevant, Brown and Forgas (1980) carried out a two-stage study of the commonly accepted elements in "religion". In the first phase a free-response procedure asked Australian students "to write down what you think are the ideas or concepts characteristic of religion and religious behaviour and beliefs". The 33 most frequently mentioned elements, expressed in the subjects' own terms, were then rated by another equivalent sample on each of a set of semantic scales, selected *a priori* to cover previously identified religious orientations. (A further recent study has found that religiously relevant adjectives elicited from a group of "Religious" subjects differed little from those used by Brown and Forgas (O'Connor, 1983).) The adjectives used to evaluate the religious elements were active–passive, formal–informal, external–internal, known–unknown, tangible–intangible, institutional–individual, plausible–implausible and orthodox–unorthodox. The elements that were rated included "experiences of God", "faith", "scriptures", "peace of mind", "Church authority", "miracles", "heaven", "revelation", "salvation", "prayer", "mystery" and "God as a being". An INDSCAL analysis of the ratings of these elements showed that the optimum solution involved three dimensions that contrasted institutional against individual orientations, positive against negative assessments and the tangible or familiar against what is intangible in religion.

While the elements that were identified in the first phase of that study go beyond the doctrinally based concepts typical of measures of religion, the dimensions that were identified converge on the religious orientations that were found in my sentence completion study (Brown, 1964). They also correspond with the results of Múthen *et al.*'s (1977) three-mode factor-analytic study of adjectival ratings of the religious concepts "altar, the conciliating Christ, love, prayer for God's help, the crucified Christ, and God", on 60 bipolar scales selected from previous work or derived empirically from completions of the phrase "the . . . crucified Christ". The analysis of those ratings yielded three factors – tradition, evaluation and familiarity – which correspond with Brown and Forgas's factors, and a fourth, activity, factor. In the person mode, in which each subject was classified as religious or not, Múthen *et al.* found a stress on the affective or untraditional, and the cognitive or traditional in religion. Their analysis of the concept mode was weaker, being based on only six concepts, but it distinguished the persons in the deity, religious or non-religious concepts, and human or divine action.

This group of studies, which has excluded specific questions about religious belief and practice, finds that religious reactions and hence attitudes involve evaluations of Christianity through contrasts between institutional or individual control, between the tangible and the intangible or mysterious, and through a primary commitment to the truth or to the usefulness of religious beliefs. A conservative fundamentalism is not the only reaction to religion.

I have recently attempted to retrieve these semantically based factors from ratings of broadly defined religious pictures, which are of course non-verbal stimuli. These reproductions, rated on the same adjectival scales used by Brown and Forgas (1980), produced a first, major factor on which paintings with recognizable religious figures, like Jesus or Moses, had the highest loadings. The second factor involved the flowing style in paintings that portrayed postures of either consolation or submission, depending on their focus. The other two factors involved a predominance of red or of yellow in the paintings. We again see here the effect of the stimuli on any results.

The "Repertory grid technique" (Fransella and Bannister, 1977), which has been offered as a method for analysing idiosyncratic or idiographic data, was used by O'Connor (1983) to explore the content and the structure of religious responses among Catholic "Religious". She found that each of her subjects readily used a free-response procedure to identify the elements that were dominant in their own systems of religious meaning. Although there are some difficulties in analysing these data, a clear finding was that females produced a greater number of elements than did males, and that the Religious produced more elements than did a control group. Furthermore, the Religious gave elements relating to God and authority more often than the control group did. A later analysis of comparable grouped data suggested that attitudes to authority might be the only personally relevant aspect of these results, in which the primary factors contrasted loving and unloving, emotional and rational, and the conventional or unconventional in religion.

These recent approaches to the structures of religion avoid direct questions about the beliefs that are held or are available, and identify basic reactions to religion. They neglect the sense of authenticity found in directly taught or apprehended beliefs, attitudes or practices, which has commonly been explored simply by assessments of the believed truth of propositions. Specific responses engendered by religious rituals, doctrines or dogma, or how any conclusion is reached that God is active in the world or in one's own life have also been neglected. We must assume that those responses depend initially on contact with others who support religious attitudes and expectations. Conflicting pressures and interests there must be resolved for any sense of religious authenticity to be achieved. At a different level, Pearce (1982, pp. 115–16) noted a conflict between the interest of tourists who visit English cathedrals reacting to their artistic, cultural and historic value, and the clergy's aim to give "priority to the sense of worship". Such reactions are probably not independent of each other and bring us back to the importance of the way religion is construed, and what it achieves.

We have noted a difference between accepting the immediate personal validity of a religious claim and asserting that it is mediated through an institution or tradition. Dittes (1969, p. 644) observed, however, that religion displays a "maximum ambiguity and minimum reinforcement of closure from objective reality". This ambiguity might be unresolved (cf. Godin, 1971). While people can be placed along a religious belief–disbelief dimension on the basis of their acceptance or rejection of religious propositions, we have already noted that there is too little evidence that dogmatism or similar personality traits consistently moderate those responses to produce an easy closure. Despite that, the indirect social or public consequences of being "religious", where an explicit commitment is required, have been less studied than has their internal structure, and the assumed psychological effects. Religious beliefs do not, however, correspond closely with religious actions or with experiences of the physical world, except through an attributional process which assigns their meaning. A recent study of attributions to God (Brown, 1984) has, however, shown with simple contrasts between church-goers and non-church-goers that God is said to be more involved in good outcomes, especially for and by regular church-goers, and that when someone does not offer expected help, that person rather than God is thought to have been responsible and to control the outcome. Although several studies of religious attributions are in progress, little has yet been published (cf. Proudfoot and Shaver, 1975, Spilka and Schmidt, 1983, Gorsuch and Smith, 1983).

It is likely that although pressures towards orthodoxy make diverse groups of subjects set their religious responses in the same way across various statements of belief, disagreements between religious groups must be expected because of confessional emphases that are theologically and socially rather than psychologically defined. That doctrinal differences between religious groups have little direct effect on behaviour may be seen in the extent to which lay Catholic attitudes to contraception have changed, bringing them into line with Protestant attitudes (Davidson and Jaccard, 1975; Westoff, 1979). Whether such changes are part of a general trend towards secularism is not yet clear, despite this being a common interpretation of the movement away from church-attendance in Britain (Currie, Gilbert and Horsley, 1977) and Australia, for example. Caplovitz and Sherrow (1977) have attributed "apostasy among college graduates", by which they mean growing up in a religious denomination and later changing to "no denomination", to poor parental relations, symptoms of maladjustment, a left political ideology and a commitment to intellectualism. Hunsberger (1980), however, failed to replicate those findings, and from an Australian study, Hunsberger and Brown (1984) argue that religious socialization, but especially a strong religious emphasis in the childhood home, is the strongest influence on maintaining a religious orientation. We nevertheless found among Australian students that about 44 per cent of Anglicans and other Protestants, 33 per cent of Catholics, 31 per cent of the Orthodox and 13 per cent of Jews had moved to a broad position of "apostasy".

It has also been assumed that God figures (the Father, Jesus, the Holy Spirit, and perhaps Mary) are not only religiously identified and offer models for behaviour, but that these concepts or images are formed projectively (rather than being introjected). Godin and Hallez (1964) and Vergote and Tamayo (1980) have shown, however, that the connotative meanings of "God the Father" align more closely with the meaning of "mother" than of "father". That is consistent with Hunsberger and Brown's (1984) finding that mothers are more important than fathers in religious socialization, which may be another instance of the extent to which social rather than deeply personal processes shape or dictate a person's religion. That connotative meanings fit with social rather than personal or idiosyncratic reactions (except for an absolute minority, although even those who focus their pathology on religion do so in a stereotyped way) might also explain why an undifferentiated acceptance of religious propositions aligns with apparently fundamentalist views.

An important feature of religious attitudes and beliefs is their linguistic or verbal encoding. They are declarations of "faith", used in conversation and to answer questions about beliefs or practice, and to identify (or conceal) a religious position. Religious talk, therefore, convinces, converts, witnesses to, and clarifies beliefs and so is grounded in social interaction. To ask catechetical questions is the most obvious way to establish what others believe, and the problems of coordinating and interpreting any replies are readily solved by accepting prepared answers. Clinical and statistical procedures offer other ways to break up the facile responses that have defined the "religious variable", and through which we use our knowledge of expected attitudes and beliefs to maintain the social order, but not to express any deep understanding or commitment. More sophisticated theoretical perspectives, like those that Deconchy considers here in Chapter 7, suggest other ways to find how religion functions.

Validating religious measures

Religion as a set of external, public or traditional structures is analogous to "la langue" in de Saussure's terms. Such systems shared by a community of speakers are seldom fully accepted, except simplistically, although they may be quite easily rejected. Individuals and institutions select from all that is available to build their own religion and establish their vocabulary of religion (forming "le parole", following de Saussure). There is tension in the answers to any questionnaire between what can be accepted and how it is to be explained or elaborated, which does not of course imply any explicit behaviour. In a recent study of religious beliefs I asked the subjects to show how they would modify each statement so that they could agree with it: 80 per cent of the statements in a questionnaire were altered to some degree, suggesting that Sherif's concept of "latitude of acceptance" and Kelly's "range of convenience" could be profitably applied to establish the salience and the ways religious propositions are accepted, as an alternative to directly scaled responses. Distinctions between obligatory and optional Christian beliefs (Thouless, 1954) or between primary and secondary beliefs (Rokeach, 1960) could also be used to understand their assumed immediacy or relevance.

Because attitudes have generally been defined as a learned predisposition to respond, they have usually been validated against explicit behaviour, although low attitude–behaviour relationships have been the norm (cf. Fishbein and Ajzen, 1975, Chapter 8). Such validation studies disregard the extent to which any attitudes can be used in "talk", which is an important but neglected form of action (cf. Harré, 1976). This aligns with the performative view of language outlined by J. L. Austin (1962), which is contrasted against descriptive speech-acts. The essential coherence of verbal statements is shown by Ostrom's (1969) finding that Likert scales which measure the affective, cognitive and conative components of religious attitudes correlate around $+0.80$, and that parallel direct self-rating scales correlate about $+0.71$. While reports of explicitly Church-related behaviour generally correlate with verbal statements of belief below $+0.30$, church attendance itself is the only actual behaviour that is predicted with reasonable accuracy (cf. Wicker, 1971). (I have already noted on page 3 that other conceptions of religious behaviour warrant detailed study.)

The talk which embodies religious attitudes and beliefs creates and maintains each person's attitudes within a social context, although religious traditions limit and control what it is possible to talk about. Nevertheless we use what others say to identify their "states of mind", including their religious beliefs, and to support judgements about anxiety or inner peace, hypocrisy or commitment, fears and hopes. Both speech and action are called on for these conclusions, together with our prejudices about the specific effects of religious expressions of traditions. These prejudices seldom recognize the ambiguity of religion, which can both comfort and challenge (Glock, Ringer and Babbie, 1967), create or resolve dependencies, and offer concrete or figurative meanings for statements of religious belief (Hunt, 1972). The resolution of these ambiguities is usually interpreted psychologically, and not as being socially or theologically based. To neglect the effects of social involvement, group identity and religious traditions in favour of a deeply psychological interpretation of religious meaning itself reflects attitudinal or ideological assumptions.

A religious commitment may also be dormant for most people; religious participation, not just at a wedding or funeral, seldom demands any assent to the truth of religious beliefs, and the reaffirmation asked of those who attend a

Baptism can be given conventionally. Although it has been found that a personal crisis is likely to make people think about religion (ITA, 1970) the internal coherence of a person's religious beliefs or attitudes offers their most robust validation.

Conclusion

Although I have been able to review only some of the ways religious beliefs and attitudes have been measured and their behavioural effects or other consequences, I have tried to show that the separate dimensions of religion identified empirically rest on prior decisions about an experiment's design, and also on the characteristics of those who are to take part in any study. It also requires that theories or assumptions about religion are shared by both experimenters and their respondents. These implicit views about religion have not yet been closely enough examined.

Granted that religion involves both public and private responses, why do some people accept its institutional character more readily than its spiritual or mystical implications? If we recognize gross differences between believers and disbelievers or between Methodists and Catholics, why have we failed to acknowledge that while religion is objectively true for some it is a hidden dimension captured fleetingly by others? Disregarding such questions could be a reason why the religion psychologists have studied has its "natural" focus on a direct, conservative fundamentalism. Contrasts between reason and revelation, orthodoxy and heterodoxy, and the nature of "faith" itself might further clarify simple distinctions between individual and institutional orientations, and help us understand the differences between those who are inconsistently pro- or anti-religious and those who would express reservations on whatever grounds.

Despite the limitations, work on religious attitudes has shown:

(1) That religion offers a general, well-focused social identity.
(2) That theistic beliefs form an apparently conservative or fundamentalist pattern that involves beliefs about social and moral control.
(3) That traditional responses to religion separate into orientations recognizing the source of its authority and the implications of a religious stance for those who accept beliefs about the transcendent, or beliefs that point to the transcendent.
(4) That personal constructions of religious beliefs and attitudes can be identified from what is said more readily than from what is done, which is directly structured by traditional social rules.
(5) That the sub-categories of religion involve institutional and individual, or consensual and committed orientations (following Allport) or stress belief, behaviour, social support and the consequences of religion (following King and Hunt). These categories of response are more heavily

loaded with what is prescribed or offered than by the way religious beliefs are realized: the approaches to our sense of God are well-formed by psychological and social theories as well as by theology or religious "faith" itself (Bowker, 1973); furthermore, we align ourselves with religious "texts" or traditions and seldom create them for ourselves.

(6) That while religion has been an important analytic tool for understanding other social attitudes, and sociological theories can explain why it survives, we have not yet fully described the range of personal responses to it. To do that requires improved techniques which allow intensive explorations of the way religion is shaped for and by individuals. We should look for issues beyond convention and authority, prejudice or dogmatism and conservatism, and even beyond religion itself to calibrate or modify religious responses. And we need to specify how recent movements have altered the contexts within which religious people operate. While religion defines a unitary variable for many people, those who are deeply involved with it seldom treat it like that.

References

ALLPORT, F. H. The J-curve hypothesis of conforming behaviour. *Journal of Social Psychology*, 1934; **5**, 141–183.

ALLPORT, G. W. *The individual and his religion*. New York: Macmillan, 1950/1962.

ALLPORT, G. W. and ROSS, J. M. Personal religious orientation and prejudice. *Journal of Personality and Social Psychology*, 1967; **5**, 432–443.

ALLPORT, G. W., VERNON, P. E. and LINDZEY, G. *The study of values: Manual*. Boston: Houghton Mifflin, 1960.

ALLEN, R. O. and SPILKA, B. Committed and consensual religion: a specification of religious prejudice relationships. *Journal for the Scientific Study of Religion*, 1967; **6**, 191–206.

AUSTIN, J. L. *How to do things with words*. Oxford: Clarendon Press, 1962.

AUSTRALIAN BUREAU OF STATISTICS. *1980 Census*. Canberra: Government Printing Service, 1981.

BENSON, J. M. The polls: a rebirth of religion? *Public Opinion Quarterly*, 1981; **45**, 576–585.

BOWKER, J. *The sense of God: sociological, anthropological, and psychological approaches to the origin of the sense of God*. Oxford: Clarendon Press, 1973.

BROWN, L. B. A study of religious belief. *British Journal of Psychology*, 1962a; **53**(3), 259–272.

BROWN, L. B. Religious belief in two student societies. *Australian Journal of Psychology*, 1962b; **14**, 202–209.

BROWN, L. B. Classifications of religious orientation. *Journal for the Scientific Study of Religion*, 1964; **4**, 91–99.

BROWN, L. B. The religionism factor after 25 years. *Journal of Psychology*, 1981a; **107**, 7–10.

BROWN, L. B. Another test of Yinger's measure of non-doctrinal religion. *Journal of Psychology*, 1981b; **107**, 3–5.

BROWN, L. B. and FORGAS, J. P. The structure of religion: a multi-dimensional scaling of informal elements. *Journal for the Scientific Study of Religion*, 1980; **19**, 423–431.

BROWN, L. B. *Attributions to God*. Paper read to a meeting of Australian Social Psychologists, Adelaide, May 1984.

CAPLOVITZ, D. and SHERROW, F. *The religious drop-outs: apostasy among college graduates*. Beverly Hills: Sage, 1977.

CAPPS, D., RAMBO, L. and RANSOHOFF, P. *Psychology of religion: a guide to information sources*. Detroit: Gale Research Company, 1976.

CLARK, W. H. *The psychology of religion: an introduction to religious experience and behaviour*. New York: Macmillan, 1958.

168   Advances in the Psychology of Religion

CLAYTON, R. R. 5-D or 1? *Journal for the Scientific Study of Religion*, 1971; **10**, 37–40.
CLAYTON, R. R. and GLADDEN, J. W. The five dimensions of religiosity: toward demythologizing a sacred artifact. *Journal for the Scientific Study of Religion*, 1974; **13**, 135–143.
CLINE, V. B. and RICHARDS, J. M. A factor analytic study of religious belief and behavior. *Journal of Personality and Social Psychology*, 1965; **1**, 569–578.
CURRIE, R., GILBERT, A. and HORSLEY, L. *Churches and Church-goers*. Oxford: Clarendon Press, 1977.
DAVIDSON, A. R. and JACCARD, J. J. Population psychology: a new look at an old problem. *Journal of Personality and Social Psychology*, 1975; **31**, 1973–1082.
DECONCHY, J-P. *Orthodoxie religieuse et sciences humaines: suivi de (Religious) orthodoxy, rationality and scientific knowledge*. The Hague: Mouton, 1980.
DEMERATH, N. J. and ROOF, W. C. Recent strands in research. *Annual Review of Sociology*, 1976; **2**, 19–33.
DITTES, J. E. Psychology of religion. In G. LINDZEY and E. ARONSON (eds), *Handbook of social psychology*, vol. V. Boston: Addison-Wesley, 1969.
DUCKER, E. N. *A Christian therapy for a neurotic world*. London: George Allen & Unwin, 1961.
EISER, J. R. *Cognitive Social Psychology*. London: McGraw-Hill, 1980.
FICHTER, J. H. *Social relations in the urban parish*. Chicago: University of Chicago Press, 1954.
FISHBEIN, M. and AJZEN, I. *Belief, attitude, intention and behaviour: an introduction to theory and research*. Reading, Mass.: Addison-Wesley, 1975.
FRANSELLA, F. and BANNISTER, D. *A manual for repertory grid technique*. London: Academic Press, 1977.
FULLERTON, J. T. and HUNSBERGER, B. E. A unidimensional measure of Christian orthodoxy. *Journal for the Scientific Study of Religion*, 1982; **21**, 317–326.
GLOCK, C. Y. On the study of religious commitment. *Religious Education Research Supplement*, 1962, pp. 98–110.
GLOCK, C. Y., RINGER, B. B. and BABBIE, E. R. *To comfort and to challenge*. Berkeley: University of California Press, 1967.
GODIN, A. Some developmental tasks in Christian education. In M. P. STROMMEN (ed.), *Research on religious development: a comprehensive handbook*. New York: Hawthorn Books, 1971, pp. 109–154.
GODIN, A. and HALLEZ, M. Parental images and divine paternity. *Lumen Vitae*, 1964; **19**, 253–284.
GORSUCH, R. L. Measurement: the boon and the bane of investigating religions. *American Psychologist*, 1984; **39**(3), 228–236.
GORSUCH, R. L. and SMITH, C. S. Attributions of responsibility to God: an interaction of religious beliefs and outcomes. *Journal for the Scientific Study of Religion*, 1983; **22**(4), 340–352.
HARRÉ, R. *Life sentences: aspects of the social role of language*. London: Wiley, 1976.
HEIST, P. and YONGE, G. *The Omnibus Personality Inventory*. New York: The Psychological Corporation, 1968.
HUNSBERGER, B. E. A reexamination of the antecedents of apostasy. *Review of Religious Research*, 1980; **21**, 158–170.
HUNSBERGER, B. E. and BROWN, L. B. Religious socialisation, apostasy and the impact of family background. *Journal for the Scientific Study of Religion*, 1984 (in press).
HUNT, R. A. Mythological–symbolic religious commitment: the LAM scales. *Journal for the Scientific Study of Religion*, 1972; **11**(1), 42–52.
ITA. *Religion in Britain and Northern Ireland: a survey of popular attitudes*. London: Independent Television Authority, 1970.
JAMES, W. *The varieties of religious experience: a study in human nature*. New York: New American Library, 1902/1958.
KEENE, J. Religious behaviour and neuroticism, spontaneity and world mindedness. *Sociometry*, 1967; **30**, 137–157.
KING, M. B. Measuring the religious variable: nine proposed dimensions. *Journal for the Scientific Study of Religion*, 1967; **6**, 173–190.
KING, M. B. and HUNT, R. A. Measuring the religious variable: National replication. *Journal for the Scientific Study of Religion*, 1975; **14**, 13–22.
KLAUSNER, S. L. Methods of data collection in studies of religion. *Journal for the Scientific Study of Religion*, 1964; **3**, 193–203.

LALLJEE, M., BROWN, L. B. and GINSBURG, G. P. Attitudes: disposition, behaviour and evaluation. *British Journal of Social Psychology*, 1984; **23**, 233–244.

LA PIERE, R. T. Attitudes vs. actions. *Social Forces*, 1934; **13**, 230–237.

MARANELL, G. M. A factor analytic study of some selected dimensions of religious attitudes. *Sociology and Social Research*, 1968; **52**(4), 430–437.

MARTIN, J. and WESTIE, F. Religious fundamentalism scale in "The tolerant personality". *American Sociological Review*, 1959; **24**, 521–528.

MICHAELS, J. A survey of empirical psychological studies of religion of the past twenty-five years. University of California, Los Angeles, 1956 (mimeo). Cited by Cline and Richards (1965).

MÚTHEN, B., OLSSON, U., PETTERSSON, T. and STAHLBERG, G. Measuring religious attitudes using the semantic differential technique: an application of three-mode factor analysis. *Journal for the Scientific Study of Religion*, 1977; **16**, 275–288.

NEW ZELAND CENSUS OF POPULATION AND DWELLINGS. *Religious professions.* Wellington, New Zealand: Department of Statistics Publication, May, 1980, Vol. 3.

N.O.P. Church-going. *N.O.P. Political Social Economic Review*, February, 1982, No. 35, pp. 20–25.

O'CONNOR, K. V. *The structure of religion: a repertory grid approach.* Ph.D. thesis, University of New South Wales, Australia, 1983.

OSTROM, T. M. The relationship between the affective, behavioral, and cognitive components of attitude. *Journal of Experimental Social Psychology*, 1969; **5**, 12–30.

PEARCE, P. L. *The social psychology of tourist behaviour.* Oxford: Pergamon Press, 1982.

POPPLETON, P. K. and PILKINGTON, G. W. The measurement of religious attitudes in a University population. *British Journal of Social and Clinical Psychology*, 1963; **2**, 20–36.

PROUDFOOT, W. and SHAVER, P. Attribution theory and the psychology of religion. *Journal for the Scientific Study of Religion*, 1975; **14**, 317–330.

RAY, J. J. Does authoritarianism of personality go with conservatism? *Australian Journal of Psychology*, 1979; **31**, 9–14.

RAY, J. J. The Protestant Ethic in Australia. *Journal of Social Psychology*, 1982; **116**, 127–138.

ROBINSON, J. P. and SHAVER, P. R. *Measures of social psychological attitudes.* Michigan: University of Michigan Survey Research Center of the Institute for Social Research, 1973.

ROKEACH, M. *The open and closed mind.* New York: Basic Books, 1960.

ROOF, W. C. Concepts and indicators of religious commitment: a critical review. In R. WUTHNOW (ed.), *The religious dimension.* New York: Academic Press, 1979, pp. 17–45.

SANAI, M. An empirical study of political, religious and social attitudes. *British Journal of Psychology* (*Statistical Section*), 1952; **5**, 81–92.

SHAW, M. E. and WRIGHT, J. M. *Scales for the measurement of attitudes.* New York: McGraw Hill, 1967.

SPILKA, B. *et al.* The treatment of religion in current psychology texts. Paper presented at the 1981 Convention of the American Psychological Association, Los Angeles, California, 25 August, 1981.

SPILKA, B. and SCHMIDT, G. General attribution theory for the psychology of religion: the influence of event-character on attributions to God. *Journal for the Scientific Study of Religion*, 1983; **22**(4), 326–339.

STARBUCK, E. D. Some aspects of religious growth. *American Journal of Psychology*, 1897; **9**, 70–124.

STROMMEN, M. P. *et al. A study of generations: report of a two-year study of 5,000 Lutherans between the ages of 15–65: their beliefs, values, attitudes, behaviour.* Minneapolis, Minn.: Augsburg Publishing House, 1972.

THOULESS, R. H. The tendency to certainty in religious belief. *British Journal of Psychology*, 1935; **26**, 16–31.

THOULESS, R. H. *Freedom and authority: some psychological problems of religious belief.* London: Hodder & Stoughton, 1954.

THURSTONE, L. L. and CHAVE, E. J. *Measurement of attitude.* Chicago: University of Chicago Press, 1929.

VERGOTE, A. and TAMAYO, A. *Parental figures and the representation of God.* The Hague: Mouton and Leuven University Press, 1980.

VERNON, G. M. Measuring religion: two methods compared. *Review of Religious Research*, 1962; **3**, 159–165.

WACH, J. *Types of religious experience, Christian and non-Christian*. Chicago: University of Chicago Press, 1951.

WEARING, A. J. and BROWN, L. B. The dimensionality of religion. *British Journal of Social and Clinical Psychology*, 1972; **11**, 143–148.

WESTOFF, C. F. The blending of Catholic reproductive behaviour. In R. WUTHNOW (ed.), *The religious dimension: new directions in quantitative research*. New York: Academic Press, 1979, pp. 231–240.

WICKER, A. W. An examination of the "other variables" explanation of attitude–behaviour inconsistency. *Journal of Personality and Social Psychology*, 1971; **19**, 18–30.

WILSON, G. D. (ed.) *The psychology of conservatism*. London: Academic Press, 1972.

YINGER, J. M. A comparative study of the substructures of religion. *Journal for the Scientific Study of Religion*, 1977; **16**, 67–86.

12

Personality and religion: theory and measurement

LESLIE J. FRANCIS

Introduction

The relationship between personality and religion is an area of enquiry of considerable interest both to the theologian and the psychologist. On the one hand, there is a whole set of questions about the impact of religion on people's lives and on their personal development, while on the other hand there is another set of questions about the kinds of people who are attracted to religion in the first place.

The attempt to raise questions about the relationship between personality and religion and to answer them in a scientific way can be traced back to those who pioneered the present traditions in the psychology of religion at the turn of the century, especially William James (1902). Although a lot of work has gone on since those early days, both at the level of theory building and at the level of empirical data collection, the present state of the field is still very untidy and far from conclusive.

When my colleagues and I began to take a systematic interest in this question (e.g. Francis *et al.*, 1981a,b), the first thing to impress itself upon us was the wide range of issues discussed by different authors under the heading of "personality and religion". After an exhaustive literature review, we were left wondering what studies like Ligon's (1975) *The psychology of Christian personality*, Roldan's (1968) *Personality types and holiness*, Sadler's (1970) anthology of readings in *Personality and religion* and Argyle and Beit-Hallahmi's (1975) chapter on personality and religion in the *Social psychology of religion* actually had in common, if anything at all. Even when we decided to narrow the field by restricting ourselves only to those studies which were concerned with the quantitative study of personality and religion, we were still overwhelmed by the multiplicity and variety of definitions employed, and the impossibility of boiling down the literature into a manageable and sensible set of conclusions.

As we came to understand the problem better, we saw that it could be traced back to the variety of standpoints that have existed in the psychological study of personality itself (Semeonoff, 1966; Lazarus and Opton, 1967; Edwards,

1970; Fransella, 1981). The problem about trying to collect and synthesize the existing mass of theory and data on personality and religion is that this material flows from a range of different, and sometimes empirically incompatible, models of personality. We decided, therefore, to begin from the other side and adopt a theory of personality, to examine how well this theory could make sense of an empirical approach to religion.

The scientific tradition to which we belong is that of measurement and psychometrics, and there are two major psychometrically based theories of personality, one developed by Eysenck in England (Eysenck and Eysenck, 1969), the other by Cattell (1973) in America. The theories differ both in terms of what counts as being within the domain of personality and in terms of the number of dimensions to which personality factors can be sensibly reduced. In both senses Cattell adopts the broader perspective, arguing that personality profiles need to be drawn in 16 inter-correlated dimensions, including such notions as intelligence. Eysenck, on the other hand, would wish to adopt a tighter definition of personality, to exclude such components as intelligence and to summarize personality differences in terms of only three or four uncorrelated dimensions.

Eysenck's personality theory

We decided to adopt Eysenck's theory as the basis from which to attempt to formulate a comprehensive description of the relationship between personality and religion, on the grounds that this theory offers the most succinct and economical account of personality differences currently available. Our aim was to examine how far empirical work based on this theory can give a coherent account of the place of religion in personal development. First, however, it is necessary to provide a clear statement of what it means to work within the boundaries of Eysenck's personality theory.

From his early work in the 1940s (Eysenck, 1947) Hans Eysenck has been working on factor-analytic studies of the interrelationships between personality-based responses. The major contribution of his earlier work, in the development of the Maudsley Medical Questionnaire, the Maudsley Personality Inventory and the Eysenck Personality Inventory (Eysenck, 1959; Eysenck and Eysenck, 1964), was the demonstration that a wide range of personality responses and personality traits could be accounted for in terms of the two underlying dimensions. He argues that all that needs to be said about personality at the most fundamental level can be in terms of the primary dimensions of introversion–extraversion and stability–neuroticism.

Although no pithy definition of neuroticism and extraversion can provide an adequate description of what Eysenck has in mind, the definitions of Saklofske and Eysenck (1978) provide a very helpful introduction to their meaning.

The dimension, Neuroticism, measures emotional lability and overreactivity, and the high scorer tends to be an anxious, worrying individual, moody, and frequently depressed and suffering from various psychosomatic disorders. The highly extraverted individual is characterised as being sociable and outgoing, a risk taker and uninhibited compared to the quiet, introspective, well-ordered, and controlled introvert.

The point to recognize about these dimensions is that they represent continuous variables, that is to say that introversion is not categorically discrete from extraversion, but that the two concepts represent opposite poles of the same continuum.

In addition to the primary scales of neuroticism and extraversion, the Eysenck Personality Inventory (Eysenck and Eysenck, 1964) contains a third scale, known as the lie scale. While originally intended to aid in the identification of respondents who tend to distort their true responses to personality questions, the lie scale has gradually assumed an identity of its own as a kind of third personality dimension, variously interpreted as measuring social acquiescence or self-insight. Finally, the Eysenck Personality Questionnaire (Eysenck and Eysenck, 1975) added a fourth scale designed to measure psychoticism, which, according to Eysenck's later theory, is a continuous personality dimension on which psychotic disorders lie towards one extreme.

Since psychoticism is a relative newcomer to Eysenck's personality theory and as yet very little work has been done on the relationship between psychoticism and religion (Kay, 1981), this chapter restricts itself to reviewing the established territory of the relationships between religion and neuroticism, extraversion and the lie scale. Each of these areas will be reviewed in turn.

Neuroticism

I shall begin with the easiest problem and look at the relationship between religion and neuroticism. As we have already seen, the neuroticism scale provides an index of emotional stability. There is a vast theoretical literature on the relationship between religion and stability, from which two conflicting psychological accounts emerge. The first suggests that religion either fosters or is an expression of instability (Vine, 1978), while the second account suggests that religion fosters stability (Allport, 1957).

It should be an easy matter for empirical studies to choose between these two interpretations, since the first would lead to hypothesizing a positive correlation between scores of neuroticism and religiosity, while the second would suggest a negative correlation. However, a review of previous empirical research only served to confuse us further. Previous research, using a variety of indices of stability, self-concept and anxiety, seem to have offered support to both of the contradictory hypotheses. For example, Brown and Lowe (1951), Bender (1958), Stanley (1964), McClain (1978) and Sturgeon and

Hamley (1971) report that religiosity is associated with greater personal stability and adjustment. On the other hand, Cowen (1954), Roberts (1965) and Wilson and Miller (1968) report that religiosity is associated with lower self-esteem, greater anxiety and higher neuroticism. Meanwhile, Brown (1962), Heintzelman and Fehr (1976) and Fehr and Heintzelman (1977) find no significant correlations in either direction. So, conflicting hypotheses are compounded by conflicting empirical information.

It needs to be noted, however, that none of the studies cited in the previous paragraph had actually employed one of Eysenck's own neuroticism scales. Indeed, in their reviews of the correlational studies in personality and religion, neither Dittes (1971) nor Argyle and Beit-Hallahmi (1975) was able to identify any studies which had explored that relationship by means of Eysenck's own scales. In order to fill this gap in the literature, my colleagues and I decided to set up a large study correlating religiosity with Eysenck's own measure of neuroticism (Francis et al., 1981a). We based the study on 15- and 16-year-old school children in state schools, because in this way we could easily sample the whole range of ability, social class, etc. One thousand and eighty-eight subjects cooperated in this project by completing the Francis scale of Attitude towards Religion Form ASC4B (Francis, 1978) and the Junior Eysenck Personality Inventory (Eysenck, 1965). Table 1 presents the mean scores for boys and girls separately, for the three personality variables and the scale of attitude towards religion.

TABLE 1 *Means and standard deviations of attitude towards religion and neuroticism, extraversion and lie scores from the Junior Eysenck personality inventory among 15- and 16-year-olds*

	Boys ($n=403$)		Girls ($n=685$)	
	Mean	SD	Mean	SD
Attitude towards religion	72.64	22.84	82.44	19.16
Neuroticism	11.50	4.84	13.77	4.97
Extraversion	17.94	4.29	17.46	4.33
Lie scale	2.09	1.80	2.24	1.86

When we first looked at our data, we found a statistically significant positive correlation between scores of neuroticism and religiosity ($r= +0.0956$, $n=1088$, $p<0.001$). Although this correlation is small and accounts for very little of the variance in the scores, it is highly significant in a statistical sense and lends clear support to the notion that religion is associated with neuroticism. However, it would be naive to allow the matter to rest with such a simple data analysis.

Closer inspection of the data revealed two other interesting phenomena. To begin with, the females in the sample obtained significantly higher scores than the males on the scale of attitude towards religion. Such a finding is hardly surprising, since it is consistent with most of the work which reports on sex differences in religions (Hyde, 1965; Povall, 1971; Francis, 1977). At the same time, the females also recorded higher scores on the scale of neuroticism. This too is consistent with the majority of work on sex differences in levels of neuroticism (Iwawaki, Eysenck and Eysenck, 1977; Saklofske and Eysenck, 1978; Powell and Stewart, 1978). Our next step was, therefore, to partial out sex differences before recalculating the correlation between neuroticism and religion. This time there ceased to be a significant correlation. The apparently significant correlation between neuroticism and religion in our data proved to be simply an artifact caused by sex difference. That finding may help to account for some of the discrepant findings in previous research.

Francis, Pearson and Kay (1983c) take the story a step further and have replicated their earlier study on a fresh sample of 1715 school children, using a more recent version of Eysenck's neuroticism scale, the Junior Eysenck Personality Questionnaire (Eysenck and Eysenck, 1975), and the same scale of Attitude towards Religion (Francis, 1978). Once again, they demonstrate that, after sex differences have been taken into account, neuroticism and religion are uncorrelated factors.

Extraversion

Although Eysenck himself has not given much attention to a specific discussion of the relationship between religion and extraversion, such a relationship is clearly at the heart of Eysenck's theory. The key to understanding this hypothesized relationship lies in Eysenck's notions of social attitudes and conditionability.

In an early study Eysenck (1954) postulated a relationship between personality and social attitudes that was explained in terms of a theory of social learning and socialization and he argued that aggressive and sexual impulses are socialized through conditioning. Empirical evidence shows that introverts condition more easily than extraverts (Eysenck, 1967) and it follows, therefore, that introverts should be more thoroughly socialized than extraverts. This high degree of socialization will be reflected in tender-minded attitudes (Eysenck, 1961). According to Eysenck, therefore, tough-minded attitudes are concerned with an immediate satisfaction of aggressive and sexual impulses, while tender-minded attitudes are concerned with "ethical and religious ideas which act as barriers to such satisfaction".

Siegman (1963) was the first person to develop the implications of Eysenck's theory of social attitudes for the relationship between personality and religion. Siegman argues that, according to this theory, introverts should be more religious. However, his own three attempts to support this hypothesis with empirical data produced conflicting evidence. The two main problems with interpreting Siegman's findings concern the smallness of the samples and the fact that his studies use a variety of indices of religiosity that are not compatible.

Siegman's first study employed one of Eysenck's early extraversion scales (Eysenck, 1956) together with his own religious attitude scale (Siegman, 1962) with 43 white male Protestant undergraduates, and found a significant correlation in the opposite direction to that hypothesized. In Siegman's second study, 32 male undergraduate students at Bar-Ilan University, Israel, completed the extraversion scale together with Thurstone and Chave's (1929) Attitude towards the Reality of God scale and Foa's (1948) Sabbath Observance scale. On this occasion the correlations between extraversion and the two measures of religiosity were in the expected direction, although only one, a negative correlation between extraversion and Foa's Sabbath Observance scale, is statistically significant. In Siegman's third study, 31 Protestant males, 55 Protestant females and 13 Jewish males completed the extraversion scale, together with a Guttman-type scale developed by Goldsen

TABLE 2   *Correlations between extraversion and religiosity from Siegman's third study*

Group scale	n	Religious belief		Church attendance	
		r	p<	r	p<
Protestant males	31	+0.35	0.05	+0.46	0.01
Protestant females	55	−0.16	NS	−0.05	NS
Jewish males	13	−0.67	0.01	−0.52	0.05

et al. (1960) to measure religious belief, and a Guttman-type scale measuring church or synagogue attendance. In that study, the relationship between extraversion and religiosity varied both according to sex and denominational background. Among Jewish males the introverts tended to be more religious, while among the Protestant males the extraverts were more religious. Among the Protestant females there was not a significant relationship between extraversion and religion.

More recently, the relationship between extraversion and religion has been explored with a subscale of the Wilson–Patterson conservatism scale (Wilson and Patterson, 1968). Once again the results are not always in the expected direction. Wilson and Brazendale (1973) report a negative relationship, Powell and Stewart (1978) found a positive relationship, and Pearson and Sheffield (1976) found no relationship. Finally, Siegman's hypothesis has been tested in Poland by Chlewinski (1981), who measured religiosity by means of the Allport, Vernon, Lindzey (1960) Study of Values inventory, and extraversion by Choynowski's (1968) Polish adaptation of the Maudsley Personality Inventory. According to this study, atheists are significantly more extraverted than are religious people.

Our own data on 1088 15–16-year-olds, employing the Junior Eysenck Personality Inventory (Eysenck, 1965) and the Francis scale of Attitude towards Religion (Francis, 1978) provides a secure basis on which to test the hypothesis that introverts are more religious (Francis *et al.*, 1981b). Here the results are quite straightforward, with a significant negative correlation between extraversion and religiosity ($r = -0.1480$, $n = 1088$, $p < 0.001$), and no interaction between sex and extraversion. The hypothesis that introverts are more religious than extraverts was therefore supported.

TABLE 3 *Means and standard deviations of attitude towards religion scores for different levels of extraversion*

Extraversion	Attitude towards religion scores		No. of subjects
	Mean	SD	
0–7	82.48	23.55	27
8–10	83.16	23.06	50
11–12	80.40	23.67	62
13–14	82.93	21.60	88
15–16	82.06	21.23	150
17–18	80.99	19.82	187
19–20	78.20	18.97	217
21–22	76.98	21.33	184
23–24	69.76	20.76	123

Although the correlation between extraversion and religion is statistically significant and in the predicted direction, the proportion of variance accounted for is small, which suggests that the relationship may not be as straightforward as the original hypothesis suggested, so it is worthwhile scrutinizing the original argument carefully. The hypothesis was advanced within the general framework of Eysenck's theory on the basis of the notions that (1) introverts condition more easily, (2) socialization is a process of conditioning, (3) socialization is reflected in tender-minded attitudes, and (4) tender-minded attitudes are concerned with ethical and religious ideas. The major problem with this argument concerns the relationship between extraversion and conditionability.

It is here the plot thickens. Eysenck and Eysenck (1963) indicate that extraversion has two main components, impulsivity and sociability, and Eysenck and Levey (1972) later proceeded to demonstrate that the impulsivity component alone is responsible for the correlation between extraversion and conditionability. Subsequently the place of impulsivity within the construct of extraversion itself has been questioned, and Eysenck and Eysenck (1977) argue that some impulsivity items correlate more highly with psychoticism than with extraversion. A consequence of this has been a shift in the item content of the extraversion scale so that in the more recent Eysenck Personality Questionnaire (Eysenck and Eysenck, 1975) extraversion is composed mainly of sociability items (Pearson, 1979; Rocklin and Revelle, 1981).

If the relationship between extraversion and religion rests mainly upon the impulsivity component in the extraversion scale, we would expect that, since this component has been reduced in later versions of that scale, the correlation between those measures of extraversion and religion would also lessen. In our original study we had employed an early measure of extraversion in the Junior Eysenck Personality Inventory (Eysenck, 1965). In the replication study on 1715 subjects, we used the later measure of extraversion in the Junior Eysenck Personality Questionnaire (Eysenck and Eysenck, 1975). This time, although the correlation between the two variables was smaller ($r = -0.0625$), introverts were still more religious (Francis, Pearson and Kay, 1983a). There seems, therefore, to be a relationship between introversion and religion.

Personality quadrants

So far we have reviewed the relationships between religion and neuroticism and between religion and extraversion as separate issues. However, a key aspect of Eysenck's theory is that these two primary personality dimensions need to be viewed together. This means that an issue we need to look at concerns the relationship between religiosity and each of the personality quadrants, of neurotic introverts, stable introverts, neurotic extraverts and stable extraverts.

By now we are quite clear, on the basis of both theory and data, that introverts tend to be more religious than extraverts, and that this relationship may be explained in terms of socialization into tender-minded social attitudes. A key question now concerns the role of neuroticism in conditioning. According to Eysenck's early theory, neuroticism was not implicated in conditioning (Franks, 1957), but as the theory developed neuroticism was considered to have a role in the conditioning process (Eysenck, 1977). It is confusing, however, that two different theories emerge as to the nature of this relationship.

On the one hand, neuroticism is regarded as a state of heightened emotionality, with emotionality a form of drive (Eysenck, 1966) that can potentiate the effect of introversion in facilitating conditioning into tender-minded attitudes, and of extraversion in resisting such conditioning. This explanation would imply a hierarchy here in which neurotic introverts would be more religious than stable introverts, and neurotic extraverts would be less religious than stable extraverts. On the other hand, regarding high neuroticism scores as an indication of anxiety (Crookes and Pearson, 1970), it could be argued that neurotic introverts and neurotic extraverts would both conform more to social norms and adopt tender-minded attitudes as a defensive function.

The only empirical data in the literature to test this question are provided by

Bagley *et al.* (1979), who found a hierarchy in which neurotic introverts have the highest religiosity scores, followed by neurotic extraverts, and then by stable introverts, with stable extraverts having the lowest religiosity scores. Those results are far from conclusive, since they are based on a small sample, significance levels are not quoted and sex differences were not taken into account. For this reason, we decided to re-examine our original data base of 1088 subjects (Francis, Pearson and Kay, 1982), and found that neuroticism *was* implicated with extraversion in predicting scores of religiosity. However, when sex differences were taken into account, the interaction between extraversion and neuroticism disappeared. This again underlines the importance of taking sex differences into account when exploring the relationships between personality and religion, and confirms Eysenck's original theory, also recently supported by Jones *et al.* (1981), that neuroticism is not implicated in any way with extraversion in developing either tender-minded attitudes in general, or religiosity in particular.

Lie scale

Finally, we turn our attention to reviewing the relationship between religion and the lie scale. Lie scales were originally introduced into personality inventories to detect the tendency of some respondents to "fake good" and so to distort the resultant personality scores (Dahlstrom and Welsh, 1960; O'Donovan, 1969). The notion of the lie scale has not, however, remained as simple as that, and their continued use has resulted in them being interpreted as a personality measure in their own right. The argument is that, since the internal consistency of a lie scale is quite independent of the motivation to dissimulate, the scale must be measuring some underlying personality dimension or set of characteristics (Eysenck and Eysenck, 1976).

Two main interpretations of the personality dimension measured by a lie scale have been offered. Dicken (1959), Eysenck, Nias and Eysenck (1971), Crookes and Buckley (1976) and Kirton (1977) suggest that the lie scale measures a lack of insight. Finlayson (1972), Eysenck and Eysenck (1976) and Powell (1977) suggest that this scale measures social acquiescence or conformity to social rules and pressures. Both these interpretations are open to criticism. It is not an easy matter, therefore, to choose between interpretations of the lie scale as measuring lack of insight, genuine conformity or a tendency to "fake good".

The majority of the empirical studies which report on the relationship between religion and lie scale scores find a significant positive relationship, which means that those who score highly on the lie scale also tend to be religious. A significant positive relationship is reported by Nias (1973a) among 11- and 12-year-olds, by Powell and Stewart (1978) among 11–15-year-olds, by Crandall and Gozali (1969) among 8–17-year-olds, by Francis, Pearson and Kay (1983b) among 15- and 16-year-olds, by Nias (1973b) among 19–25-year-olds, and by Wilson and Brazendale (1973) among 18–34-year-olds. On the other hand, no such relationship was found by Nias (1973b) among the general population or by Pearson and Sheffield (1976) among 18–30-year-old student nurses. We came across no study which reported a significant negative correlation between religion and lie scale scores.

The positive relationship between religion and lie scale scores has been interpreted in the literature in two different ways. On one hand, the development of personality characteristics has been interpreted as a function of religious influence by Crandall and Gozali (1969), who explain the higher lie scale scores among 8–17-year-old children from a religious background in terms of their defensive denial behaviour. They argue that religiosity leads to the repression or denial of actual, but unacceptable, thoughts and behaviour, so that religiosity may make a child less able to allow into consciousness the recognition that he has deviated from demanding standards of conduct.

On the other hand, a majority of commentators have hypothesized that religiosity scores are a dependent variable. For example, Nias (1973a) accepts the notion that the lie scale measures social acquiescence or conformity to social rules and pressures, and argues that the more socially acquiescent children will also be more religious on the grounds that children pick up the attitudes of the group upon which they are dependent and that they internalize the values of their parents and teachers. Taking another view, Francis, Pearson and Kay (1983b) accept the notion that the lie scale measures lack of insight, and argue that an implication of this is that the more insight the 15- and 16-year-olds in their sample have into their own thoughts and behaviour, the less favourably they are disposed towards religious items. Since insight and self-knowledge can be regarded as signs of maturity (Eysenck, Nias and Eysenck, 1971) this interpretation is consistent with the notion of religiosity as an expression of immaturity (Pohier, 1965).

Summary

This chapter has adopted the theory of personality, proposed by Hans Eysenck, to examine the extent to which it can elucidate the relationship between personality and religion. The main conclusions, granted that females are more religious than males, are (1) that introverts tend to be more religious than extraverts; (2) that those who score high on the neuroticism scale tend to be neither more nor less religious than those who score low on this dimension; (3) that neuroticism does not interact with either introversion or extraversion, whether to foster religion or reject it; and (4) that those who score high on the lie scale tend to be more religious than are those who score low on this measure.

By carefully exploring the empirical location of religion within Eysenck's theory of personality, this chapter has demonstrated that there is indeed a tendency for an association to exist between religion and a certain kind of personality. While such an association clearly exists, it is far too loose either to explain religion as a function of personality, or to delimit the wide range of personality and individual differences likely to be found within the community of adherents to one religious faith.

References

ALLPORT, G. W. *The individual and his religion.* New York: Macmillan, 1957.
ALLPORT, G. W., VERNON, P. E. and LINDZEY, G. *A study of values.* Boston: Houghton Mifflin, 1960.
ALLSOPP, J. F. and FELDMAN, M. P. Extraversion, neuroticism, psychoticism and antisocial behaviour in schoolgirls. *Social Behaviour and Personality,* 1974; **2,** 184–190.
ARGYLE, M. and BEIT-HALLAHMI, B. *The social psychology of religion.* London: Routledge & Kegan Paul, 1975.
BAGLEY, C., VERMA, G. K., MALLICK, K. and YOUNG, L. *Personality, self-esteem and prejudice.* Farnborough: Saxon House, 1979.
BENDER, I. E. Changes in religious interest: a retest after 15 years. *Journal of Abnormal and Social Psychology,* 1958; **57,** 41–46.
BROWN, D. G. and LOWE, W. L. Religious beliefs and personality characteristics of college students. *Journal of Social Psychology,* 1951: **33,** 103–129.
BROWN, L. B. A study of religious belief. *British Journal of Psychology,* 1962; **53,** 259–272.
BURGESS, P. K. Eysenck's theory of criminality, a new approach. *British Journal of Criminology,* 1972; **12,** 74–82.
CATTELL, R. B. *Personality and mood by questionnaire.* San Francisco: Jossey-Bass, 1973.
CHLEWINSKI, Z. Personality and attitude towards religion in Poland. *Personality and Individual Differences,* 1981: **2,** 243–245.
CHOYNOWSKI, M. An elaboration of the Polish adaptation of H. J. Eysenck's MPI. *Biul. Psychomet.,* 1968; **2,** 52–95.
COWEN, E. L. The negative concept as a personality measure. *Journal of Consulting Psychology,* 1954; **18,** 138–142.
CRANDALL, V. C. and GOZALI, J. Social desirability responses of children of four religious-cultural groups. *Child Development,* 1969; **40,** 751–762.
CROOKES, T. G. and BUCKLEY, S. J. Lie score and insight. *Irish Journal of Psychology,* 1976; **3,** 134–136.
CROOKES, T. G. and PEARSON, P. R. The relationship between EPI scores and 16PF second-order factors in a clinical group. *British Journal of Social and Clinical Psychology,* 1970; **9,** 189–190.
DAHLSTROM, W. G. and WELSH, G. S. *An MMPI Handbook.* Minnesota: University Press, 1960.
DICKEN, C. F. Simulated patterns on the Edwards Personal Preference Schedule. *Journal of Applied Psychology,* 1959; **43,** 372–378.
DITTES, J. E. Religion, prejudice and personality. In M. STROMMEN (ed.), *Research on religious development: a comprehensive handbook.* New York: Hawthorn, 1971, pp. 355–390.
EDWARDS, A. L. *The measurement of personality traits by scales and inventories.* New York: Holt Rinehart, 1970.
EYSENCK, H. J. *Dimensions of personality.* London: Routledge & Kegan Paul, 1947.
EYSENCK, H. J. *The psychology of politics.* London: Routledge & Kegan Paul, 1954.
EYSENCK, H. J. The questionnaire measurement of neuroticism and extraversion. *Rivista di Psicologia,* 1956; **50,** 113–140.
EYSENCK, H. J. *Manual for the Maudsley Personality Inventory.* London: University of London Press, 1959.
EYSENCK, H. J. Personality and social attitudes. *Journal of Social Psychology,* 1961; **53,** 243–248.
EYSENCK, H. J. *Crime and personality.* London: Routledge & Kegan Paul, 1964.
EYSENCK, H. J. Personality and experimental psychology. *Bulletin of the British Psychological Society,* 1966; **19,** 1–28.

EYSENCK, H. J. *The biological basis of personality*. Springfield, Illinois: Charles C. Thomas, 1967.

EYSENCK, H. J. *Crime and personality* (3rd edn). St Albans: Paladin, 1977.

EYSENCK, H. J. and EYSENCK, S. B. G. *Manual of the Eysenck Personality Inventory*. London: University of London Press, 1964.

EYSENCK, H. J. and EYSENCK, S. B. G. *Personality Structure and Measurement*. London: Routledge & Kegan Paul, 1969.

EYSENCK, H. J. and EYSENCK, S. B. G. *Manual of the Eysenck Personality Questionnaire*. London: Hodder & Stoughton, 1975.

EYSENCK, H. J. and EYSENCK, S. B. G. *Psychoticism as a dimension of personality*. London: Hodder & Stoughton, 1976.

EYSENCK, H. J. and LEVEY, A. Conditioning, introversion-extraversion and the strength of the nervous system. In V. D. NEBLITZYN and J. A. GRAY (eds), *Biological bases of individual behaviour*. New York: Academic Press, 1972.

EYSENCK, H. J. and WILSON, G. D. *The psychological basis of ideology*. Lancaster: Medical and Technical Publications, 1978.

EYSENCK, S. B. G. *Manual of the Junior Eysenck Personality Inventory*. London: University of London Press, 1965.

EYSENCK, S. B. G. and EYSENCK, H. J. On the dual nature of extraversion. *British Journal of Social and Clinical Psychology*, 1963; **2**, 46–55.

EYSENCK, S. B. G. and EYSENCK, H. J. The place of impulsiveness in a dimensional system of personality description. *British Journal of Social and Clinical Psychology*, 1977; **16**, 57–68.

EYSENCK, S. B. G., NIAS, D. K. B. and EYSENCK, H. J. Interpretation of children's lie scale scores. *British Journal of Educational Psychology*, 1971; **41**, 23–31.

FEHR, L. A. and HEINTZELMAN, M. E. Personality and attitude correlates of religiosity – source of controversy. *Journal of Psychology*, 1977; **59**, 63–66.

FINLAYSON, D. S. Towards the interpretation of children's lie scale scores. *British Journal of Educational Psychology*, 1972; **42**, 290–293.

FOA, U. G. An equal interval scale for the measurement of attitudes towards Sabbath observance. *Journal of Social Psychology*, 1948; **27**, 273–276.

FRANCIS, L. J. Readiness for research in religion. *Learning for Living*, 1977; **16**, 109–114.

FRANCIS, L. J. Attitude and longitude: a study in measurement. *Character Potential*, 1978; **8**, 119–130.

FRANCIS, L. J., PEARSON, P. R., CARTER, M. and KAY, W. K. The relationship between neuroticism and religiosity among English 15 and 16 year olds. *Journal of Social Psychology*, 1981a; **114**, 99–102.

FRANCIS, L. J., PEARSON, P. R., CARTER, M. and KAY, W. K. Are introverts more religious? *British Journal of Social Psychology*, 1981b; **20**, 101–104.

FRANCIS, L. J., PEARSON, P. R. and KAY, W. K. Eysenck's personality quadrants and religiosity. *British Journal of Social Psychology*, 1982; **21**, 262–264.

FRANCIS, L. J., PEARSON, P. R. and KAY, W. K. Are introverts still more religious? *Personality and Individual Differences*, 1983a; **4**, 211–212.

FRANCIS, L. J., PEARSON, P. R. and KAY, W. K. Are religious children bigger liars? *Psychological Reports*, 1983b; **52**, 551–554.

FRANCIS, L. J., PEARSON, P. R. and KAY, W. K. Neuroticism and religiosity: among English school children. *Journal of Social Psychology*, 1983c; **121**, 149–150.

FRANKS, C. M. Personality factors and the rate of conditioning. *British Journal of Psychology*, 1957; **48**, 119–126.

FRANSELLA, F. (ed.). *Personality theory: measurement and research*. London: Methuen, 1981.

GOLDSEN, R. K., ROSENBERG, M., WILLIAMS, R. M. Jr. and SUCHMAN, E. A. *What college students think*. Princeton, New Jersey: Van Nostrand, 1960.

HEINTZELMAN, M. E. and FEHR, L. A. Relationship between religious orthodoxy and three personality variables. *Psychological Reports*, 1976; **38**, 756–758.

HYDE, K. E. *Religious learning in adolescence*. London: Oliver & Boyd, 1965.

IWAWAKI, S., EYSENCK, S. B. G. and EYSENCK, H. J. Differences in personality between Japanese and English. *Journal of Social Psychology*, 1977; **102**, 27–33.

JAMES, W. *The varieties of religious experience*. New York: Longman, 1902.

JONES, J., EYSENCK, H. J., MARTIN, Z. and LEVEY, A. B. Personality and the topography of the conditioned eyelid response. *Personality and Individual Differences*, 1981; **2**, 61–83.

KAY, W. K. Psychoticism and attitude to religion. *Personality and Individual Differences*, 1981; **2**, 249–252.

KIRTON, N. J. Characteristics of high lie scores. *Psychological Reports*, 1977; **40**, 279–280.

LAZARUS, R. S. and OPTON, E. M. (eds). *Personality*. Harmondsworth: Penguin, 1967.

LIGON, E. M. *The psychology of Christian personality*. Schenectady, New York: Character Research Press, 1975.

McCLAIN, E. W. Personality differences between intrinsically religious and non-religious students – Factor Analytic Study. *Journal of Personality Assessment*, 1978; **42**, 159–166.

NIAS, D. K. B. Measurement and structure of children's attitudes. In G. D. WILSON (ed.), *The psychology of conservatism*, Chapter 6. London: Academic Press, 1973a.

NIAS, D. K. B. Attitudes to the Common Market: A case study in conservatism. In G. D. WILSON (ed.), *The psychology of conservatism*, Chapter 16. London: Academic Press, 1973b.

NIE, N. H., HULL, C. H., JENKINS, J. G., STEINBRENNER, K. and BENT, D. H. *Statistical package for the social sciences* (2nd edn). New York: McGraw-Hill, 1975.

O'DONOVAN, D. An historical review of the Lie Scale – with particular reference to Maudsley Personality Inventory. *Papers in Psychology*, 1969; **3**, 13–19.

PEARSON, P. R. How comparable are Eysenck's Personality Measures? *International Research and Communication System*, 1979; **7**, 258.

PEARSON, P. R. and SHEFFIELD, B. F. Is Personality related to social attitudes?: an attempt at replication. *Social Behaviour and Personality*, 1976; **4**, 109–111.

POHIER, J. M. Religious mentality and infantile mentality. In A. GODIN (ed.), *Child and adult before God*. Chicago: Loyola University Press, 1965, pp. 19–42.

POVALL, C. H. Some factors affecting pupils' attitudes to religious education. Unpublished M.Ed. dissertation. University of Manchester, 1971.

POWELL, G. E. Psychoticism and social deviancy in children. *Advances in Behaviour Research and Therapy*, 1977; **1**, 27–57.

POWELL, G. E. and STEWART, R. A. The relationship of age, sex and personality to social attitudes in children aged 8–15 years. *British Journal of Social and Clinical Psychology*, 1978; **17**(4), 307–317.

ROBERTS, F. J. Some psychological factors in religious conversion. *British Journal of Social and Clinical Psychology*, 1965; **13**, 157–182.

ROCKLIN, T. and REVELLE, W. The measurement of extraversion: a comparison of the Eysenck Personality Inventory and the Eysenck Personality Questionnaire. *British Journal of Social Psychology*, 1981; **20**, 279–284.

ROLDAN, A. *Personality types and Holiness*. New York: St Paul Publications, 1968.

SADLER, W. A. (ed.). *Personality and religion*. London: SCM Press, 1970.

SAKLOFSKE, D. H. and EYSENCK, S. B. G. Cross cultural comparison of personality: New Zealand children and English children. *Psychological Reports*, 1978; **42**, 1111–1116.

SEMEONOFF, B. (ed.). *Personality assessment*. Harmondsworth: Penguin, 1966.

SIEGMAN, A. W. A cross-cultural investigation of the relationship between religiosity, ethnic prejudice and authoritarianism. *Psychological Reports*, 1962; **11**, 419–427.

SIEGMAN, A. W. A cross-cultural investigation of the relationship between introversion, social attitudes and social behaviour. *British Journal of Social and Clinical Psychology*, 1963; **2**, 196–208.

STANLEY, G. Personality and attitude correlates of religious conversion. *Journal for the Scientific Study of Religion*, 1964; **4**, 60–63.

STURGEON, R. S. and HAMLEY, R. W. Religiosity and anxiety. *Journal of Social Psychology*, 1971; **108**, 137–138.

THURSTONE, L. L. and CHAVE, E. J. *The measurement of attitudes*. Chicago: Chicago University Press, 1929.

VINE, I. Facts and values in the psychology of religion. *The Bulletin of the British Psychological Society*, 1978; **31**, 414–417.

WILSON, G. D. and BRAZENDALE, A. H. Social attitude correlates of Eysenck's Personality Dimensions. *Social Behaviour and Personality*, 1973; **1**, 115–118.

WILSON, G. D. and PATTERSON, G. A new measure of conservatism. *British Journal of Social and Clinical Psychology*, 1968; **7**, 264–269.

WILSON, G. D. A dynamic theory of conservatism. In G. D. WILSON (ed.), *The psychology of conservatism*, Chapter 17. London: Academic Press, 1973.
WILSON, W. and MILLER, H. L. Fear, anxiety and religiousness. *Journal for the Scientific Study of Religion*, 1968; **7**, 111.

Acknowledgement

I gratefully acknowledge the help of Paul R. Pearson, William K. Kay and Marian Carter in the collection of the data and the analysis of the theory on which this chapter is based.

13

Brotherly love or self-concern?: behavioural consequences of religion[1]

C. DANIEL BATSON, PATRICIA A. SCHOENRADE
AND VIRGINIA PYCH

SOME version of the Golden Rule, "Do unto others as you would have others do unto you", is known to all major religions, East and West. The faithful are admonished to love neighbour as self. And who is one's neighbour?

Jesus replied, "A man was going down from Jerusalem to Jericho, and he fell among robbers, who stripped him and beat him, and departed, leaving him half-dead. Now by chance a priest was going down that road; and when he saw him he passed by on the other side. So likewise a Levite, when he came to the place and saw him, passed by on the other side. But a Samaritan, as he journeyed, came to where he was; and when he saw him, he had compassion, and went to him and bound up his wounds, pouring on oil and wine; then he set him on his own beast and brought him to an inn, and took care of him. And the next day he took out two denarii and gave them to the innkeeper, saying, 'Take care of him; and whatever more you spend, I will repay you when I come back.' Which of these three, do you think, proved neighbour to the man who fell among the robbers?" (Luke 10:30–36).

The answer is obvious.

There are even frequent admonitions to extend the scope of brotherly love beyond strangers in need, to enemies as well: "Love your enemies, do good to those who hate you, bless those who curse you. . . . If you love those who love you, what credit is that to you? For even sinners love those who love them . . ." (Luke 6:27–32). Similarly, the Buddhist is taught in the *Sutta Nipata*:

> Just as with her own life
> a mother shields from hurt
> her own, her only, child –
> let all-embracing thoughts
> for all that lives be thine.
>
> An all-embracing love
> for all the universe
> in all its heights and depths
> and breadth – unstinted love,
> unmarred by hate within,
> not rousing enmity.

[1] The notes to this chapter are on pages 207–8.

The universal brotherly love advocated in such teachings is often considered to be a defining feature of world religions, in contrast to tribal religions. In the words of Edwin Burtt (1957):

> A conviction of moral obligation toward all men, simply because they are men, is born. The wall that circumscribed sympathetic feeling and kept it within the tribe is broken down, and the sense of community is encouraged to open out beyond that limit; the idea takes root that we are essentially members of a society embracing all human beings on the same terms and in which therefore all men are brothers. This involves a radical and decisive transcendence of customary morality and of the attitudes which pervade it (p. 108).

Such an impulse toward universal brotherly love is clearly manifest in the lives of deeply religious individuals like Albert Schweitzer, Mahatma Gandhi, Martin Luther King, Jr, and Mother Theresa of Calcutta. It was also shown by the many unnamed Christians in Holland and Belgium who sheltered Jews from the Nazis during World War II, and by the freedom riders who risked their lives to further racial justice in the southern United States during the early 1960s.

But at the same time that we can think of cases in which religion has served as a driving force for universal love, acceptance, and tolerance, we can also think of cases in which it has produced self-righteousness, pious elitism, and cruel, inhuman behaviour. Religion provided much of the justification if not the instigating motivation for the Crusades, Inquisition, and witch hunts, for missionaries' insensitive oppression of native cultures, and even for slavery.

There appears to be a tragic, unintended corollary to knowing that one is among God's elect. If some are the "elect", "sheep", "chosen people", "family of God", then others are the "damned", "goats", "outcasts", "infidels". Far from encouraging universal brotherly love, such labels are likely to encourage rejection and intolerance. As Robert Brannon (1970) has noted, "Some critics of religion have gone so far as to charge that racial and ethnic intolerance is a natural extension of religious precepts" (p. 42). When one thinks back over the role of religion in Western civilization, this charge does not seem as extreme as Brannon implies. Instances in which religious institutions and doctrines have encouraged racial and ethnic intolerance, as well as other forms of callousness to the needs and rights of others, are at least as prevalent as instances in which religion has provoked loving compassion and tolerance.

The possibility that religion can encourage callous self-concern is, in fact, clearly recognized in the parable of the Good Samaritan. For, at the same time that the parable extols the compassion of the neighbourly Samaritan, encouraging the faithful to go and do likewise, it condemns the piety of the priest and the Levite, suggesting that it was their very religiousness that led them to pass by on the other side. One can imagine the unhelpful priest and Levite looking with disdainful pity upon the man who fell among thieves; clearly, he was not the sort of riffraff with whom upstanding, moral pillars of the religious community like themselves should get involved. One can also imagine this priest and Levite among those who, when called upon to account for their actions, would say, "Lord, when did we see thee hungry or thirsty or a stranger or naked or sick or in prison, and did not minister to thee?" (Matthew 25:44). They would willingly have helped the right person, but they never saw him in need; all they saw were the poor, lonely, downtrodden, and distressed.

As even this brief overview reveals, by selecting extreme examples one can justify quite contradictory views of the behavioural consequences of religion – the consequences are wonderfully positive; they are horribly negative. To arrive at a more balanced view, we would suggest moving beyond extreme examples to look at the attitudes and behaviour of more typical religious individuals. We would also suggest seeking more objective, empirical evidence. To organize our review of this evidence, we shall subdivide the question of the behavioural consequences of religion. First, we will ask whether religion discourages antisocial attitudes and behaviour, such as intolerance, racial prejudice, and discrimination. Then we will ask whether it encourages prosocial attitudes and behaviour, such as compassion and help for the lonely, sick, and downtrodden.

Effects of religion on antisocial attitudes and behaviour

There is much empirical research concerning the effect of religion on antisocial attitudes and behaviour; in fact, this is probably the most extensively researched topic in the psychology of religion. In evaluating this research it is important to keep three points in mind. First, a variety of measures of intolerance, prejudice, and bigotry have been used. These measures include ethnocentrism, racism, anti-Semitism, and what might be called general prejudice (i.e., prejudice against any of a number of other ethnic or national groups such as Chicanos, Puerto Ricans, and Orientals). Second, the research tends to focus upon the relationship between religion and prejudice among white, middle-class Christians in the United States. This is both because of the accessibility of such individuals and because prejudice within this group has been a major social issue during the past four decades. Third, the research is correlational, so, strictly speaking, it does not assess the influence of religion on prejudice but only the relationship between the two. This relationship could result from the influence of prejudice on religion as well as the influence of religion on prejudice, or from the influence of some third variable on both.

Batson and Ventis (1982) recently presented a review of more than 80 different findings based on over 60 different studies of the religion–prejudice relationship. In their review they included tables that report the number of findings suggesting one or another relationship. Therefore, rather than looking at individual studies, we will rely on these line scores to give a summary overview of the research on the religion–prejudice relationship.

Prejudice and amount of religious involvement

When persons are more religious, are they less prejudiced, more prejudiced, or is there no difference? Based on the research to date, an answer is all too clear. Contrary to what religions preach about universal brotherhood, the more religious an individual is, the *more* prejudiced he or she is likely to be. In early studies, for example, Allport and Kramer (1946) found that Protestant and Catholic students were more likely than those with no religious affiliation to be prejudiced against blacks. Adorno and his associates (1950) reported that both authoritarianism and ethnocentrism were higher among church attenders than among non-attenders. Kirkpatrick (1949) found that religious people had more punitive attitudes than non-religious people toward criminals, delinquents, prostitutes, drug addicts, and those in need of psychiatric treatment. Stouffer (1955) demonstrated that among a representative sample of American church members, those who had attended church within the past month were more intolerant of nonconformists, socialists, and communists than were those who had not attended.

More generally, Table 1 reproduces Batson and Ventis's line score summary of 44 different findings relevant to the relationship between four types of intolerance and prejudice (ethnocentrism, racial prejudice, anti-Semitism, and general prejudice) and various indices of amount of religious involvement. These findings were obtained from 36 different studies conducted between 1940 and 1975.

As you can see, the score in Table 1 is very lopsided. Overall, 34 of the 44 findings show a positive relationship between amount of prejudice and amount of interest in, involvement in, or adherence to religion. Eight findings show no clear relationship – most of these come from the northern United

TABLE 1   *Line score on research examining the relationship between prejudice and amount of religious involvement*

	Index of religious involvement										
	Membership or attendance			Religious attitudes			Orthodoxy or conservatism			Total		
Index of prejudice	+	?	−	+	?	−	+	?	−	+	?	−
Ethnocentrism	3	0	0	3	0	1	2	0	0	8	0	1
Racism	6	2	0	3	0	0	4	2	0	13	4	0
Anti-Semitism	4	1	0	0	1	0	4	1	0	8	3	0
Other measures	2	0	0	1	0	0	2	1	1	5	1	1
Total	15	3	0	7	1	1	12	4	1	34	8	2

Note: Column entries in the table indicate, first, the number of reports of a positive relationship between prejudice and amount of religious involvement; second, the number of reports of no relationship; and third, the number of reports of a negative relationship.

From Batson and Ventis (1982).

States. Only two show a negative relationship – one of these tested preadolescents (Nias, 1972) and the other tested preadolescents and adolescents (Strommen, 1967). The pattern of results is highly consistent regardless of how prejudice or religion is measured. We seem to be faced with a very clear, if unsettling conclusion: at least for white, middle-class Christians in the US *religion is not associated with increased love and acceptance but with increased intolerance, prejudice, and bigotry.*

But you may object to this conclusion, recognizing a basic flaw in these studies. All of the white, middle-class people who identify themselves as Christian are lumped together. Gordon Allport and others have argued that it is not enough to measure whether or even to what degree a person is involved in religion; it is also necessary to measure how the person is religious.

Prejudice and different ways of being religious: the extrinsic–intrinsic distinction

Allport (1950) made a distinction between immature and mature religion and later (1966), between extrinsic and intrinsic orientations to religion. Adorno *et al.* (1950) made a similar distinction between neutralized religion and taking religion seriously. Spilka distinguished between consensual and committed religion (Allen and Spilka, 1967). In general, each of these researchers suggests two different ways of being religious – one in which religion is used as an extrinsic means to reach self-serving ends and another in which it is taken seriously as an intrinsic end in itself. Moreover, each of these researchers insists that some such distinction is essential in understanding the relationship between religion and prejudice; they contend that although an extrinsic, means orientation may be associated with prejudice, an intrinsic, end orientation is not.

Are they right? To find out it is necessary, first, to have some measure of these two ways of being religious. The most popular measure has been to type individuals as extrinsic or intrinsic based on scores on the Allport and Ross (1967) Religious Orientation Scale (or some similar instrument). But another measure has also been used. Gorsuch and McFarland (1972) have noted that a fairly reliable measure of the distinction between extrinsic and intrinsic orientations can be obtained simply by asking people about the frequency of their involvement in religious activities. The extrinsically oriented should limit their involvement to a moderate level, since for them religion is subsumed under more important values and goals. The intrinsically oriented, on the other hand, should be highly involved, since religion is the master motive in their lives. Employing this logic, a number of researchers have compared three levels of involvement in religious activities as an index of religious orientation: no or low involvement (e.g., less than four times a year), moderate involvement (e.g., less than weekly), and high involvement (e.g., at least weekly). These three levels have been assumed to identify the non-religious, extrinsically religious, and intrinsically religious, respectively.

Equipped with these two ways of measuring the extrinsic versus intrinsic distinction, we can turn to empirical research on the relationship between each of these orientations and prejudice. Table 2 contains Batson and Ventis's (1982) line score summary of 40 different findings obtained across 31 studies conducted between 1945 and 1977. The first three columns summarize 14 findings from 12 studies that used some form of questionnaire or interview data to distinguish between the extrinsic and intrinsic orientations. The next three columns summarize 26 findings from 22 studies that broke the amount of religious activity either into low (L), moderate (M), and high (H), or into moderate (M) and high (H).

TABLE 2   *Line score on research examining the relationship between prejudice and extrinsic versus intrinsic religion*

	Index of religious orientation						Total		
	Extrinsic vs. intrinsic			Moderate vs. high					
Index of prejudice	E<I	E=I	E>I	M<H	M=H	M>H		Total	
Ethnocentrism	0	0	1	0	0	2	0	0	3
Racism	0	0	6	0	2	10	0	2	16
Anti-Semitism	0	0	3	0	0	6	0	0	9
Other measures	0	0	4	0	0	6	0	0	10
Total	0	0	14	0	2	24	0	2	38

Note: Column entries in the table indicate, first, the number of reports that E<I (extrinsic less prejudiced than intrinsic) or M<H (moderate attenders less prejudiced than high attenders); second, the number of reports of no difference; and third, the number of reports that E>I or M>H.

From Batson and Ventis (1982).

The pattern of results in Table 2 is extremely clear. As predicted by Allport and others, the way one is religious seems to make a great difference; the more intrinsically religious are consistently found to be less prejudiced than are the extrinsically religious. In all 14 findings based on questionnaire measures, those who were classified as intrinsic scored lower on prejudice, however measured, than those classified as extrinsic. And in 24 of the 26 findings based on involvement in religious activities, the highly involved scored lower on prejudice, however measured, than did those who were only moderately involved. The remaining two studies found no difference. But in one of these, attitudes toward political issues concerning minority rights were measured, not prejudice (Rokeach, 1969b). In the other, racial attitudes of white Catholics who had recently migrated from the North and were members of an integrated church in Florida were assessed (Liu, 1961). Self-selection as a migrant to the Deep South could easily account for the lack of difference in this study. Overall, it is difficult to conceive of obtaining stronger evidence that the way one is religious affects the religion–prejudice relationship.

It would seem that the earlier conclusion that there is a positive relationship between religious involvement and prejudice needs to be revised. Apparently, in the studies measuring amount of involvement, the relatively low prejudice of the intrinsically religious minority was masked by the high prejudice of the extrinsically religious majority. When these different ways of being religious are taken into account, the more appropriate conclusion would seem to be that *although the extrinsically religious may be high in intolerance and prejudice, the intrinsically religious are relatively low.*

This revised conclusion has been widely accepted among psychologists interested in religion. For example, Allport (1966) asserted that "Both prejudice and religion are subjective formulations within the personal life. One of these formulations (the extrinsic) is entirely compatible with prejudice; the other (the intrinsic) rules out enmity, contempt, and bigotry" (p. 456). Similarly, Gorsuch and Aleshire (1974), after an extensive review of research on the relationship between religion and prejudice, concluded that

> The extrinsically oriented person, i.e., one who supports religion for what he can get from it, tends to be prejudiced. On the other hand, a person who is intrinsically committed to his religious position, i.e., supports religion for the sake of religion itself, . . . tends to be less prejudiced (p. 284).

The question of the relationship between religion and antisocial attitudes seems to be neatly answered. Even though being more religious is associated with being more intolerant and prejudiced, this is true only among those who have emasculated the more profound claims of their religion and are using it as an extrinsic means to self-serving ends. Those who take their religion seriously, as an intrinsic end in itself, are not more intolerant. Although there is no clear evidence that the intrinsically religious are *less* prejudiced than are those not involved in religion at all (see Batson and Ventis, 1982), there is at least no clear evidence that they are more so. And they are clearly less prejudiced than the large segment of the population that is involved in religion in a nominal, extrinsic way.

More doubts: social desirability, intrinsic religion, and reduced prejudice

Perhaps because this revised conclusion has been so satisfying to researchers interested in religion, it has seldom been questioned. There has been much debate over the best way to measure extrinsic and intrinsic religion, but virtually none over the conclusion that intrinsic religion is associated with relatively low prejudice. We believe, however, that this conclusion must also be questioned. For, as pointed out by Batson and Ventis (1982), a respondent's wish to present him or herself in a socially desirable light may account for the observed relationship between intrinsic religion and relatively low prejudice.

There is preliminary evidence that individuals who report being highly active and devout in their religion (i.e. intrinsic) give socially desirable responses when asked about their behaviour in other areas of life (Crandall and Gozali, 1969). There is also evidence that most individuals adjust their responses in a socially desirable direction when answering questions about prejudice (see Batson, 1976; Karlins, Coffman and Walters, 1969; Sigall and Page, 1971; Silverman, 1974).

Combining these observations, it is easy to see how a concern to look good might account for the association between intrinsic religion and low prejudice. People especially concerned about appearing socially desirable would be more likely to be classified as intrinsic and unprejudiced; people less concerned about social desirability would be more likely to be classified as extrinsic and more prejudiced. If this occurred, then it would create exactly the pattern of results observed in Table 2, even if there were no association between intrinsic religion and low prejudice, except as each is affected by social desirability.

Because of the likelihood that respondents will give socially desirable responses when asked to report their prejudice, a more appropriate measure of prejudice is to observe their behaviour. Regrettably, in studies of the religion–prejudice relationship this has rarely been done. Thirty of the 31 studies summarized in Table 2 employed self-report questionnaire or interview measures of prejudice, making social desirability a plausible alternative explanation of the results. The one study that employed a behavioural measure was conducted by Robert Brannon (1970). Unfortunately, there is an important confound in Brannon's study that clouds interpretation of the results. What appeared as greater racial tolerance on the part of his intrinsically religious subjects may, in fact, have been nothing more than greater loyalty to their home church.

Given this confound, Brannon's study also fails to provide clear evidence that intrinsic religion is associated with greater racial tolerance. And since his was the only study among those summarized in Table 2 that controlled for social desirability and so could provide clear evidence, we are left with none. The mountain of evidence for the highly popular, revised conclusion that intrinsic religion is associated with low prejudice has completely melted away.

The relationship between religious orientation and prejudice when social desirability is controlled

Where does this leave us? Are we back to the initial conclusion that religion and prejudice are positively correlated? No, we are not. We are two important steps beyond that point. First, we still have the hypothesis proposed by Allport, Adorno and Spilka that the way one is religious influences the religion–prejudice relationship. To suggest, as we have, that none of the mass of research summarized in Table 2 provides clear evidence for this hypothesis is not to suggest that there is clear evidence against it. The hypothesis may still be true; it has not yet been adequately tested. Second, we know at least one obstacle that must be overcome if an adequate test is to be made; when assessing the religion–prejudice relationship, we must take account of the respondents' tendency to give socially desirable responses. Having taken these two steps, the next step is obvious. We need additional data assessing the relationship between prejudice and religious orientation, and in collecting these data we need to control for social desirability.

Batson, Naifeh, and Pate (1978) reported a study designed to provide such data, not only for the extrinsic, means orientation and the intrinsic, end orientation but for a third orientation to religion as well. This third orientation, called "religion as quest", involves an open-ended, questioning, self-critical approach to religion. The quest orientation has been found in factor-analytic studies to be independent of both the extrinsic, means orientation and the intrinsic, end orientation. (See Batson, 1976, and Batson and Ventis, 1982, for a discussion of the three-dimensional model of religious orientations as a means, end, and quest.) The study of Batson, Naifeh and Pate (1978) was the first to consider the relationship between the quest orientation and prejudice.

In that study, subjects (51 undergraduates interested in religion) completed not only the racial prejudice questionnaire used by Allport and Ross (1967), but also the Marlowe–Crowne Social Desirability scale (Crowne and Marlowe, 1964). In addition, a behavioural measure of prejudice was taken.

To obtain the behavioural measure undergraduates were put in a situation in which their expressed readiness to interact with a black individual would have clear behavioural consequences. This was done by telling them that later in the study they would be interviewed in depth about their religious views. They were then given an opportunity to indicate which of the available interviewers they would like to have interview them. As a basis for their judgement they were provided information sheets describing each interviewer. The sheets differed in particulars, but each described a well-rounded college graduate, interested in religion, who had grown up in a middle-class Protestant Church. Clipped to each information sheet was a photograph. The photographs revealed that one interviewer was white, the other black.

After reading the information sheets, subjects were asked to indicate how much they would like each interviewer to interview them. A difference score was created by subtracting the rating of the black interviewer from the rating of the white. Relative preference for the white over the black interviewer on this difference score reflected a preference to interact with one person rather than another solely on the basis of race, providing an index of racial prejudice. (Information sheets and photographs were counterbalanced, and photographs of two different individuals of each race were used to insure that effects were not simply the result of idiosyncratic characteristics of particular individuals.)

Previous research by Silverman (1974) had indicated that in such a situation a prejudiced person's wish to avoid contact with a minority-group member would temper his or her wish to present socially desirable responses. As a result, it would be possible to obtain more honest responses than on the typical prejudice questionnaire, which carried no implications for future behaviour.

Results of the study by Batson *et al.* (1978) revealed, first, that scores on the means orientation correlated positively with scores on the prejudice questionnaire, while scores on both the end and quest orientations correlated negatively with prejudice. Recapitulating the findings in the first part of Table 2, the end orientation correlated significantly more negatively with scores on the prejudice questionnaire than did measures of the means orientation ($p < 0.02$). The quest orientation also correlated significantly more negatively than did the means orientation ($p < 0.02$).

Second, the end orientation correlated positively with scores on the Social Desirability scale ($p < 0.01$), while the means and quest orientations did not. This pattern further documented the need to control social desirability when assessing the relationship between an end orientation to religion and racial prejudice.

The importance of social desirability in this relationship was further suggested by results on the behavioural measure of prejudice. Not only did the means orientation correlate positively with this measure of prejudice, the end orientation did too. The end orientation had showed a negative correlation with prejudice measured by questionnaire. But when the effect of social desirability was controlled by employing a behavioural measure of prejudice, the relationship became positive. This shift in the relationship was highly significant ($p < 0.005$). In contrast, the quest orientation correlated negatively with prejudice even when social desirability was controlled. This orientation correlated more negatively with the behavioural measure than either the means ($p < 0.10$) or end ($p < 0.03$) orientations.

Overall, these results seem quite consistent with the possibility that the previously reported association between an intrinsic, end orientation to religion and reduced racial prejudice could be an artifact of social desirability. Rather than indicating that intrinsic religion rules out enmity, contempt, and bigotry, as Allport claimed, these results suggest that intrinsic religion relates to a desire to present oneself as righteous in society's eyes – indeed, as more righteous than one actually is. In contrast, the quest orientation related to decreased prejudice not only on self-reports, but also at a behavioural level.

Based on these results, it may seem that we should adopt a re-revised conclusion concerning the religion–prejudice relationship: *a quest orientation to religion is related to low prejudice, while an intrinsic, end orientation is related instead only to the appearance of low prejudice.* Batson and Ventis

(1982) have, in fact, suggested just such a re-revised conclusion. At the same time, they have cautioned that the results of one study cannot be considered sufficient evidence for it. But if we turn our attention from the antisocial to the prosocial effects of religion, we can find more evidence.

Effect of religion on prosocial attitudes and behaviour

Does religion produce increased concern for others in need? We noted earlier that all major religions, East and West, preach love and compassion. But as with antisocial attitudes and behaviour, there often seems to be little relationship between the prosocial values a religion seeks to instill and the behaviour of followers of that religion. Once again, we must turn to empirical evidence if we are to learn how being religious affects people's actual response to the needs of others.

When we turn to the empirical evidence concerning prosocial effects, we find there is relatively little of it, far less than for antisocial effects.[2] Yet, in spite of the lack of evidence, it is commonly assumed that religion promotes prosocial behaviour. For example, in his presidential address to the American Psychological Association, Donald Campbell (1975) suggested that religion is important because it inculcates more stringent moral standards, leading individuals to think not only of their own needs but also of the needs of others. And Campbell was not the first American president to make such an argument. In his Farewell Address in 1797, George Washington declared:

> Religion and morality are indispensable supports. ... These great pillars of human happiness [are the] firmest props of the duties of men and citizens. ... A volume could not trace all their connections with private and public felicity. ... And let us with caution indulge the supposition that morality can be maintained without religion.

There are two steps in the argument proposed by Campbell and by Washington: (a) religion inculcates more stringent moral standards, and (b) as a result, it leads people to act with more concern for others. Such an argument is both plausible and popular, but is it sound? To find an answer, we need to examine the empirical evidence for each step.

Moral standards, prosocial behaviour, and amount of religious involvement

The eight studies summarized in Table 3 suggest that the first step in this argument is sound; being more religious does seem to lead a person to adhere to more stringent moral standards. Those who are more involved in religion more strongly espouse values that involve curbing personal desire and gain in order to benefit others and society at large.[3] But do the faithful actually

TABLE 3 *Summary of research examining the relationship between moral standards and amount of religious involvement*

Study	Sample population	Location	Measure of religion	Measure of moral standards	Relationship reported
Gorer (1955)	5000 (approx.) adults, nationwide sample	England	Frequency of church attendance and prayer	Judgement of various actions as immoral	Respondents who were more religious judged more actions wrong and judged them more wrong
Goldsen *et al.* (1960)	1600 (approx.) undergraduates	Cornell University	Religiousness scale, measuring belief in God and importance of religion	Self-report of frequency of drinking, cutting classes, and premarital sex	Respondents who were more religious reported less drinking, less cutting of classes, and less acceptance of premarital sex
Boehm (1962)	110 children (ages 6–9) attending Catholic schools; 112 attending state schools	Brooklyn, NY: Natick. Mass.	Attendance at Catholic or state school	Test of use of intent rather than result as basis for moral evaluation	More children in Catholic school distinguished between intent and result, and they did so younger
Middleton and Putney (1962)	554 undergraduates in social science classes	Florida State University; San José State College	Self-report of belief in God, frequency of church attendance, and importance of religion	Self-report of feeling of violation of own ethical standards if engaged in personal "sins" (e.g. gambling, smoking, drinking, sex) and social "sins" (e.g. stealing, lying, cheating)	For all three measures of religion, more religious were much more likely to view personal sins as violation of their standards and were less likely to report engaging in them; no reliable differences for social sins

Klinger, Albaum and Hetherington (1964)	72 introductory psychology students	University of Wisconsin	Religious vs. economic or political as highest value on Allport, Vernon, and Lindzey Survey of Values	Degree of condemnation of hypothetical parent who intentionally did not report some income in order to use the extra money to send child to college	Respondents whose highest value was religious most opposed the parent's behaviour, although they were not significantly more opposed than those whose highest value was economic
Wright and Cox (1967)	2276 sixth form (i.e. secondary school students, ages 16–18)	England	Self-report of orthodoxy of belief and frequency of church attendance	Rating of wrongness of various behaviours (e.g. gambling, drunkenness, smoking, lying, stealing, premarital sex)	Respondents who were more religious adopted stricter moral stance on most behaviours, especially on personal as opposed to social "sins"
Berkowitz and Lutterman (1968)	766 adults	Wisconsin	Church membership; contribution to religious organizations	Score on Berkowitz's Social Responsibility Scale	Positive correlation for both measures of religious involvement
Haan, Smith and Block (1968)	Over 900 college students and Peace Corps volunteers	San Francisco Bay area	Religious affiliation; frequency of church attendance	Level of moral reasoning using Kohlberg's stages	Protestant and Catholic respondents were more likely to make moral judgements by appeal to social convention; agnostic, atheist, or areligious respondents were more likely to appeal to internalized principles; more frequent church attendance was associated with more reliance on social convention

From Batson and Ventis (1982).

practise what they preach; do they show more loving concern for those in need at a behavioural level? The 13 findings from 12 studies presented in Table 4 provide data relevant to this question. In each study, some measure of religious involvement was associated with some measure of compassionate helping of those in need. Table 4 is divided into two sections. In the first are eight findings from seven studies that employed either respondents' self-reports or ratings of the respondents by someone else to provide a measure of helping. In the second section are five studies that employed behavioural measures of helping.

We have separated these two types of studies, because we fear that studies of the first type might be contaminated by social desirability. Paralleling the effect of social desirability on self-reports of reduced prejudice, it seems likely that social desirability could affect self-reports of increased helpfulness, since helpfulness is a desirable trait in our society. Even ratings of a person's helpfulness that are made by someone else appear subject to contamination by social desirability, for Dennis Krebs (1970) has noted that people who are rated as more likeable and sociable tend also to be rated as more helpful, even when they are not. All the studies in the second section of Table 4 used relatively unobtrusive behavioural measures of helping, so they should be less subject to contamination by social desirability.

When we look at the results of the studies summarized in Table 4, we find a dramatic difference between those in the first and second sections. The eight findings from the studies that used self-report or rating measures suggest that there is a positive, if rather weak, correlation between involvement in religion and helpfulness. But results of the studies in the second section, the studies that control for social desirability by using behavioural measures, reveal a very different pattern. Not one of the five studies provides any evidence that the more religious are more helpful.

It seems that the argument that religion undergirds prosocial behaviour stumbles and falls on the second step. Although the highly religious have more stringent moral standards, there is no evidence that they are any more likely than the less religious to help someone in need. The more religious may *see* themselves as more helpful and caring; they may even be seen this way by others. But when it comes to action, there is no evidence that they are more helpful.

Earlier we found that increased religious involvement was associated with more rather than less prejudice and discrimination; now we find that it is associated with no real increase in helpfulness. Of course, advocates of religion might point out that the evidence concerning prosocial effects is not as discouraging as the evidence concerning antisocial effects; it does not show that religious involvement makes a person *less* helpful. But to rejoice at this lack of evidence for a clear detrimental effect would seem to be grasping at straws. There is, however, a more sound reason for not being discouraged by the evidence that involvement in religion does not increase helpfulness.

TABLE 4 *Summary of research examining the relationship between helping and amount of religious involvement*

Study	Sample population	Location	Measure of religion	Measure of helping	Relationship reported
1. Studies using self-report ratings by self, peer, or researcher to measure helping					
Hartshorne and May (1929)	Children	US	Frequency of church attendance	Various tests of service	Very slight tendency for frequent church attenders to score higher on service
Clark and Warner (1955)	72 well-known community members	Village in upper New York state	Church attendance	Average rating of person's kindness and honesty by 14 community members	Positive correlations for both kindness ($r=0.41$) and honesty ($r=0.64$)
Friedrichs (1960)	280 fraternity members	Columbia University, New York	Frequency of church attendance; belief in God	Rating of altruism by self and by others in fraternity; self-report of helpfulness in response to hypothetical need situations	Both church attendance and belief in God showed low positive correlations with self-report of helpfulness, r's=0.20 and 0.24, $p<0.01$, but neither were related to either self or other ratings of altruism
Cline and Richards (1965)	155 adults, male and female (72% Mormons)	Salt Lake City, Utah	Belief in God, religious activity, and importance of religion based on "depth" interview; self-report of religious involvement on questionnaire	Rating by "depth" interviewer as showing "love and compassion" for others and "being a Good Samaritan"	For males and females, belief in God was not related to either helpfulness rating; religious activity, importance of religion, and self-reported involvement were all positively related (r's ranging from 0.21 to 0.50)
Rokeach (1969a)	Nationwide survey of 1406 adults	US	Religious affiliation; church attendance	Ranking "helpful" as an important personal value	No significant relation with religious affiliation, but significant positive relation with church attendance

TABLE 4—*continued*

Study	Sample population	Location	Measure of religion	Measure of helping	Relationship reported
Rokeach (1969a)	298 college students	Michigan	Church attendance; importance of religion	Ranking "helpful" as important personal value	Significant positive relation with both church attendance and importance of religion
Gallup Poll (Sept. 1973; see Langford and Langford, 1974)	Nationwide survey of adults	US	Attending church during previous seven days	Self-report of "taking concrete action on behalf of others"	59% of those who had attended said that they "almost always" did; only 31% of non-attenders claimed this
Nelson and Dynes (1976)	482 male adults returning a mail questionnaire	Medium-sized city in south-western US	Self-report of regular prayer, church attendance, and regular involvement in religion	Self-report of helping through social service agencies	Significant but low positive correlations (most r's between 0.10 and 0.20); when correlations adjusted for helping *through* church as well as for income and age, they drop to close to zero

2. Studies using a behavioural measure of helping

Study	Sample population	Location	Measure of religion	Measure of helping	Relationship reported
Forbes, TeVault, and Gromoll (1971)	People in church doorway or parking lot after Sunday morning service	Medium-sized city in mid-western US	Type of church; conservative versus liberal Protestant and Catholic	Mailing an addressed, unstamped "lost letter" dropped in church doorway or parking lot	No differences in rate of return (approximately 40% for each location), but more letters dropped outside conservative churches were returned unstamped with postage due

Smith, Wheeler and Diener (1975)	402 introductory psychology students	University of Washington, Seattle	Self-report on questionnaire as evangelical, other religious, non-religious, or atheist	Volunteering five hours to work with a profoundly retarded child	No reliable differences in rates of volunteering for different groups (overall, 16% volunteered)
Annis (1975)	68 introductory psychology students	Western Carolina University	Religious value score on Allport, Vernon, and Lindzey scale	Attempting to help after hearing a ladder fall, possibly injuring a young woman	No reliable difference between helpers and non-helpers in religious value score
Annis (1976)	71 introductory psychology students	University of Mississippi	Self-report of orthodoxy, frequency of prayer, and frequency of church attendance; religious value score on Allport, Vernon, and Lindzey scale	Attempting to help after hearing a ladder fall, possibly injuring a young woman	No reliable differences in rate of helping as a result of any of the measures of religious involvement (overall, 48% attempted to help)
McKenna (1976)	Adults in clergy and non-clergy homes who answered telephone	Selected urban and rural settings in US	Clergy versus non-clergy home	Calling garage for stranded female motorist who mistakenly called the home with her last dime	No reliable difference in rate of calling the garage from clergy and non-clergy homes; in the rural setting both rates were very high, so differences may have been obscured

From Batson and Ventis (1982).

Prosocial behaviour and different ways of being religious

When considering the effect of religion on antisocial attitudes and behaviour, we found that the initial conclusion of a positive relationship between the amount of religious involvement and prejudice could not be accepted because it failed to take account of different ways of being religious. That experience should make us cautious about hasty acceptance of the conclusion that religious involvement is not associated with more prosocial behaviour. Any valid conclusion probably needs to take account of the ways different orientations to religion might affect prosocial behaviour. Two such conclusions have been proposed.

First, paralleling his revised conclusion about the antisocial effects of different ways of being religious, Gordon Allport reasoned that although the extrinsic orientation might lead a person to be self-centred, only looking out for "Number One", the intrinsic orientation should lead a person to transcend self-centredness and display true compassion and brotherly love (Allport, 1966). Second, paralleling their re-revised conclusion about antisocial effects, Batson and Ventis (1982) have suggested a very different possibility, that the quest orientation relates to increased compassion, while the intrinsic, end orientation relates only to the *appearance* of compassion. Which, if either, of these views is correct?

A study by Tate and Miller (1971) provided some evidence consistent with both views. They found that intrinsically religious individuals (those who scored above the mean on the Intrinsic scale and below the mean on the Extrinsic scale) considered the values *helpful*, *loving*, and *responsible* to be of greater personal importance than did extrinsically religious individuals (who scored above the mean on the Extrinsic scale and below the mean on the Intrinsic scale). For the values *helpful* and *loving* the difference in ranking by the two groups was statistically reliable; for *responsible* it was not.

So intrinsically religious individuals value helpfulness. But do they practise what they preach? That is, do their more prosocial values lead them to show greater compassion for those in need? Allport's view is that they do; Batson and Ventis's view is that they do not, that only the quest orientation is associated with greater compassion at a behavioural level. There are three studies in the literature that have considered the relationship between different ways of being religious and behavioural response to the needs of others, and the results of these studies are more consistent with Batson and Ventis's view than with Allport's.[4]

First, in a quasi-experimental study based on the parable of the Good Samaritan and using seminary students as subjects, Darley and Batson (1973) found that the end orientation to religion correlated positively with a persistent form of helping, while the quest orientation correlated positively with more tentative forms ($p < 0.05$). When the more devout, end-oriented seminarians encountered a young man in need, it seemed to trigger a preprogrammed response (e.g. taking him for coffee, to the infirmary, or praying for his welfare), and this response was little modified by his statements about his needs. In contrast, the tentative helping associated with higher scores on the quest orientation seemed more attuned to the young man's statement that he was all right and, ultimately, wished to be left alone. It seemed less a response to an external need to be helpful and more to the young man's expressed needs.

Second, Batson (1976) reported an experiment in which male under-graduates were asked to adopt the hypothetical role of a lay referral counsellor. They heard excerpts from tape-recorded referral interviews for six male clients, each client clearly expressing that he felt his social situation was the source of his problem. After hearing each client discuss his problem, the undergraduates were asked to fill out a referral form on which they indicated whether they thought the client's problem lay with the client as a person or with his social situation. The quest orientation correlated significantly more positively ($p < 0.05$) with a situational perception of clients' problems – the perception that the clients themselves expressed – than did the end orientation.

Finally, Batson and Gray (1981) reported an experiment in which female undergraduates were confronted with a lonely young woman, Janet, who said either that she did or did not want help. Batson and Gray reasoned that attempts to help Janet when she said that she did not want it would indicate helping that was a response to an internal need to be helpful rather than to Janet's expressed need.

Results of this study revealed, first, that scores on the end orientation were positively correlated with *self-reports* of greater helpfulness ($p < 0.05$) and concern ($p < 0.01$), suggesting a desire to be helpful or at least to be seen as helpful. Scores on the quest orientation did not correlate reliably with these self-reports.

But on helping *behaviour*, a very different pattern appeared. Scores on the end orientation showed a low positive correlation with helping ($p < 0.04$), suggesting that this orientation did produce some motivation to help. Yet the correlation between this orientation and helping was just as strong when Janet said that she did not want help as when she said that she did. This pattern of correlations suggested that the underlying motivation was to respond to one's own need to be helpful, rather than to Janet's expressed needs. In contrast, scores on the quest orientation correlated positively with helping when Janet said that she wanted help ($p < 0.05$) and negatively when she said that she did not ($p < 0.09$). The difference between these correlations was highly significant ($p < 0.01$), suggesting motivation to respond to Janet's expressed needs.

Putting the pieces together into a general conclusion

The results of these three studies seem quite consistent with Batson and Ventis's (1982) view that the quest orientation related to increased compassion, while the intrinsic, end orientation relates only to the appearance of compassion. And when the results of these three studies are considered along with the results reported by Batson, Naifeh and Pate (1978) on the relationship between religious orientation and prejudice, a general pattern begins to emerge. The intrinsic, end orientation to religion seems to be associated with a desire to present oneself as less antisocial and more prosocial, but it is not associated with less antisocial or more prosocial action. This orientation seems to be associated with increased concern to be *seen* as concerned, which would seem to be nothing more than a socialized form of self-concern. In contrast, the quest orientation seems to be associated with action that reflects a genuine tolerance and compassion for others, not just a concern to appear concerned.

Faced with this general pattern of results, we believe that the time has come to adopt, at least tentatively, a general and further revised conclusion. *A quest orientation to religion is related to reduced intolerance and increased sensitivity to the needs of others, while an intrinsic, end orientation is related instead only to the appearance of these social benefits.* This conclusion is very much at odds with the popular revised conclusion – that a devout, intrinsic orientation to religion reduces antisocial and increases prosocial attitudes and behaviour. But we believe that the empirical evidence does not support the popular view. Instead, we believe that it supports our further revised conclusion.

To underscore the difference between the conclusion that we are proposing and the currently popular one with a somewhat fanciful prospect, the popular conclusion seems to assume that the Good Samaritan was intrinsically religious. In the light of our review of the available evidence, however, we are inclined to wonder whether, had someone been nearby to give them questionnaires, it might have been the priest and the Levite – who for all their appearance of goodness did nothing – who would have scored high on the intrinsic, end orientation to religion. In contrast, the Samaritan might have scored high on the quest orientation.

A qualification: institutional versus individual responses to others' needs

An intrinsic, end orientation to religion is closely associated with high involvement in institutional religion (see Batson and Ventis, 1982; Gorsuch and McFarland, 1972). Does our re-revised conclusion imply, then, that active involvement in institutional religion does not lead to greater tolerance of and compassion for the poor, sick, and downtrodden? Not necessarily, because our conclusion and the related research apply only to the way a person responds as an individual. Although an individual response to others in need is clearly covered by religious teachings like the parable of the Good Samaritan, needs in our society are often dealt with at an institutional rather than individual level. And religious institutions have been among the most likely to respond, whether with Thanksgiving and Christmas baskets for the poor, visits to the sick and elderly, or financial contributions to one or another defence or relief fund.

Given that religious institutions are an important channel for meeting needs in our society, we seem to be faced with an interesting dilemma. The sensitivity to the expressed needs of others shown by those scoring higher on the quest orientation would seem to reflect a desirable form of individual response. But, if anything, those scoring higher on this orientation are less likely to be involved in institutional religion (Batson and Ventis, 1982). Thus, they are less likely to participate in this important channel for institutional response to others' needs.

In contrast, the relative insensitivity to the wishes of individuals in apparent need shown by those scoring higher on the end orientation would seem to reflect a less desirable form of individual response. But those scoring higher on this orientation are more likely to be involved in religious institutions (Gorsuch and McFarland, 1972) and in helping others through these institutions (Nelson and Dynes, 1976). Paralleling the apparent insensitivity of the more end-oriented individuals to Janet in the Batson and Gray (1981) study, the help that religious institutions provide may not always be sensitive to the wishes of the needy. Yet it is doubtful whether those in need, or society at large, would be better off without it.

Still, to recognize that the needy benefit from the institutional response of the intrinsically religious does not resolve the dilemma; indeed, it sharpens it. For we may take our fanciful reflection on the parable of the Good Samaritan a step further and ask, "even if we were to learn that the priest and Levite passed by on the other side because they were taking contributions from the Temple in Jerusalem to an orphanage down the road, would we excuse their insensitivity to the needs of the man who fell among thieves?"

References

ADORNO, T. W., FRENKEL-BRUNSWIK, E., LEVINSON, D. J. and SANFORD, R. N. *The authoritarian personality*. New York: Norton, 1950.
ALLEN, R. D. and SPILKA, B. Committed and consensual religion: a specification of religion–prejudice relationships. *Journal for the Scientific Study of Religion*, 1967; **6**, 191–206.
ALLPORT, G. W. *The individual and his religion*. New York: Macmillan, 1950.
ALLPORT, G. W. Religious context of prejudice. *Journal for the Scientific Study of Religion*, 1966; **5**, 447–457.
ALLPORT, G. W. and KRAMER, B. M. Some roots of prejudice. *Journal of Psychology*, 1946; **22**, 9–30.
ALLPORT, G. W. and ROSS, J. M. Personal religious orientation and prejudice. *Journal of Personality and Social Psychology*, 1967; **5**, 432–443.
ALLPORT, G. W., VERNON, P. E. and LINDZEY, G. *A study of values*. Boston: Houghton Mifflin, 1960.
ANNIS, L. V. Study of values as a predictor of helping behavior. *Psychological Reports*, 1975; **37**, 717–718.
ANNIS, L. V. Emergency helping and religious behavior. *Psychological Reports*, 1976; **39**, 151–158.

BATSON, C. D. Religion as prosocial: Agent or double agent? *Journal for the Scientific Study of Religion*, 1976; **15**, 29–45.

BATSON, C. D. and GRAY, R. A. Religious orientation and helping behaviour: Responding to one's own or to the victim's needs? *Journal of Personality and Social Psychology*, 1981; **40**, 511–520.

BATSON, C. D., NAIFEH, S. J. and PATE, S. Social desirability, religious orientation, and racial prejudice. *Journal for the Scientific Study of Religion*, 1978; **17**, 31–41.

BATSON, C. D. and VENTIS, W. L. *The religious experience: A social-psychological perspective.* New York: Oxford University Press, 1982.

BERKOWITZ, L. and LUTTERMAN, K. G. The traditional socially responsible personality. *Public Opinion Quarterly*, 1968; **32**, 169–185.

BOEHM, L. The development of conscience: A comparison of students in Catholic parochial schools and in public schools. *Child Development*, 1962; **33**, 591–602.

BRANNON, R. C. L. Gimme that old-time racism. *Psychology Today*, 1970; **3**, 42–44.

BURTT, E. A. *Man seeks the divine: A study in the history and comparison of religions.* New York: Harper, 1957.

CAMPBELL, D. T. On the conflicts between biological and social evolution and between psychology and moral tradition. *American Psychologist*, 1975; **30**, 1103–1126.

CLARK, W. H. and WARNER, C. M. The relation of church attendance to honesty and kindness in a small community. *Religious Education*, 1955; **50**, 340–342.

CLINE, V. B. and RICHARDS, J. M. A factor-analytic study of religious belief and behavior. *Journal of Personality and Social Psychology*, 1965; **1**, 569–578.

CRANDALL, V. C. and GOZALI, J. The social desirability responses of children of four religious-cultural groups. *Child Development*, 1969; **40**, 751–762.

CROWNE, D. and MARLOWE, D. *The approval motive.* New York: Wiley, 1964.

DARLEY, J. and BATSON, C. D. From Jerusalem to Jericho: a study of situational and dispositional variables in helping behaviour. *Journal of Personality and Social Psychology*, 1973; **27**, 100–108.

FORBES, G. B., TEVAULT, R. K. and GROMOLL, H. F. Willingness to help strangers as a function of liberal, conservative or Catholic church membership: a field study with the lost-letter technique. *Psychological Reports*, 1971; **28**, 947–949.

FRIEDRICHS, R. W. Alter versus ego: an explanatory assessment of altruism. *American Sociological Review*, 1960; **25**, 496–508.

GALLUP, G. H. *The Gallup poll: Public opinion 1972–1977.* Wilmington, Del.: Scholarly Resources, 1978.

GOLDSEN, R. K., ROSENBERG, M., WILLIAMS, R. M. Jr. and SUCHMAN, E. A. *What college students think.* New York: Van Nostrand, 1960.

GORER, G. *Exploring English character.* London: Cresset, 1955.

GORSUCH, R. L. and ALESHIRE, D. Christian faith and ethnic prejudice: A review and interpretation of research. *Journal for the Scientific Study of Religion*, 1974; **13**, 281–307.

GORSUCH, R. L. and MCFARLAND, S. Single- vs. multiple-item scales for measuring religious values. *Journal for the Scientific Study of Religion*, 1972; **11**, 53–65.

HAAN, N., SMITH, B. and BLOCK, J. Moral reasoning of young adults. *Journal of Personality and Social Psychology*, 1968; **10**, 183–201.

HARTSHORNE, H. and MAY, M. A. *Studies in service and self-control.* New York: Macmillan, 1929.

KARLINS, M., COFFMAN, T. L. and WALTERS, S. G. On the fading of social stereotypes: Studies in three generations of college students. *Journal of Personality and Social Psychology*, 1969; **13**, 1–16.

KIRKPATRICK, C. Religion and humanitarianism: a study of institutional implications. *Psychological Monographs*, 1949; **63**, No. 304.

KLINGER, E., ALBAUM, A. and HETHERINGTON, M. Factors influencing the severity of moral judgments. *Journal of Social Psychology*, 1964; **63**, 319–326.

KOHLBERG, L. Moral stages and moralization: The cognitive-developmental approach. In T. LICKONA (ed.), *Moral development and behavior: theory, research, and social issues.* New York: Holt, Rinehart & Winston, 1976.

KREBS, D. L. Altruism: an examination of the concept and a review of the literature. *Psychological Bulletin*, 1970; **73**, 258–302.

LANGFORD, B. J. and LANGFORD, C. C. Church attendance and self-perceived altruism. *Journal for the Scientific Study of Religion*, 1974; **13**, 221–222.

LIU, W. T. The community reference system, religiosity, and race attitudes. *Social Forces*, 1961; **39**, 324–328.

MCKENNA, R. Good Samaritans in rural and urban settings: A non-reactive comparison of helping behavior of clergy and control subjects. *Representative Research in Social Psychology*, 1976; **7**, 58–65.

MIDDLETON, R. and PUTNEY, S. Religion, normative standards, and behavior. *Sociometry*, 1962; **25**, 141–152.

NELSON, L. D. and DYNES, R. The impact of devotionalism and attendance on ordinary and emergency helping behavior. *Journal for the Scientific Study of Religion*, 1976; **15**, 47–59.

NIAS, D. K. B. The structuring of social attitudes in children. *Child Development*, 1972; **43**, 211–219.

ROKEACH, M. Value systems and religion. *Review of Religious Research*, 1969a; **11**, 2–23.

ROKEACH, M. Religious values and social compassion. *Review of Religious Research*, 1969b; **11**, 24–38.

SIGALL, H. and PAGE, R. Current stereotypes: a little fading, a little faking. *Journal of Personality and Social Psychology*, 1971; **18**, 247–255.

SILVERMAN, B. I. Consequences, racial discrimination, and the principle of belief congruence. *Journal of Personality and Social Psychology*, 1974; **29**, 497–508.

SMITH, R., WHEELER, G. and DIENER, E. Faith without works: Jesus people, resistance to temptation, and altruism. *Journal of Applied Social Psychology*, 1975; **5**, 320–330.

STOUFFER, S. A. *Communism, conformity, and civil liberties*. New York: Doubleday, 1955.

STROMMEN, M. P. Religious education and the problem of prejudice. *Religious Education*, 1967; **62**, 52–59.

TATE, E. D. and MILLER, G. R. Differences in value systems of persons with varying religious orientations. *Journal for the Scientific Study of Religion*, 1971; **10**, 357–365.

WRIGHT, D. and COX, E. A study of the relationship between moral judgment and religious belief in a sample of English adolescents. *Journal of Social Psychology*, 1967; **72**, 135–144.

Notes

1. This chapter is, in large measure, a condensation and revision of Chapter 8 of Batson and Ventis (1982).
2. There would seem to be two historical reasons for this. First, early psychologists devoted most of their efforts to trying to understand and overcome problems in living – neurosis, psychosis, learning dysfunctions, and antisocial behaviour. This focus on problems and on attempts to alleviate them was, perhaps natural. When something does not work well it attracts our attention; when it works better than expected we are not likely to notice. Only in the last few decades have psychologists paid much attention to more positive aspects of human behaviour, such as going out of one's way to help someone in need.

   A second reason for the lack of attention to possible prosocial effects of religion is that many early psychologists shared Freud's negative view of religion; they believed that it had a pernicious influence on the human spirit and that this influence should be exposed. Such a belief led them to look for evidence of negative rather than positive effects of religion and, as the research summarized in Table 1 reveals, they had little difficulty finding it. Indeed, the negative evidence was so strong that psychologists more sympathetic to religion found themselves preoccupied with rebutting it; the hypothesis that religion increases brotherly love was seldom even entertained.
3. We should also note two qualifications on this conclusion. First, in several of the studies summarized in Table 3, a distinction is made between personal "sins" such as gambling, drinking and premarital sex, and social "sins" such as stealing, lying and cheating. The effect of religion on standards concerning personal sins appears to be considerably stronger than its effect on standards concerning social sins. This may be because the behaviours classed as social sin are generally considered more serious and so are more likely to be condemned by everyone.

   The second qualification concerns the nature of the moral standards that the more religious adopt. If we look closely at the results summarized in Table 3, an interesting pattern emerges.

The study by Boehm (1962) suggests that children in religious (Catholic) schools are more sophisticated earlier in their thinking about moral issues than are children in state schools. But the study by Haan, Smith and Block (1968) suggests that religious young adults are more likely to appeal to the conventional standards of society than to internalized moral principles when justifying their moral decisions. Lawrence Kohlberg (1976), a well-known expert on the development of moral thinking, has argued that appealing to conventional standards is a less sophisticated way of thinking about moral issues than appealing to internalized principles. Thus, although religion may inculcate more stringent moral standards, and even more sophisticated thought about moral issues in the child, by the time the child grows up these standards may inhibit more sophisticated moral thinking. Religion may facilitate moral development up to the point of adherence to conventional moral standards but retard development beyond that point.

4. Since Batson was involved in conducting each of these studies, you may justifiably be concerned that the dice were loaded. To find out, we would encourage the interested reader to consult the original research reports.

14

Psychological and psychiatric studies of new religions

JAMES T. RICHARDSON

Introduction

THIS CHAPTER attempts to summarize and integrate the growing literature in the areas of psychological and psychiatric studies of new religions. This literature has had several foci including (1) characterizing members and new converts in terms of their mental health before and after joining; (2) assessing members and converts in terms of certain personality characteristics and syndromes; and (3) examining the effects of membership by studying people who have left these groups either voluntarily or by forceful means. A number of studies from both sides of the Atlantic will be included in the review.

We will focus on strictly psychological and psychiatric studies, but will also of necessity offer interpretations of this work to place it in a broader social psychological and sociological context. This broad contextual analysis is necessary because of rather severe disagreements within the psychological and psychiatric literature in the area. New religions have become quite controversial in America and in some other societies, and members of the several disciplines involved in the study of new religions are arrayed on both sides of the controversy. Considerable differences in interpretation have arisen, and explaining those differences is almost as interesting as studying the phenomenon of new religions itself.

Before delving into the personality and mental health assessment data, some attention should be given to locating participants in "social space", and discussing the implications of such information. This information will be useful in interpreting the psychological data, and in understanding why so much controversy has surrounded the new religions. It is noteworthy that this basic information on social location is the one area of new religion research on which virtually all scholars agree.

Participants in the new religions are typically male, single, Caucasian, and from the middle to upper-middle classes of society. The typical members are relatively well educated and usually half or more have done at least some college or university work. A sizeable majority has been involved in drug usage prior to affiliation, many quite heavily. Similar comments can be made about involvement with alcohol use and their sexual behaviour.

There is considerable variation in these characteristics by time period, location, and group or social movement. As one would suspect, there are demographic and spatial limits on member recruitment to new religions (they can't recruit people who do not exist or who have not heard of their group). Also, there is an interaction between the type of group and type of potential recruit, with certain types of groups being prone to attract certain types of members (Wuthnow, 1976). But even those considerations do not alter the overall picture of a typical recruit described above. Additional data on time period and location of recruitment, and on group characteristics, only sharpens the view we have of the usual membership characteristics.

Major personality assessment findings

Results will be presented from some selected studies that have made explicit efforts to use standardized instruments to assess the personality characteristics of the members and the recruits to new religions. Innumerable studies have used more impressionistic, qualitative and social survey methods to describe members and recruits, most of which will not be systematically surveyed, except when it helps to interpret other results.

A communal Jesus Movement organization

First, some research in which I have been directly involved will be discussed. Early in the 1970s, two graduate students and I developed a large research project focusing on one of the major Jesus Movement (JM) organizations in America. This group had at the time over 1000 full-time members located in communes in about 30 states. We gathered considerable information by administering survey questionnaires to many members, in depth open-ended interviews with some leaders, content analysis of the organization's publications, participant observation of many different group settings, and by standardized personality assessment instruments. Robert Simmonds, who was particularly interested in personality assessment and change, selected the Adjective Check List (ACL) and the State Trait Anxiety Index (STAI). The ACL was administered on three different occasions and the STAI was administered twice. Two administrations of both were given to 53 people, separated in time by about 10 weeks. This part of the study was designed to assess personality change over time, which was the focus of Simmonds' dissertation (Simmonds, 1977).

No significant differences were found over this time period, perhaps because of its shortness. However, the personality pattern discerned with these two instruments in both applications was quite striking when compared with the groups of "normals" used to produce norms for these instruments. No significant differences were found on the "state anxiety" scores, which indicates that at the time of that assessment the members were not different from "normals" in their level of anxiety. However, we did find a significant difference in the "trait anxiety" scores, with the JM group showing higher scores.

The ACL comparison was even more striking (see Simmonds *et al.*, 1976, and Simmonds, 1977 and 1978). Members in each group taking the ACL were significantly ($p < 0.001$) lower on variables of defensiveness, number of favourable adjectives checked, self-confidence, self-control, personal adjustment, achievement, dominance, endurance, order, intraception, affiliation, heterosexuality, change, and in the total number of adjectives checked. Members were significantly higher than "normals" on the number of unfavourable adjectives checked and on succorance and counselling-readiness. An administration a year previously had revealed that males were significantly higher on abasement, while the second and third administrations showed the sample significantly lower on nurturance. On the first administration females were significantly *lower* on counselling-readiness.

These results suggested a "dependency-prone" personality type which was either attracted to and/or fostered by the group. Simmonds (1978) referred to this general pattern as *maladaptive* and suggested that participation in the group was a form of addiction similar to drug addiction. However, second thoughts fostered mainly by our continuing participant observation called such interpretations into question (see Richardson and Simmonds, 1977). It seemed obvious that the large majority of those in the group were functioning well, *within the context of the organization*, even if our data suggested that they might not be able to function as well in a "normal setting". This observation led us to consider seriously the problems associated with using instruments developed in one context (such as the individualistic, competitive American culture, as exemplified by university students) in a vastly different context (such as a communal, more collectively oriented religious group stressing basic values of love, caring, submission, etc.). We concluded that we were uncovering dramatic *situational* differences by using individualized measurement techniques, and that this crucial point should not be obscured by assumptions about the monolithic nature and ultimate value of the dominant American culture. This conclusion should be kept in mind in assessing the following research results.

Some data in support of the general notion of being careful about concluding that such groups were maladaptive were gathered using survey methods. Simmonds (1977) reported that although there had been high involvements in the use of drugs (97 per cent), alcohol (91 per cent), and tobacco (76 per cent) prior to joining, use of these substances dropped to near zero afterwards, according to self-report data. Drug use had been frequent (59 per cent daily) and hard drug (opiates) use high (40 per cent), making the record of rehabilitation especially impressive. Also, these commune members, who were plainly functioning well individually and as a social unit, reported that over half had previously been "in trouble with the law", and 38 per cent said they had seen a psychologist or psychiatrist in a therapeutic situation. Nineteen per cent claimed to have made a suicide attempt some time before joining as well. Although the members had a history of high levels of sexual activity and a number of the women had illegitimate children, they were well integrated into the group (as were their children), and sexual behaviour was strictly regulated in traditional ways. Many people were also acquiring useful job skills through training given in the group. These results corroborated earlier work on the same group (see Richardson *et al.*, 1979). Thus it seems plain that, although our personality instruments taken alone indicated some deviance, *the entire context seemed to be one of healing, rehabilitation and reintegration of these members into a society.*

An Eastern-oriented Organization

Another significant study of a new religion that included personality assessment is Nordquist's study of an Eastern-oriented group, Ananda Cooperative Village, located in California. Some of these results are reported in Nordquist (1978) and Rosen and Nordquist (1980).

Nordquist used three previously developed assessment instruments, two newly developed attitude assessment scales, plus a biographical survey questionnaire and a lengthy period of participant observation with the group at its location outside of Grass Valley, California, during 1975–76. He used the Loevinger *et al.* (1970) Sentence Completion Test (SCT), a form of the well-known Rokeach Value Survey (RVS) (Rokeach, 1973), the Counter-Cultural Attitude Scale (CCAS) developed by Musgrove (1974), a Social Compassion Scale derived from Rokeach (1969) and an Estrangement–Unalienated Scale developed by Rosen based on Andrew Rigby's work (1974) on communes in Britain (the result of this last scale will not be discussed here). Twenty-eight members completed this array of instruments. They fit the general pattern already described in terms of "social location of origin", although Nordquist's particular sample was about half female and half married. He also had deliberately selected older, more long-term members and leaders of the group.

The SCT revealed that members were arrayed from the "conformist" through the "individualistic" levels, the modal category being the "self-aware" level, which is a transitional level between the "conformist" stage and the "conscientious" stage (the modal category for females was "conformist"). The "self-aware" stage is defined (Rosen and Nordquist, 1980) as

a transitional level between the conformist and conscientious stages. At this level there is a lessening of group adherence, a growing sense of self-awareness, and a clearer distinction of self from non-self. The person begins to see different possible ways of acting and relies less on dichotomies. The person becomes increasingly aware of the fact that exceptions from rules are tolerable and that one does not always (have to) live up to expectations. Group norms are changing into an appreciation for individual differences in human action. According to Loevinger (1976), this is probably the modal level for adults in the USA.

Quite revealing results came from the use of the Rokeach Value Survey. Because Ananda is an Eastern-oriented group, Nordquist made one major modification in the survey instrument, substituting "self-realization" for "salvation" as one of the values respondents were to rank. Highest ranked "terminal" values were (in order), "self-realization", "inner harmony", "happiness", "wisdom", and "freedom". Lowest ranks were given to "pleasure", "national security", "social recognition", "a comfortable life", and "an exciting life". There were no significant differences by sex on the terminal value choices.

Highest ranking "instrumental" values were "loving", "cheerful", "honest", "forgiving", and "self-controlled". Lowest rankings were assigned to "logical", "clean", "intellectual", "polite", and "obedient". Females ranked "loving", "forgiving", "imaginative", and "ambitious" higher than did males, and males ranked "self-control" higher than did females. Correlations of the results for both types of values with data from Rokeach's original "religiously committed college students" (1969) indicated a "high degree of similarity".

Data from the Musgrove scale revealed that the Ananda group ranked at the top of the "medium" category used by Musgrove, indicating general similarity with the student group of some 600 reported in Musgrove (1974). The Ananda group was ". . . More strongly oriented toward an estheticism and mysticism and against technology and bureaucracy than it was oriented toward political activism" (Rosen and Nordquist, 1980). Nordquist (1978) had earlier been more specific by saying that these results:

> . . . revealed very high concern for the ecology, a contemplative Eastern way of life, simple forms of living, handicrafts instead of mass production, and opposing the Establishment through an alternative way of life. They did not agree with statements supporting work as pure fun, drugs, obscenity, or statements against authority.

The most intriguing results came from examining the variable, *social compassion*. In 1969 Rokeach reported results that caused a stir among many religionists and students of religion when he claimed to have found a negative relationship between a scale of "social compassion" and the terminal value "salvation". Since Nordquist substituted "self-realization" for "salvation" in his study, he used only ten items from Rokeach's social compassion scale, and since his sample is small, the results must be considered as tentative. Nonetheless, they are striking. On eight of the items the Ananda members responded positively. They were undecided on one item and unfavourable on another. The overall pattern is definitely in a "direction of compassion" (Nordquist, 1978).

Taken as a whole, these results do not suggest personality disorders or major psychopathologies. They reflect a different setting and lifestyle centred around values of self-realization and even altruism. Nordquist (1978) says this lifestyle sharply contrasts with "accomplishment–achievement" orientation of American culture. He also found similar results to those discussed earlier on rehabilitation from drug usage among members. Thus, it seems reasonable again to draw attention to the functional usefulness of a given social context for people who reside in that setting. Nordquist's careful attention to the selection and development of instruments has yielded considerable information about the effects of this group at least on its members. Admittedly his sample was small, but his measure, in combination with a year of participant observation, makes the study notable.

A comparative study in Germany

Another study of note has been done by Wolfgang Kuner of the University of Tübingen in Germany. Kuner presented some preliminary results in Spring 1981 in Lincoln, England at a conference on "New Religions" sponsored by the Sociology of Religion Study group of the British Sociological Association (Kuner, 1981). Kuner focused on the question of the mental health of members of selected new religious groups in The Federal Republic of Germany. He also examined the relationship between length of membership and mental health.

Kuner used the German version of the MMPI, which is made up of 550 items comprising a number of different scales for assessing personality status and emotional adjustment. He gained the cooperation of leaders and members of the Children of God (COG), Ananda Marga (AM) and the Unification Church (UC), and succeeded in getting instruments completed by 42 COG, 303 UC, and 47 AM members, along with a control group of 125 students at the University of Tübingen. These numbers represented sizeable proportions of all the full-time members in Germany, as ascertained by Kuner (COG, 84 per cent; UC, 57 per cent, AM, 47 per cent). Slightly over half the subjects were female, but only the UC group actually had a majority of female members.

This brief report can only refer to some of Kuner's major conclusions. First, he looked at internal validity and concluded that no serious restrictions on the data were needed. Male UC members (and, to a lesser extent, females) were high on the "Lie" scale, which was designed ". . . to identify deliberate or intentional efforts to evade answering the test frankly and honestly . . .". UC members seemed to want to present themselves in a more favourable light. Kuner concluded that this was not a surprising result, and cites a statement by those who developed the MMPI that elevated lie-scale values may occur with "highly religious and moralistic individuals who rigidly control any overt expression of anti-social or unethical impulses" (Dahlstrom and Welsh 1960). Kuner also attributed this apparent defensiveness to the enmity shown by society toward the Unification Church.

Although there were some significant differences among and between the groups (which cannot be examined here), Kuner stated that overall "the average group profiles score within the 'normal' range", with no significant numbers of members indicating poor mental health. He added ". . . altogether [members] show better scores than the control group; [they] seem to live with less worries and under less psychic stress".

When examining the relationship between the time in the group to mental health, Kuner found a positive relationship between scores on the lie-scale and time in the AM and UC groups, and concluded that, ". . . the longer membership lasts, the stronger the identification with the movement's rules", a not too surprising idea. The data revealed that "no significant linear correlation was detected between elevated scale values [clinical cases] and time of membership". Also that "the longer the membership lasted the higher the probability to achieve a value within the narrow normal range". One particularly interesting interaction was found between sex and time in the group. Female UC members were more prone toward depression over time, while male UC members increased self-confidence. Kuner suggests this may relate to the better career prospects for males in this male-dominated group.

Kuner's comparison of several groups, and his use of a control group makes this a valuable study. He has collected the only personality assessment data with standardized instruments on the AM and the COG, and his is the only such information available on members of new religions outside America of which I am aware (although Nordquist is now gathering data in Sweden). Kuner concluded his study by stating,

> As far as an influence on mental state and psycho-social development can be traced, the [new religious movements] prove themselves rather 'therapeutic and/or resocialization groups' for socially alienated. The results . . . give little support for the Anti-Cult Movement's point of view.

Deprogramming and personality assessment

Another important study has been done by Ungerleider and Wellisch (1979), who did research involving four groups: two members of some new religions who feared deprogramming (FD), nine people who had been deprogrammed and left the group (DL), eleven people who had been deprogrammed and returned to the group, and a group of eight ex-members who had voluntarily left their group (V). The sample was small, and made up of volunteers; therefore the results, though interesting, should be viewed cautiously. The analysis also suffered from a failure to understand the propensity for most people to develop justificatory and excusatory accounts for what they do and have done (Beckford, 1978; Scott and Lyman, 1968). This comment applies especially to Ungerleider and Wellisch's interpretation of information given by those subjects who had been deprogrammed and had not returned to their membership groups. Solomon's (1981) research shows quite clearly that those who have been deprogrammed are more prone to adopt a "brain-washing" interpretation of what they have experienced (also see Singer, 1979, who admitted that 75 per cent of her "subjects" [patients] had not left the group completely of their own volition). Ungerleider and Wellisch's results in general suggest a similar pattern to that found in other groups. "All persons tested were normal on all aspects of the mental status examination" (Ungerleider and Wellisch, 1979). Ungerleider and Wellisch analysed the "love/hate" variable of the Interpersonal Check List, and found that "The nonreturnee (DL), returnee (DR) and concerned member (FD) groups viewed themselves as having become significantly more emotionally affiliative while in the cult, whereas the voluntary ex-members saw themselves as almost unchanged on the variable" (1979, p. 280). This means a shift from distant and unemotional ways of relating, to more emotional involvement with others in the group.

On the MMPI, all groups fell within the normal range with those still in the group (FD and DRs) showing an elevated score on the lie scale, as did Kuner's UC members. As noted earlier, this could result from overt efforts at positive self-presentation or from an acceptance of the group's creed. Ungerleider and Wellisch also found high levels of repressed hostility, especially among those still in the groups. They concluded that this hostility probably predated involvement in the group, was focused especially on the family (from which they feared or had actually experienced deprogramming), and that this response may have derived directly from a fear of deprogramming.

The "account" interpretation offered to aid in understanding Ungerleider and Wellisch's data from deprogrammed subjects gains indirect support from several areas. All those who were DRs said their deprogramming experience was "not gentle", while 88 per cent of the DL group viewed it as "gentle". The DLs indicated that they had become submissive during membership. Ungerleider and Wellisch also state that the DLs seemed to counterbalance the attractions of affiliation with the group with a "negative reaction to a sense of being dominated and forced into an unendurably submissive role" (1979, p. 282). They also note that those who remained in the group did not feel dominated but actually felt dominant, a finding they attempt to discount using a "cognitive-dissonance model", and asserting that "their perceptions appear to differ from the reality that all of the cults function on a hierarchical model of power" (*ibid.*). This assertion does not stand scrutiny in the light of research by those who have made participant observations in such groups (see Davis and Richardson, 1976, on the COG). Ungerleider and Wellisch concluded that,

> No data emerged, either from intellectual, personality, or mental status testing to suggest that any of these subjects were unable or even limited in their ability to make legal judgements. Rather the groups all emerged as intellectually capable on testing. They revealed clinically an intellectual and philosophical bent which resembles what Lifton has termed "strong ideological hunger" regardless of status in relation to the cult. These cults appear to

provide, at least for a time, nourishment for these theological hungers as well as relief from the internal turmoil of ambivalence.

They also noted (1979) "that forcible removal of individuals from any group to which they have belonged for more than 12 months is exceedingly difficult". All those "successfully" deprogrammed in their sample from the Divine Light Mission had been in for less than one year. *But*, for the group of eight voluntary leavers, three (38 per cent) had been in less than a year and five (62 per cent) had been in *more* than one year, a finding consonant with the high drop-out rates found by Eileen Barker (1981) in her thorough study of the Unification Church in Britain and elsewhere.

Galanter's study of the "relief effect"

Marc Galanter, a psychiatrist, has completed significant research on members of the Unification Church and Divine Light Mission to test the idea that new religions furnish a biologically based "relief effect" to members. Galanter uses a sociobiological perspective to suggest that individuals without roots in a social group will exhibit "neurotic distress symptoms". The "adaptive value of this vulnerability" derives from the fact that it assures integration into a social group. These symptoms can be alleviated by participation in a social group such as a religious sect. Galanter's studies of both the UC and the DLM were developed to test whether or not participation in such groups lowered neurotic distress scores among members.

In one article Galanter *et al.* (1979) focused on the Unification Church and compared a sample of 237 members to a control and comparison group of 305 people. In another paper, Galanter (1980) followed a cohort of 104 people through the 3-week training programme of the Church in one of its training centres in California. Galanter used several of the same instruments in both studies, which enables valuable comparisons. Some of his findings included lower "general well-being" scores for long-term members and joiners, when compared to a control group from a stable environment, with the lowest scores being for those who chose to join. Those who joined seemed to have more affiliative ties within the group, and fewer ties outside the group. Galanter concluded that those who join may have had some "neurotic distress" before joining, but that this distress was ameliorated by membership in the group. (He also notes that several people who were participating in the workshop were asked to leave because of "psychological instability".) He cited literature indicating "an apparent therapeutic response" from joining self-help groups, religious sects and other groups, and he suggests that some features of the setting might well be directly useful to the induction process in conventional mental health settings.

In the 1979 paper, Galanter *et al.* found that 90 per cent of the 237 members reported a history of prior commitments to other new religions, illustrating the concept of conversion careers (see Richardson, 1980a). This and other results are even more significant because his sample was representative of all the Church's members in one large area. Galanter also reported on prior drug use, which was very high, a factor related to the neurotic distress scores, which were also high for the period before joining. He cited the facts that one-quarter had serious drug problems before joining, that 30 per cent had required professional care and 6 per cent had been hospitalized as indicating that the population from which members were drawn had a higher likelihood of psychiatric illness than the general population, and he concluded (p. 168):

> Affiliation with the Unification Church apparently provided considerable and sustained relief from neurotic distress. Although improvement was ubiquitous, a greater religious commitment was reported by those who indicated the most improvement.

Galanter's work on Divine Light Mission members (Galanter, 1978; Galanter and Buckley, 1978), was based on a random sample of 119 "premies" attending a national festival who were asked to fill out a 170-item questionnaire. Included in it were questions about group functions, psychiatric symptoms, drug use, and meditation. The members were similar to members of the Unification Church: typically single, white, in their 20s, and they had been members for about 2 years on the average (UC long-term members in his 1979 study had been members nearly twice as long). The DLM members also had a very high incidence of prior drug use. Members displayed a "strong sense of cohesiveness and communal sharing" (p. 687) and strong feelings of trust were felt towards other members. A dramatic decline in psychiatric symptoms was found, using a multiple regression analysis involving variables such as group cohesiveness, group activity (participation), and meditation time. Having "transcendental experiences" was also found to be a predictor of symptomatic relief. Galanter and Buckley (1978) noted (p. 689) that "Clear parallels exist between DLM religious approaches and traditional psychotherapy", and they are impressed with the DLM as a setting for therapy. They say (p. 690),

> The diversity of specific psychological symptoms alleviated here is notable. A decline was reported in symptoms affected by behavioral norms, such as drug taking and job trouble; it was also found in subjectively experienced symptoms, such as anxiety, not readily regulated.

They close this paper by commenting on the way the DLM has apparently been able to restructure the peer group in a manner that stopped drug use, instead of encouraging it, as is usually the case.

In a related paper, Galanter (1981) focused particularly on the effects that participation in the UC and the DLM had on alcohol consumption. He concluded that such affiliation contributed significantly to a drop in alcohol use, and offered a sociobiologically based model to explain this, suggesting that "There is a positive relationship between psychological well-being and feelings of cohesiveness in a large group" (1981, p. 71). He further suggested that ". . . psychological well-being is also correlated with adherence to group norms", and tied these ideas together by stating, "when joining a large group, an individual experiences a 'relief effect' in his level of neurotic distress, a process closely associated with social cohesiveness and the acceptance of group norms" (1981, p. 73). Galanter concluded this paper with a discussion of the rise in recent years of the "intense, cohesive, large-group experience" as a "mental health modality which has gained widespread recognition in recent decades" (1981, p. 76) and identified some of the characteristics of large-group therapy for alcoholics and others. Included in it were,

> (a) large-group versus small-group size; (b) a high level of social cohesiveness; (c) an intense, nonrational or anti-rational belief system; (d) a correlation of members psychological well-being with cohesiveness and with a consensual belief system; (e) group determination of major behavioural norms (such as drinking). Other aspects of such groups not addressed here, but observed during field work with these groups are (f) an explicit system of totem and ritual . . . and (g) the dependence of social role and status on the relationship to normative beliefs . . .

The similarity of many features of the new religions to this list is obvious, and Galanter has explicitly suggested that therapists have things to learn from some of the newer religious groups which have been very successful at changing their participants' behaviours.

Fundamentalism on campus

A study by the psychiatrist Armand Nicholi (1974) also deserves mention. His data are of particular interest because his subjects were a sample of Harvard and Radcliffe students who did not belong to a "cult", but who were apparently "normal" college students who had recently experienced conversion to a Biblical faith and participated in a campus group involved in Bible studies (probably Campus Crusade). These young people (17 in all) were given "intensive interviews" covering a number of subjects. They reported that their parents had little influence over their spiritual interests, but that peers had got them interested in religion. These students had used drugs, but not to the extent that has been described for the DLM or the Moonies. Thus, the relationship between taking drugs and participating in religion seems somewhat different in this case. Nicholi suggests that his subjects seemed interested in filling a spiritual void left by the absence of religious instruction during their early years. They expressed concern in the area of personal and sexual relations, and suffered from what Nicholi called "existential despair". After joining the Bible study group the subjects stopped using drugs, cigarettes and alcohol. They expressed more self-esteem, and more concern for others. Their personal relationships were improved, including those with their parents. Chastity became the rule in sexual matters, and general affect was positive. Performance at their studies was higher, and the students expressed less fear of death. Also, a number of them made career-plan changes involving a move into the helping professions. Nicholi summarizes his findings by saying that conversion resulted in ". . . a marked improvement in ego functioning" (1974, p. 400).

Negative views of new religions

All the work just cited that presents data on personality assessment of members of the newer religious groups seems at odds with the reports of a few members of the psychiatric community who are publicly opposed to participation in the newer religions. These reports, by such people as Margaret Singer and John Clark, focus mainly on conclusions drawn from studies of some people who have left certain of the newer groups, many apparently involuntarily. These differences in research site or focus, coupled with a difference in research perspective, has contributed to major differences in findings. Others who have studied people who have left these groups have indicated some adjustment problems, but most have not concluded that the experience of being in the groups is totally deleterious (see Wright, 1983; Beckford, 1978; Skonovd, 1982; Derks and Van der Lans, 1982). However, Singer (1979) and Clark (1979) have drawn that conclusion. Since this is the case, the results of what is perhaps the most cited article – that of Singer in *Psychology Today* (1979) – will be summarized to contrast with the data already discussed.

Singer paints an extremely negative picture of life in the cults, based on the accounts given by a number of people she has interviewed after they left the groups. She fails to appreciate that the accounts she is hearing are possibly biased, as these individuals are trying to work out acceptable explanations of why they spent time in the groups. She also does not recognize the possible impact of the fact that 75 per cent of her interviewees ". . . had left the cults not entirely of their own volition . . ." (1979, p. 80). Singer did not report in the 1979 paper data derived from the application of any standard personality assessment instruments. However, based on her clinical interviews with a number of people who had left, she claims that most people who join do so as a reaction to periods of depression and confusion, and that the cults use intense social and psychological pressures to induce and maintain membership. She discusses the submissiveness of converts and the altered state of consciousness which many experience. She further discusses the problems faced by people who leave these groups including depression, indecisiveness, loneliness, "uncritical passivity", and a "blurring of mental activity". Singer points out that some of the people experience difficulties in explaining what they were doing during their time in the cult, and that they experience guilt over the time they spent in such activities. In sum, life in the cults is described by Singer as hellish, while life after them is probably worse. Nowhere does she directly face the fact that her work serves a legitimating function for those opposed to membership in the new groups. She also does not address the competition *between* psychotherapy and the new religions (see Kilbourne and Richardson, 1984).

Conclusions

This paper is not the proper place to furnish a detailed discussion of the political and social context that has contributed to the controversy about new religions (see Anthony, Robbins and McCarthy, 1980; Bromley and Richardson, 1983; Richardson, 1982; Shupe and Bromley, 1980). However, taking most of the data presented herein at face value causes some difficulty in understanding why such a hue and cry about the new religions has arisen in some quarters. Virtually all the studies that have focused on members of the newer religious groups reveal that some younger representatives of America's more educated and affluent classes have decided to "try out" a different lifestyle, at least temporarily.

But therein lies a major problem. The tremendous interest by the media and others in our society in new religions, and the controversy about them, derives in large part from the *social location* of most of their recruits. They are part of the most educated generation in history, and they are from relatively affluent family circumstances. Not many people cared about those who joined the infamous People's Temple group that met its tragic end in the jungles of Guyana. Most members of that group (which is not "new" in the sense we mean by the term, since it started in the 1950s; see Richardson, 1980b) were poor and black. It included nearly 200 young children and a similar number of elderly people. But most members of the Moonies, the Hare Krishna and many other new groups are as we have described them. And the decision of many such people to be *voluntarily downwardly mobile* and leave the "appointed place" in society for which their families have worked long and hard has led to understandable grief and consternation in thousands of families. The high level of concern of some (but not all) such families has helped give impetus to what is called "the Anti-cult Movement" in America and elsewhere, and we have even seen the development of a new quasi-professional occupation of deprogrammer to help family members who are upset extract and rehabilitate their young members from new religious groups (see Shupe and Bromley, 1980). Other factors (such as the interests of professional psychiatry and organized traditional religious groups) must also be taken into account for a full understanding of these developments that seem to be contradicted by what is revealed in most of the systematic and thorough research on the new religions.

The personality assessments of these group members reveal that life in the new religions is often therapeutic instead of harmful. Other information suggests that these young people are *affirming* their idealism by virtue of their involvement in such groups. Certainly there is some "submerging of personality" in groups which are communal or collective, simply because they do not foster the individualistic and competitive lifestyle to which we are accustomed, particularly in American society. However, there is little data to support the almost completely negative picture painted by a few psychiatrists who have been involved in the controversy over new religions.

The above comments are not meant to dismiss totally the work of those who take a negative view of the new religions, just as it is not meant to support completely the work of those who appear to have a positive view about the experience of participation in them. Both types of work have values, and both have limitations. No single piece of research can answer every question about the meaning of the new religions. It is hoped, however, that reviews such as this will contribute to answering questions about new religions by encouraging more systematic study of them with comparisons of those who remain in the groups and those who leave, including those who are extracted for deprogramming. Only with more and better information can we properly understand the meaning of the contemporary phenomenon of new religions.

References

ANTHONY, D., ROBBINS, T. and MCCARTHY, J. Legitimating repression. *Society*, 1980; **17**(3), 39–42.

BARKER, E. Who'd be a Moonie? A comparative study of those who join the Unification Church in Britain. In B. WILSON (ed.), *The social impact of new religious movements*. New York: Rose of Sharon Press, 1981.

BECKFORD, J. A. Accounting for conversion. *British Journal of Sociology*, 1978; **29**(2), 249–262.

BROMLEY, D. and RICHARDSON, J. T. *The brainwashing/deprogramming controversy*. Toronto: Edwin Mellen Press, 1983.

CLARK, J. Cults. *Journal of the American Medical Association*, 1979; **24**(3), 281–299.

DAHLSTROM, W. G. and WELSH, G. S. *An MMPI Handbook; a guide to use in clinical practice*. Minneapolis: University of Minneapolis Press, 1960.

DAVIS, R. and RICHARDSON, J. T. The organization and functioning of the Children of God. *Sociological Analysis*, 1976; **37**(4), 320–341.

DERKS, F. and VAN DER LANS, J. The post-cult syndrome: fact or fiction? Paper presented at Conference of Psychologists of Religion, Catholic University, Nijmegen. The Netherlands, 1982.

GALANTER, M. The "relief effect": a sociobiological model of neurotic distress and large-group therapy. *American Journal of Psychiatry*, 1978; **135**, 588–591.

GALANTER, M. Psychological induction into the larger group: findings from a modern religious sect. *American Journal of Psychiatry*, 1980; **137**, 1574–1579.

GALANTER, M. Sociobiology and informal social controls of drinking: findings from two charismatic sects. *Journal of Studies of Alcohol*, 1981; **42**(1), 64–79.

GALANTER, M. Charismatic religious sects and psychology. *American Journal of Psychology*, 1982; **139**(12), 1539–1548.

GALANTER, M. and BUCKLEY, P. Evangelical religion and meditation: psychological effects. *Journal of Nervous and Mental Disease*, 1978; **166**(10), 685–691.

GALANTER, M., RABKIN, R., RABKIN, J. and DEUTCH, A. The 'Moonies': a psychological study. *American Journal of Psychiatry*, 1979; **136**(2), 165–170.

KILBOURNE, B. and RICHARDSON, J. T. Psychotherapy and new religions in a pluralistic society. *American Psychologist*, 1984; **39**(3), 237–251.

KUNER, W. New religious movements and mental health. Empirical research into three NRMs in the Federal Republic of Germany. Paper presented at Conference on New Religions, Lincoln, England, 1981.

LOEVINGER, J., WESSLER, R. and REDMORE, C. *Measuring ego development* (2 volumes). San Francisco: Jossey-Bass, 1970.

LOEVINGER, J. *Ego development: Conceptions and theories*, San Francisco: Jossey-Bass, 1976.

MUSGROVE, F. *Ecstasy and holiness: counterculture and the open society.* London: Methuen, 1974.

NICHOLI, A. A new dimension of the youth culture. *American Journal of Psychiatry*, 1974; **131**(4), 396–401.

NORDQUIST, T. *Ananda cooperative village: a study in the beliefs, values, and attitudes of a New Age religious community.* Uppsala University: Religionshistoriska Institutionen Monograph Series, 1978, p. 16.

RICHARDSON, J. T. Conversion careers. *Society*, 1980a; **17**(3), 47–50.

RICHARDSON, J. T. People's Temple: a comparison and corrective critique. *Journal for the Scientific Study of Religion*, 1980b; **19**(3), 239–255.

RICHARDSON, J. T. Conversion, deprogramming, and brainwashing. *The Center Magazine*, 1982; **15**(2), 18–24.

RICHARDSON, J. T. and SIMMONDS, R. B. Problems of interpretation of personality assessment data from members of communal new religions. Paper presented at the meeting of the International Association of Psychologists of Religion, Uppsala, Sweden, 1977.

RICHARDSON, J. T. and SIMMONDS, R. B. *Organized miracles: A sociological study of a Jesus Movement organization.* New Brunswick, NJ: Transaction Books, 1979.

RIGBY, A. *Alternative realities: A study of communes and their members.* London: Routledge & Kegan Paul, 1974.

ROBBINS, T. and ANTHONY, D. (eds). *In Gods we trust.* New Brunswick, NJ: Transaction Books, 1981.

ROKEACH, M. Value systems in religion. *Review of Religious Research*, 1969; **11**, 3–39.

ROKEACH, M. *The nature of human values.* New York: The Free Press, 1973.

ROSEN, A. and NORDQUIST, T. Ego developmental level and values in a yogic community. *Journal of Personality and Social Psychology*, 1980; **39**(6), 1152–1160.

SCOTT, M. and LYMAN, S. Accounts. *American Sociological Review*, 1968; **33**(10), 46–61.

SHUPE, A., Jr and BROMLEY, D. *The new vigilantes: Deprogrammers, anticultists, and the new religions.* Beverly Hills, Ca.: Sage, 1980.

SIMMONDS, R. B., RICHARDSON, J. T. and HARDER, M. A Jesus Movement group: An Adjective Check-list assessment. *Journal for the Scientic Study of Religion*, 1976; **15**, 323–337.

SIMMONDS, R. B. The people of the Jesus Movement: A personality assessment of members of a fundamentalist religious community. Unpublished PhD dissertation, University of Nevada, Reno, 1977.

SIMMONDS, R. B. Conversion or addiction: consequences of joining a Jesus Movement group. In J. T. RICHARDSON (ed.), *Conversion careers.* Beverly Hills, Ca.: Sage, 1978.

SINGER, M. T. Coming out of the cults. *Psychology Today*, 2979, **12**, 72–82.

SKONOVD, N. Apostasy: the process of defection from religious totalism. In D. BROMLEY and J. RICHARDSON (eds), *The brainwashing/deprogramming controversy.* Toronto: Edwin Mellen Press, 1983.

SOLOMON, T. Integrating the 'Moonie' experience: a survey of ex-members of the Unification Church. In T. ROBBINS and D. ANTHONY (eds), *In Gods we trust.* New Brunswick, NJ: Transaction Books, 1981.

UNGERLEIDER, J. T. and WELLISCH, D. K. Coercive persuasion (brainwashing), religious cults and deprogramming. *American Journal of Psychiatry*, 1979; **136**, 279–282.

WRIGHT, S. Defection from new religious movements: a test of some theoretical propositions. In D. G. BROMLEY and J. T. RICHARDSON (eds), *The brainwashing/deprogramming controversy.* Toronto: Edwin Mellen Press, 1983.

WUTHNOW, R. *The consciousness reformation.* Berkeley, Ca.: University of California Press, 1976.

Name Index

Italic numbers are to References

Subject Index